THE HEART OF A
BUSINESS ETHIC

WITH AN INTRODUCTION AND AFTERWORD BY
C. William Pollard
Foreword by Warren Bennis

Edited by Donald D. Holt

UNIVERSITY PRESS OF AMERICA,® INC.
Lanham • Boulder • New York • Toronto • Oxford

University Press of America,® Inc.
4501 Forbes Boulevard
Suite 200
Lanham, Maryland 20706
UPA Acquisitions Department (301) 459-3366

PO Box 317
Oxford
OX2 9RU, UK

Library of Congress Control Number: 2005930958
ISBN 0-7618-3188-6 (paperback : alk. ppr.)

♾™ The paper used in this publication meets the minimum
requirements of American National Standard for Information
Sciences—Permanence of Paper for Printed Library Materials,
ANSI Z39.48—1984

Ken Wessner and Ken Hansen

HANSEN-WESSNER
LECTURESHIP VOLUME

ABOUT THIS VOLUME

This book is based on the Hansen-Wessner Lectureship Series established by The ServiceMaster Foundation to consider the source of moral authority and ethical behavior in business. The eight lectures in the inaugural series from 1995 to 2002 honored the memory of Ken Hansen and Ken Wessner, former Chief Executives of ServiceMaster. They were my predecessors at the company, and also my mentors in life. For them, the business firm was not only an economic entity to maximize profits, but also a vehicle for the development and growth of the people who served together to provide value for customers and shareholders.

The lectures were held at major universities in the United States and Britain that also have leading graduate schools of business. Faculty members at each institution gave responses. The lecturers are people who know and understand business and who, in their personal and professional lives, have provided an example of moral and ethical behavior. A special thanks to Don Holt, former Editor of *Fortune Magazine*'s international edition, for applying his expertise in business and the written word in editing these lectures for publication and to Richard Chewning who was the Chavanne Professor of Christain Ethics at Baylor University.

C. William Pollard
Chairman Emeritus
The ServiceMaster Company

CONTENTS

FOREWORD

The rancorous public debate over business ethics and corporate reform has lacked a few crucial ingredients: A genuine love for business and human enterprise, the confidence that the American corporation is "worth saving," a sense that it is fully worthy of our loftiest ideals and most focused energies.

Gratefully, this is precisely what Peter Drucker, Max De Pree, James Baker, Michael Novak and their distinguished colleagues offer us in *The Heart of a Business Ethic.*

Their contribution is substantial and timely. A *CBS/New York Times* poll a few short years ago revealed that only about one in six persons expressed much faith in American business. A full two-thirds of Americans suspect most corporate leaders to be dishonest.

Evidence of how low reputations have sunk comes from the accolades received by a Canadian-produced documentary, "The Corporation," in which a psychiatrist who works with the FBI in pursuing psychopathic criminals announces: "In many respects, corporations are the prototypical psychopath."

Forgotten in recent discussions has been the fragrant sense of possibility that business and enterprise represent, as exemplified by a corporation working at its fullest capacities. It is a corporation that can offer thousands of women and men the opportunity to discover and exercise their gifts; it is the corporation that fuels innovation; it is the corporation that forges countless leaders who later shape the worlds of government, academia, philanthropy and civic life.

"A life committed to business," Michael Novak writes in these pages, "is a noble vocation." What an opportune time to take those words seriously, and to accept along with those words the exhilarating moral exhortations offered herein as a means to unleash the capacious potentials of persons, organizations and entire societies.

The essays in this volume are weighty and inspiring, but I would like to add an observation having to do with bridging the gap between inspiration and reality. So much lip service is paid to the issue of business ethics; but how does one in fact build an organization distinguished by tangible integrity, moral vision, and transparency? I have found that the key is a commitment on the part of the corporate leader to establish a culture of candor, in which followers feel free to speak truth to power and leaders are bold enough to hear such truth—and act upon it.

A first step for an organization seeking to create this manner of culture is to examine its current culture unblinkingly—without falling back on defining myths of superiority that build internal cohesion, but stifle the ability to self-critique.

Another key step is to listen to your contrarians. If you don't have any, recruit them. Both of these steps are more difficult than they sound. It is human nature to surround oneself with encouragers and enablers who remind you of how brilliant you are.

True contrarians are usually shunned as "not being with the program," far more likely to be fired than rewarded. But they are the wise leader's secret treasure. You can choose to hear how great you are from a paid subordinate or from the judgment of history. You decide.

A challenge also exists for the rest of us, followers, lieutenants and board members: Avoiding being blinded by the "shimmer effect" of an organization's top leader. From history's first light, followers have "given the benefit of the doubt" to top leaders, confusing their position with heroism and losing all perspective in the process. The act of good leadership is a shared responsibility, and nowhere is this truer than in the task of cultivating accountability in the workplace and boardroom.

It is fashionable to sneer at the modern business organization, this alleged sociopath. Yet James Baker, by way of Adam Smith, notes in the concluding essay that our economic system's genius is in how it turns naked self-interest into something that benefits a myriad people. This does not happen in some vast ocean of theory, but rather in tangible, human organizations of every size, shape and hue. What results is a dance of collaboration, a life-giving movement that can bring value to each person involved.

We should be grateful to the contributors to this essay collection for rekindling in us that glad sense of possibility.

Warren Bennis
Distinguished Professor of Business Administration
University of Southern California

INTRODUCTION

By C. William Pollard

As we conduct business in a pluralistic society, can we agree on a source of moral authority? Would that source be relevant to a business firm's success or to the way it performed its role in society? Is there a moral basis for the ethos of the firm—a spirit of community that helps to guide and constrain what might otherwise become a fragmented center of self-interests? Can a business be successful on a sustainable basis and be morally bankrupt? Would leadership make a difference? Would it make a difference if a firm had ethical leaders who knew the source of their moral authority, had the courage of their convictions and provided a living example of right behavior?

These questions come at a significant moment. In the very recent past we have had far too many examples of financial *and* moral failures in business. The *Financial Times* once reported on what it called the Barons of Bankruptcy—a privileged group of top business leaders who made extraordinary fortunes even as their companies were heading for disaster. The newspaper examined 25 business collapses since the start of 2001 and, according to its figures, the executives and directors of those doomed companies walked away with over $3.3 billion in compensation and proceeds from stock sales while their companies were heading into bankruptcy.

How do we explain such a result? The answers could include just another explosion of corporate greed, coupled with gross negligence by boards and incompetence or culpability by outside auditors. Current incentive systems, including stock options or the way we account for them, have been contributing factors, as has the manic focus on quarter-by-quarter performance along with the assumption that business growth and value can be accurately reported and measured within a three-month time horizon. And underlying all of it was a lapse in moral leadership. The reality is that all these factors converged into what we might call "The Perfect Storm"—a storm that contributed, along with a down economic cycle, to an overall loss in market value of over $6 trillion. People have been hurt. Savings and provisions for retirement plans have been extinguished. Jobs have been lost. One of the world's largest accounting firms, whose reputation was once like sterling on silver, is gone. Some corporate leaders and directors will go to jail, and others should.

Some might argue that these events are just another bump, albeit a big one, in the evolution of understanding how best to manage and balance those ever-present human factors of greed, self-interest, bias, power, and deceit with appropriate checks and balances of government supervision, control and more rules and regulation. I strongly believe that there is something more at work here that is fundamental to understanding human behavior and that is essential to the development of moral and ethical leadership. We need nothing less than a radical reformation of thought and action to include a renewed focus on the development of the character and integrity of the business leader, determination of a source for moral authority, and a standard of right behavior that cannot be waived or modified. Unfortunately, little of that is happening. In American business today we are running pell-mell down the road of trying to solve ethical business issues with more legislative answers and more rules of compliance. From my experience as a director of several public companies, I know that senior managers and board members are consumed right now with trying to understand and respond to all the new rules and issues of process, structure, and compliance. While many of these new rules will help clarify the boundaries of right and wrong business practices, they cannot do the whole job. The ethical and moral judgments of business leaders in changing, dynamic markets cannot be solely determined by a set of rules nor can a right result always be achieved by following a particular process. While rules may bring a higher standard of accountability and add the "stick" of more penalties, they cannot determine the honesty, character, or integrity of the people involved.

Thus the crucial question becomes, how do these virtues become a part of who a person is and how he or she acts, as a business leader, a parent, or a neighbor? In a series of articles in the *Chicago Tribune* on the state of our economy, the headline was: "Have We Sold Our Souls?" The writer concluded that many corporate leaders no longer were able to define reality and have lied to themselves, their employees, and their shareholders because they have become detached from a life of genuineness, meaning, and purpose. Effective and responsible leadership starts with the ability of leaders to define reality and in so doing to understand the essence of their own human nature and the human nature of the people they are leading. It is important for the business leader not only to be concerned about what employees do and how they do it, but also to ask the deeper question of *why* people do their work and who they are becoming in the process.

Our humanity cannot be defined solely by its physical or rational nature. The uniqueness of our nature is that it also has a spiritual side. It is this spiritual side that influences our character, our ability to determine right and wrong, to recognize good and evil, to make moral judgments, to love or to hate. It allows us to develop a philosophy of life, a world view that can provide a moral and ethical framework and standard that is not relative and functions even when there are no prescribed rules. Henry Ford once famously said: "Why do I always get a whole person when all that I wanted was a pair of hands?" Often, that is the way we look at people in business. We talk about people as being units of production or the cost of labor in a profit and loss statement. As we downsize or re-engineer an organization, can we downsize or re-engineer people? They do not come to us as just a pair of hands. People come to us as whole people, and they must be understood and led as such.

We know that the wealth creation formula for now and in the future will be dependent more on human capital than on the availability of land or reproducible assets. The human capital factor is estimated by most economists to have a value that is twice as great as any physical resources. But are we providing a meaningful purpose along with a standard for responsible and moral behavior for this human capital? Robert Fogel, an economist at the University of Chicago and a 1993 Nobel Prize winner, recently wrote a book entitled *The Fourth Great Awakening* in which he traced the history of religious faith in America from pre-Revolutionary times to the present. As he analyzed the effect of religion on our society and economy, he concluded that the biggest issue in our culture today was not the lack of employment opportunities or even the distribution of economic resources. Nor, in his judgment, was it a lack of diversity or equal opportunity. In his opinion, the major issue was simply a lack of the distribution of what he referred to as spiritual resources or spiritual assets. There is, he concluded, a void in our society in the development of the character of people and a provision for their spiritual needs. In his book *The Death of Character*, James Hunter, a noted sociologist from the University of Virginia, concluded that while Americans are innately as capable of developing character as they were in the past, there are now few cultural or institutional guidelines in our society that call for its cultivation or maintenance. The reason, he suggested, was because there was no consensus of moral authority. What these two authors, along with the lecturers in this series, are saying strongly suggests a root cause for the current ethical crises. Since human capital is so important to the future of our economy, and if there is a void in the development of character and a lack of consensus of moral authority, then the most pressing question we face is how do we nurture and develop the ethos of the firm and the spirit of its community?

In his classic work, *The Gulag Archipelago*, Alexander Solzhenitsyn argued that the line between good and evil passes through every human heart. He asserted that even within hearts overwhelmed by evil there was one small bridgehead of good and, even in the best of hearts, there remained a small corner of evil. His conclusion was that it was impossible to expel evil from the world in its entirety, but it was possible to recognize it and constrain it. For Solzhenitsyn, the source of truth and constraint came from God, an authority beyond himself.

In a commencement address at Harvard University, he reminded students of the misery and evil of life under a communist regime and the consequences for a society without a moral compass. He also noted, however, that he was increasingly finding in the West a growing dependence upon no other scale but a legal one. Such a society, he said, would never reach for anything higher than a set of rules and the letter of the law and would not take advantage of the high level of human potential and possibility. In such a culture, he concluded, there would be nothing more than moral mediocrity, paralyzing the noblest of impulses.

Thus our goal should be clear. The business firm of the twenty-first century must develop a spirit of community that is focused on the dignity and worth of every person. It must become a community with a soul, where truth is not an option but a mandate. This community would expect of its leaders truth and transparency in the conduct of their personal as well as their business lives and a commitment to serve the interest of others over their own self-interest. Finally, this community would be a place where, in the process of serving customers and making money, it would be okay to raise the question of God as a source of moral authority.

As we mix the skills and talents of people at work, and work becomes a place where we attempt to correct society's imbalances regarding economic opportunity, race, and gender, can we also be about the process of developing the whole person, including nurturing character and spiritual development? This should be a major social responsibility of business. The following chapters, summarized below, offer thoughtful variations on these themes. As you reflect on the meaning for you of what has been said in these lectures, consider whether there is truth to be found here, and, if so, how will you apply it to the way you lead and to the way you live.

THE BUSINESS OF VALUES

Brian Griffiths, a member of the British House of Lords and Senior Advisor of Goldman Sachs, hit all of these points in the inaugural lecture at the Peter F. Drucker Management Center of the Claremont Graduate School in California. He issued a clarion call for business leaders to create an ethos for the firm based on clearly defined core values—values that would permeate all aspects of business, including governance, compensation, incentives, stock ownership, accounting policies, quality and performance, and ethical conduct and behavior. He argued that when such values become the heart and soul of the firm, the marketplace responds and the firm will develop a competitive edge. But for this to occur, he noted, there must be leadership. He called for leaders who can articulate the values and set an example by their behavior, who have the heart and practice of a servant, who are committed to truth, and who understand human authenticity. Such leadership, he suggested, develops high-trust cultures with shared values, resulting in a consistency of habit or behavior—what he called the "people's language of good and evil."

While he cited numerous examples of successful business firms that have been so led in the past, he warned against value systems that are subjective or relativistic, incorporating a post-modern world view that denies the existence of God, objective truth, and the reality of the spiritual dimension of life. We cannot, he said, do without moral absolutes. In examining the question of a source of such absolutes, he first referred to the writing of C. S. Lewis in the *Abolition of Man*. After examining the great religions of the world and classical Greek and Roman philosophers, Lewis concluded that there is a common theme or belief within human experience that recognizes certain things to be true and others to be false and condemns behavior that is unjust or harmful to others. Griffiths then referred to the Abrahamic covenant of God as a more specific source of moral, ethical and spiritual values—"a source that starts with God as the creator of a world with people made in His image and with a divine mandate to take responsibility for the earth and to be productive." The themes and values that emerge from such a source, he suggested, are respect for the individual, the importance of truth, and the binding reality of the covenants or promises people make with each other. Companies that embody these values are rewarded in the marketplace. They excel, he said, in the "business" of making money, creating shareholder value, and serving customers. This he refers to as "The Business of Values." Griffiths finds this particularly significant at a time when so many traditional repositories of values, such as the family, churches and schools, have weakened or, in some cases, given up their roles. Thus, he argues, the business firm has an opportunity to become an important carrier of values. This, he asserts, may well be one of the business firm's most important social responsibilities.

He concluded his lecture with two warnings and one reminder for leaders of companies with strong values. "First," he said, "don't allow values to become cultic, with no room for difference or diversity. Second, don't allow values to limit the firm from responding to the changing demands of customers or cause the firm to ignore the dangers of the arrogance of success. And remember," he said, "that leadership is responsible for implementing the values of the firm, an obligation that cannot be delegated."

In his response, Peter Drucker added an intriguing idea. While he agreed that firms with strong values have a better opportunity to win in the marketplace, he said they also would be better able to weather adversity. "For if the right values are absent at such a time," Drucker said, "there is no incentive for human beings to walk the extra mile, to make the extra commitment, to do the hard work of rethinking and rebuilding the firm." Drucker concluded by reminding us that values without actions are nothing more than good intentions. One of the best ways, he said, to determine if the appointed leader will be effective in implementing the right values is to view how he or she makes personnel decisions—hiring and firing, promoting and demoting, praising and punishing, rewarding and compensating. These seemingly routine actions, Drucker insisted, tell volumes about a leader and what he or she really believes.

CORPORATE SOULCRAFT IN THE AGE OF BRUTAL MARKETS

The second lecture, at the Kellogg Graduate School of Management at Northwestern University, proved to be remarkably predictive. Elmer Johnson, a respected attorney and former Executive Vice President of General Motors, spoke during the early exuberant stages of the historic business expansion of the 1990s, when no heights of prosperity seemed out of reach. It was well before the "perfect storm" of corporate scandals crashed upon us wiping out so much, but he clearly saw the dark clouds gathering on a not-so-distant horizon.

On the positive side, Johnson further developed the idea of the business firm as a carrier of values, a theme he had passionately pursued as an executive and director of GM. He affirmed the importance of a firm's role in providing a necessary moral dimension within the free market system and society as a whole. The business firm, he said, should serve as one of society's chief mediating structures and should, like the family, church, and community, stand between the individual and the state. As the firm produces goods and services for profit, he argued, it should also be a moral community that helps shape human character and behavior. To do so, the firm needs a good society within which to function and it is dependent upon truth to survive. He asserted that the central lesson of the Jewish and Christian faiths, as well as classical Greek tradition, is that moral behavior with truth as its core is the key to a good life and a good society. The business firm, he suggested, should be about soul craft and should be judged by the qualities of human character it nurtures and develops. The work of the firm, he said, not only can provide dignity for the individual, but also can teach virtue to the whole community. He noted the encouraging trend among business firms to expand employee participation in decision-making and ownership. In so doing, he said, the organization recognizes the dignity and worth of people at all levels.

Johnson also warned, however, about what he saw as growing market and cultural forces encouraging selfish tendencies. There are, he said, too few effective institutions nurturing people to be "other" oriented. The dangerous trends he saw included excessive executive compensation, lack of governance accountability, and insensitive implementation of corporate restructurings. These actions, he asserted, reflected an overall short-term mindset that fed personal self-interest and greed. "We are at a crossroads in corporate America," he said. "We must rediscover the power of a turned-on community of employees led by a new kind of corporate manager who is motivated much less by money and much more by pride in the products produced and by the joy of unleashing the employees' talents and energies and tapping their potential for personal growth and team cooperation."

He gave specific suggestions for what firms should do to begin the process of building a moral community, including:

1. Refashion economic incentives to encourage a longer-term perspective and an environment of trust and respect for the dignity and worth of people.
2. Exclude from executive positions those who are occupied with their own self-interest and pay plans and instead select those who are not only competent but also have a spiritual inner strength and depth of character.

As he concluded, he asked the penetrating question of how bad must things become before there is a critical mass of leadership with the courage to speak up and begin the process of change and awareness for the development of the firm as a moral community to help shape human character and behavior. I would assert that we have come to that point. Things *have* gotten so bad in corporate leadership that it is time to speak up and provide something more than added rules and regulations. It is time, as Johnson suggested, for us to heed the words of T. S. Eliot in *Choruses from the Rock*, as he says: "What life have you if you have not life together? There is no life that is not in community and no community not lived in praise of God."

Professor Lawrence G. Lavengood, in his response, commended Johnson for raising issues of soul craft, moral purpose, community, and virtue within the context of the function and purpose of the business firm. He acknowledged that too often the principles behind these ideas have not been adequately discussed or considered in the educational process of an MBA student. He shared Johnson's concern for a lack of moral reflection and action.

But he utterly failed to anticipate, presumably out of optimism and hope, the approaching storm. He argued that within the market system competition acts as a check against excessive self-interest, as do the regulatory actions of government as a representative of the public good. Since a well-managed corporation depends on trust for its performance, Lavengood concluded that it has no option but to be a moral community to shape human character and behavior. This role, he suggested, extends to the community outside the walls of the corporation as well as inside. And when there is conflict, the public interest also should always prevail. Since the business firm is made up of people for people, and since all people have a moral dimension, he concluded that the business firm must be managed consistent with this reality or it will fail.

Would that his quite solid analysis had reflected what really was going on in board room after board room. But we now know that many firms did not manage according to a moral dimension, and many did fail.

REFLECTIONS ON SOME PRESERVING PRINCIPLES OF CAPITALISM IN A DEMOCRACY

The third lecture was given before faculty and students of the Harvard Business School and the Harvard Divinity School by Max De Pree, former Chairman and CEO of Herman Miller and author of several books on management and leadership including the bestseller *Leadership Is an Art*. He reflected on what he called the preserving principles of capitalism in a democracy, which he defined as hope, common good, moral purpose, education, accountability, and hospitality.

Hope, he said, is a cardinal virtue—an important ingredient of well-being and necessary for a vision of the future. In a free-market system, hope derives from a feeling of acceptance as an authentic and legitimate person in the community and from having equitable access to things like health, education, and a good job.

In a healthy democracy and a growing market, the extent of individual liberties, exercise of self-interest, and enactment of laws must all be measured in terms of the common good. In developing this point, De Pree pointed out that there "may be no smaller packages in this world than people wrapped up in themselves."

Moral purpose in our lives and in the life of an organization, he suggested, is like the fire that was kept burning in every church and monastery in Celtic Britain and Ireland as a sign of God's presence. Moral purpose provides the basis for human development and action that looks beyond self-interest and promotes diversity, creativity, and trust. It allows leaders to make themselves vulnerable, to deal equitably with systems for distributing the results of the firm, and to exercise prudence and self-restraint. For De Pree, these are the signs of God's presence at work in the business firm.

In discussing the importance of education as a preserving principle, De Pree cited Toqueville's conclusion: "In the United States, the instruction of the people powerfully contributes to the support of the democratic republic, where the instruction which enlightens the understanding is not separated from the moral education which amends the heart." But De Pree questioned whether moral education was still part of American public education, suggesting that the current system would benefit from becoming part of the free market. He asserted that the monopolistic forces in public education may well be a deterrent to quality education as well as moral enlightenment.

Leadership, he said, often amounts to serious meddling in the lives of people. So leaders must be accountable for their direction or misdirection. They must, he concluded, stand alone, take the heat, bear the pain, tell the truth, and do what is right.

Hospitality, his final preserving principle, is the essence of what we can give to others. What can democratic capitalism give to people? Freedom? Opportunity? Acceptance? Trust? Yes, all of these. Inhospitable cultures or organizations are afraid of these concepts. Capitalism, he pointed out, can be both hospitable and inhospitable, especially as it works through the role of competition or lack thereof. Leaders can encourage or discourage hospitality. As they learn to be hospitable, to give and serve those they lead, they open up the organization to new and different people and new and more creative ideas. In so doing, they also are better able to understand and assume the responsibility for reconciliation when differences or disagreement occurs.

Said De Pree: "Our greatest challenge in the end will be to *do* what we say and believe in. Or as Marion Wade, the founder of ServiceMaster, used to say: 'If you don't live it, you don't believe it.'"

Professor Lynn Sharp Paine of the Harvard Business School commended De Pree for reminding us that democratic capitalism is not solely an economic enterprise but is also a moral enterprise and that ethical principles are as essential to its effective functioning as economic principles. However, she argued that enlarging the space for ethics within democratic capitalism is easier said than done. There is a tendency, she suggested, to see economics and ethics, money and morals as antagonists occupying separate and more or less self-contained realms. Such bifurcation, she emphasized, is not helpful or constructive in responding to the issues of today. For better or for worse, we live in a world where ethics and economics are intertwined at every juncture and business leaders, as well as philosophers, theologians, and ethicists, should be encouraged to develop more leaders who, in her terms, are multilogical—leaders who are comfortable in the realms of ethics as well as economics and can inject the question of what is right and wrong into the strategies and tactics of a business or any organizational behavior. We must, she suggested, develop more leaders who can speak with conviction in both ethical and economic terms and only then will we realize the full potential of democratic capitalism.

THE INTERNATIONAL VOCATION OF
AMERICAN BUSINESS

The fourth lecture was held at Notre Dame University and was given by Michael Novak, a prolific writer, theologian, former U. S. Ambassador and the Chair in Religion and Public Policy at the American Enterprise Institute. As he began the lecture, Novak not only affirmed the principles discussed in previous lectures, but also asserted that business should be seen as a calling — a noble vocation propelled by moral ideals without which democratic capitalism could not endure. He suggested, however, that many nations and cultures still find it difficult to root themselves in capitalism, democracy, and moral purposes. What then, he asked, is the proper conduct for American business with respect to such countries? What is the *international* calling of American business? Can the U. S. business firm have a "constructive engagement" that will help to expand the principles of democratic capitalism and moral ideals? His backdrop for a response to these questions was a fictional case study of a U. S. technology company working in a country that was still operating under a totalitarian political system but at the same time was seeking economic growth by being more open in the areas of commerce and market systems.

The political processes were infected with corruption and imposed restrictions on foreign firms that required them to use certain suppliers and make payments to officials. They were also required to expose all national employees to political indoctrination, and limit reference or expression to any religious or faith principles in the workplace. As he further developed his response to the ethical and moral issues represented in the case study, Novak reminded us of two basic ambiguities or tensions of life related to human behavior in commerce. First, business, as a moral occupation, is practiced by people who are capable of both moral and immoral acts. Second, while the promotion of commerce is essential to the prosperity and well-being of a culture, the preoccupation with commerce and with the physical pleasures it can bring can dry out the moral soul of the person. The cistern will crack, he suggested, and there will be no living water.

Because of this, he issued a stern warning to American business, in an imperative tone as if he were speaking directly to each American CEO doing business abroad. "Be careful as you proceed in your constructive engagement or international vocation. Know your own moral identity and purpose and train your people in the reason and rationale for your moral ideals (as we have recently learned, also a very good idea when doing business at home). Don't sell yourself short. Be prepared to negotiate for the preservation of your values so that you can truly serve as a wedge or avant garde for the development of a more healthy civil and moral society. Finally, and perhaps most importantly, be prepared to say no to what may look like a good economic opportunity in a country that is not prepared to engage and consider change."

As leaders in the world economy, Novak said, American business firms must fulfill their responsibility to be carriers of moral values and principles of a free society. As such, they can truly be agents for change with commercial integrity, providing human opportunity, generating economic growth, being a catalyst for new and better pathways for the poor, and encouraging the development of character and moral behavior. If they fail in so doing, he suggested that they risk the possibility of becoming nothing more than bought and paid-for economic prostitutes serving the interests of foreign tyranny. In conclusion, he reminded us that business leadership today should be a highly moral profession. The bad news is that one can fail; the good news is that one can succeed. This, he suggested, is the drama of life.

Nathan Hatch, former Provost of Notre Dame, provided a thoughtful response by suggesting that the potential for morality or immorality in business, or in any profession, may not be so much dependent upon the nature of the activity, but rather more related to the complicated and often contradictory actions of human behavior. As an example, he pointed to John D. Rockefeller, whom he described as "a complicated enigma of devout principle and scheming manipulation."

The danger, he suggested, is for one to get off course because of lack of a moral compass that transcends a business or other professional activity.

He asked whether our society has ample wellsprings of training or encouragement for the restraint of self-interest and the monitoring of actions for the common good. Do we fully understand the unintended consequences of size in our global companies or the growing trend of the work function becoming a free agency instead of being part of a community that encourages loyalty and trust? He warned of the ever-present danger that our good words about moral purpose or direction may become nothing more than rhetorical veneer. The challenge of providing moral leadership in business, he suggested, may be more straight and narrow than Novak conceives and fewer there will be that find it.

THE ROLE OF THE BUSINESS CORPORATION
AS A MORAL COMMUNITY

For the fifth lecture, we moved overseas to Oxford University to consider anew the source of moral behavior by the business firm, but this time in a decidedly global context, with added emphasis on the role of government in supporting or mandating such behavior. Once again, Brian Griffiths provided the lead lecture, with an added view and response from Ram Gidoomal, Chairman of the South Asian Development Partnership.

In this lecture, Lord Griffiths considered the question of a source for the moral standards of a business firm within the context of a global market that is becoming more secular and pluralistic. While recognizing that a business firm could operate within the law but have little or no concern for seeking to adhere to a higher moral principle, he concluded that such an environment would become cold, bleak, and insecure. Self-interest would prevail; truth would be compromised; and there would be little or no development of trust, loyalty, or concern for the interests of others.

Inevitably, he suggested, the competition of a free market would penalize such a firm because its cost of operation would be higher and the quality of the product or service it produced would be lower. So, if the adherence to and practice of moral standards enhances the effectiveness and value of a firm, to where does it turn for such a standard? Is the "self-interest" of the market all that is needed? Will the business firm encourage honesty, civility, integrity, quality, fairness, and truth because it will be more competitive and create greater value for its owners if it does so? Is the bottom line or the competition of a free market a sufficient source?

No, said Griffiths, because there is a difference between one who thinks honesty is the best policy and one who is honest. "The crooked timber of humanity in which self-interest resides," said Griffiths, invoking Immanuel Kant's famous phrase, "is too insecure a foundation on which to build lasting moral standards." If the firm and its leadership recognize certain moral standards only when it is economically expedient to do so, there would be a lack of integrity at the heart of the management. That, in turn, would encourage the abandonment of such standards of honesty or fairness when no one is looking or when there is a perception or conclusion that it would be economically advantageous to do so. Such a double standard would be destructive for the people of the firm, he suggested, as well as for the public good and social order.

Griffiths then pointed out that some have suggested that a global ethic or a moral standard be concocted that incorporates the views of all the world's religions and ethical traditions. He noted that there have been several attempts within a business context that would emphasize responsibility to the stakeholder and the basic values of human dignity, truth, fairness, mutual respect, service, and a sense of moderation and honesty. The strength of such an approach, he suggested, is that it accepts pluralism and secularism. The weakness is one of personal motivation and the lack of a conviction of faith or belief. A global ethic can become the lowest common denominator of values between the religious and non-religious. In his view, it can never provide a motivating force such as an individual's commitment an all-powerful but all-loving God.

So then, is the answer for an ultimate source for moral authority to be found in a revealed monotheistic religion such as Judaism, Islam or Christianity? In response, Griffiths reminded us that the Judeo-Christian heritage has been an important influence on the morality of business conduct, especially in Britain and America. Although the force of secularism and post-modern thought may have dampened the influence, it still remains strong in public life. He also suggested that while there may be more than one answer to the question of where the firm secures its moral authority and standards, those standards, to be meaningful, must be concrete, robust, and able to stand the test of time. They must both encourage good behavior and sanction bad behavior. He concluded that any religion in which business is seen as a calling or vocation, with a career in business viewed as a life of service before God, is the most powerful source from which to establish and derive absolute moral standards in the life of the business firm. For him, the Christian faith provides such a source.

He cautioned, however, that for moral standards to be effective, they must be implemented. They must be accepted by those who work for the firm. People must own the standards and they must see them in the reality of the way leaders live and make decisions. They must become "habits" of the firm and are often tested in the way leaders make decisions about people. Lord Griffiths concluded his lecture by recognizing that the concept of the corporation as a moral community is only one facet of business life and, unfortunately, is rarely high on the agenda. But he asserted again that such a concept, if managed properly, can bring significant benefits to the firm, its employees, owners, and customers.

Ram Gidoomal tackled the difficult issue of the role of government in encouraging ethical and moral behavior of business. He noted that more often than not, the most effective way for government to act is by the use of what he referred to as non-legislative levers, incentives and benefits for right behavior, rather than a list of do's and don'ts resulting in a legalism that encourages "the least compliance you can get away with." He recognized, however, that government can work to create a level playing field on which both small and large business firms can compete. And government can be effective in assuring a good working environment and promoting equal opportunities for all workers, including minorities.

There also is a role for government to play as part of the globalization of markets that includes support of economic initiatives for developing countries and care for the environment.

But morality, he suggested, is more than the law. While the law may seek to define some of the rights and wrongs in running a business, morality and ethics define what right and wrong mean. For government to be effective in encouraging right behavior, it must legislate under the authority of a "higher law." Although Gidoomal described himself as a Hindu follower of Christ, he did not suggest government should look for a "higher law" based exclusively upon Christianity. It must have a broader framework, he suggested, because of the make-up of the societies being governed.

As he concluded, Gidoomal noted, however, that the growing lack of a Judeo-Christian heritage as a distinctive in many democracies will eventually lead to more multi-cultural societies with a narrowing range of agreement on core values. In his judgment, this will result in a growing limitation of governmental influence on the moral standards of a business. Thus, defining the role of government in supporting and promoting moral standards will become more and more challenging in the future.

THE NATURE OF THE EXERCISE OF AUTHORITY

The sixth lecture was back in the United States at Yale University and was given by David Young, the founder and president of Oxford Analytica, a global information and consulting firm in Oxford, England. Young was a special assistant to President Nixon during the Watergate years.

In addressing the ethical framework for a leader in government or in business, Young spoke to the reality of the battle between the forces of good and evil in the use of power. In particular, he drew on his experience in the White House during a time when there was not only the use of power but also the abuse of power. While his remarks primarily focused on political leadership, he stressed that the issues and principles apply equally to business. He characterized the conflict that is inherent in the exercise of power as a spiritual battle that tests the character and beliefs and exposes the vulnerability of a leader. He called it the non-rational side of the exercise of power that is seldom talked about and doesn't fit within the often-confident self-image portrayed by a leader.

As he reflected on his White House years in the Nixon administration, especially during the period leading up to Watergate, Young discussed the tension between the exercise of power and corruption. The potential for corruption, he suggested, is more than dishonest dealing. It can result in the leader losing his or her way, divorced from reality and behaving in a way that he or she would not want the public or followers to know about. If this occurs, there is a resort to secrecy and the control and misuse of information, which creates an atmosphere of intrigue, often resulting in the use of people as scapegoats. The end result is an absence of truth and trust. When the forces of evil take over, lies are not just used to protect the public good, but instead to maintain the power and protect the image of the leader.

Young cited both Nietsche and the Apostle Paul to buttress his contention that the exercise of power involves spiritual warfare. Young, like the Apostle Paul, would conclude that the power and presence of God as a source of strength and direction is needed to overcome evil and maintain a moral compass and direction. In commenting on the application of his thesis to business, Young recognized, as I did in my book *The Soul of the Firm*, that power in business is suspect. He suggested that business leaders are subject to the same demands and temptations faced by politicians, including the use and control of information and the practice of the art of financial reporting to protect and preserve the status and power of the business leader at the expense of the employees and shareholders.

In the end, Young concluded that it is the character of the leader that will make the difference—a character that will not only withstand the forces of evil, but also those conflicting desires to put the preservation of power and self-interest ahead of the interest of others. This type of character, he suggested, is shaped not only by the physical and rational dimensions of one's humanity, but also by the spiritual dimension. It requires the acknowledgement of both the mystery and authority of God as a power beyond ourselves.

In his response, Professor Donald Gibson of the Yale School of Management also recognized the importance of human spirituality in understanding effective leadership and the exercise of power. He pointed out that while many authorities on management would prefer to ignore or leave at home the messy spiritual side of people, there is a growing interest in seeking to understand the role of spirituality in the corporate environment. Gibson concluded by suggesting that this renewed interest in spirituality should be used by business leaders to encourage a renewal in corporate America for the development of communities based on trust and commitment to extend beyond self-interest.

Thomas Ogletree, a professor of theological ethics at Yale Divinity School, suggested in his response that we consider moving beyond the discussion of spiritual warfare to consider how leaders can practically encourage core moral themes and attributes, such as truth-telling, integrity, and right behavior. He recognized that when leaders devote themselves to moral practices, there will be spiritual battles and that evil and corruption will always be present for us. This, he suggested, should not dissuade our involvement in promoting moral attributes in business leadership and our commitment to integrity and right behavior.

Miroslav Volf, the Henry B. Wright Professor of Divinity at Yale Divinity School, commended Young for raising the spiritual dimension in considering how power is exercised. He cited two very different revolutionary leaders—Martin Luther and Nelson Mandela—to emphasize the importance of not only the spiritual character of a leader, but also the moral vision of a leader—a vision that should include the development, enhancement, and welfare of the community as a whole.

THE INTEGRATION OF FAITH IN THE WORKPLACE

In the seventh lecture, held at the University of Southern California, Donald Soderquist, retired Vice Chairman and Chief Operating Officer of Wal-Mart, called upon business leaders who are people of faith to boldly integrate that faith in their work. At the same time, he encouraged the entire business community to make room for God in consideration of the matter of ethical conduct in business. He defined character as the real you—the person behind the mask; ethics as the things you do, especially in the way you treat people; values as characteristics that are desirable because they are intrinsically good; and faith as a set of beliefs rooted in a solid foundation. As he reviewed the landscape of ethical conduct over the past 15 years, including surveys reflecting the attitudes of young people, he saw a growing ambiguity in the definition of right and wrong. He asserted that as the idea of absolutes has been largely rejected, historical standards are ignored, and there is a lack in the development and teaching of character. Perhaps his most important point was that moral values have to be rediscovered over time to be vital and meaningful in a society. This rediscovery process, he concluded, begins with leadership—ethical leadership that places a high value on integrity, honesty, promise-keeping, fairness, respect for the dignity and worth of people, excellence, and truth.

When Don Soderquist joined Wal-Mart more than twenty years ago, the retail company had $1.25 billion in annual sales. When he retired as vice chairman, the annual sales volume was over $190 billion and Wal-Mart was reaching to become the largest company in the world. As he looked back upon those years of remarkable growth, he concluded that the most important part of Wal-Mart's success was the company's ethical conduct and sound set of core values based upon Judeo-Christian principles. Wal-Mart had established a culture of trust among a work force of 1.2 million people and a loyalty among its customer base that resulted in a consistent pattern of repeat purchasing, which on average resulted in a 90 percent market penetration per store.

Like every organization made up of people, Wal-Mart is not perfect and has had its share of mistakes. At times, associates or officers have done the wrong thing. However, because of its focus on the dignity and worth of people and a passion to satisfy the needs of customers, Wal-Mart has been able to accomplish what no other company has been able to do and what some said was impossible.

In executing their business strategy, the leaders of the company have sought to keep the focus on the value and the worth of people, and in so doing, have developed a continuing process within the company of rediscovering the core values of integrity, honesty, truth, trustworthiness, fairness, excellence, keeping promises and respecting individuals. Though Wal-Mart's core values reflect Judeo-Christian principles, Soderquist acknowledged that talking about God in the workplace, even at Wal-Mart, makes people nervous. "You can talk about values and ethics, but just don't talk about God," he said. But for Soderquist, the role of God and one's faith is an integral part of understanding and applying ethical standards. Because of his faith as a Christian, God and His Word are the most important source and foundation for his ethical standards and the practice of right behavior. Though he made clear in his lecture that he felt strongly that it was not his role as a business leader to impose his faith on anyone, he felt equally strongly that he did have an obligation to explain how his faith governed his actions and provided a moral compass and source of direction. For Soderquist, that meant recognizing the reality of a loving God, the dignity and worth of people created in his image, the importance of living an honorable and productive life and defending truth at all cost. For him, faith is not only a religious belief, but is also a way of life, a source of strength of direction for leading, nurturing, and caring for people.

In responding, Warren Bennis, noted author and authority on leadership and professor at the University of Southern California, applauded the example of ethical cultures created by both Wal-Mart and ServiceMaster. While he was not as pessimistic as Soderquist about the condition of deteriorating values, especially among young people, Bennis did recognize the need for a stronger emphasis on the role of meaning and values in leadership and in work and the importance of a moral compass for a leader. But most of his response consisted of three questions for Soderquist: First, since we are all made of warped wood, born in sin, how do you imbed ethical principles into a company the size of Wal-Mart; how do you create such a culture where people not only believe but act upon such ethical principles?

Bennis's second question related to the integration of faith and work. Since religious faiths can be exclusive in their application and since the world is becoming increasing pluralistic, how can you implement a Judeo-Christian ethic and be inclusive?

His third question related to the growth of Wal-Mart and the criticism by some that it has brought about an eclipse of local communities by eliminating small Ma and Pa stores.

Soderquist responded to the first question by emphasizing the importance of the beliefs and actions of leaders in setting an example of right behavior for people to follow, getting out and about to understand and relate to the people on the front line who are serving the customer, and making the tough decisions that have to be made when the standards are violated. He addressed the inclusiveness by pointing out that his message of integration was not to promote a faith or to exclude those of a different faith, but instead to raise the fundamental question of a source or authority for ethical behavior and for the common core values of an organization, as well as to provide an understanding of the basis of agreement and alignment among different people with different faiths.

In response to Bennis's third question, Soderquist noted the forces of a free market and also noted that Wal-Mart does better in a community when small businesses survive. They typically provide a specialty function that Wal-Mart does not do well, and in the process, attract more customers to the community to do their shopping.

BUSINESS ETHICS IN SKEPTICAL TIMES

The eighth and final lecture was by former Secretary of State James Baker at the University of Michigan Business School. The lecture was given during the spring of 2002 when the financial scandals at Enron, Tyco, World-Com, and others had been front-page news for months. There was reason for people to be skeptical and to distrust business and business leaders. For Baker, it was a time to study and learn from what had occurred. As a corporate director of several companies, Baker's primary focus related to the ethical conduct and responsibility of those in governance and in leadership. First of all, he suggested that with respect to business, we should always be skeptical. "Healthy skepticism is an essential element of both a sound market economy and a mature ethical perspective," he said. The free market and the businesses that operate within it need the checks and balances of the rule of law or what he referred to as institutionalized skepticism, as well as the prudent skepticism of shareholders and board members. We live, he suggested, in an imperfect world. People will fail. The market and business can be fertile ground for the growth and development of excessive greed and self-interest. It is all part of being human.

But as Baker also pointed out, one of the geniuses of the free-market system is to provide a competitive check and balance and, on a collective basis, turn the forces of greed (with the help of what Adam Smith referred to as that invisible hand) into a benefit for society as a whole. Although the free market system, like democracy, is not perfect, Baker suggested that it has self-correcting forces within it. He wants to move carefully in seeking to avoid another Enron. Baker believes, as I do, that we should resist adopting rules and reforms that are inconsistent or that weaken our economic system and structure. Here he drew on his political and governmental experience, post-Watergate, and commented on the unrealistic and deeply flawed laws relating to campaign financing and the establishment of the office of independent prosecutors.

He suggested that if in our response to the current failures, we move too far in the direction of new rules, regulations, requirements, and more process, we will, so burden our economy and business units that the result will be more harm than benefit. For my part, I also worry that leaders will grow timid and overly cautious, and avoid bold entrepreneurial actions that have been an important part of the success of our system. For Baker, reform should be directed at strengthening the self-correcting mechanisms of the market and to support and not weaken what he called the inherent ethical nature within the system itself. In that case, one could ask Baker what, if anything, we can learn from current events? What should be our focus for change of individual and corporate conduct to avoid or limit the virus that infected the Enrons of the world? It starts, he suggested, with a focus on representing the interest of shareholders and requiring true independence, competence, and integrity from board members. This independence should not be simply measured by a lack of "other relationships" with the company, but instead by the character and integrity of the director and his or her willingness to cross or disagree with management when necessary—to tell it like it is.

It will also require, in Baker's judgment, a complete review of executive compensation, including the use of and accounting for stock options. In his view, accounting standards should also be reviewed. Some of the accounting rules, he suggested, are so esoteric and difficult to understand and apply that they encourage multiple interpretations and confusion, often generating technical responses that fail to provide meaningful disclosure or reporting of the substantive results of the company with the inevitable result of a hidden surprise and a loss of credibility.

As Baker ended his remarks, he opened up the floor for questions from students, faculty and others who were in attendance. This open forum was ended with this question from a faculty member who taught ethics at the University of Michigan Business School. "Secretary Baker, what was your source of strength and courage to be able to cross or confront the boss or the authority system when you knew that what was being proposed was wrong or was against your moral or ethical standards?" In response, Baker reflected on the importance of his family upbringing and his Christian faith and conviction which, for him, provided both a compass for direction and a courage to stand up for what was right.

Claremont

GRADUATE UNIVERSITY

CHAPTER ONE

THE BUSINESS OF VALUES

By Lord Griffiths of Fforestfach

Brian Griffiths was Economic Advisor to British Prime Minister Margaret Thatcher. He subsequently became Lord Griffiths. He has served on numerous corporate boards and as an international advisor to Goldman Sachs in London. He also has been a professor at the London School of Economics, Dean of the City University Business School and a director of the Bank of England. His published works on ethics include the book Morality in the Market Place. *This lecture was given at the Peter F. Drucker Graduate Management School at Claremont College in California.*

THE BUSINESS OF VALUES

What I call the business of values implies a conscious decision by the senior managers of a company to create an ethos based on clearly defined core values. These then become the standard for everything done in the company. This should not be confused with an earlier debate on the social aspects of business, which dealt with the responsibility of a company to the community and the environment, typically in such matters as charitable giving, job creation, environmental protection and so on. Neither should it be confused with business ethics, which involves moral judgments and the standards of behavior expected in business, especially in connection with export contracts. The business of values includes both of these, but it is a much larger subject and in particular is directly relevant to the day-to-day running of a company.

This subject is important for a number of reasons. It is one that the early leaders of the ServiceMaster company wrestled with a great deal. Out of that came two intriguing legacies: the double-entendre in the name ServiceMaster (being very good at providing services to customers and serving a higher Master, God), and the four objectives of the company—*to honor God in all we do, to help people develop, to pursue excellence and to grow profitably.*

It is also an issue that interests me personally. My experience as a non-executive director of a number of companies and as an adviser to various organizations convinces me that the ethos that management develops permeates all aspects of business—the style of leadership; the governance of the company; issues of incentives, compensation and stock ownership; accounting policy and the work of the audit committee; and what is right and what is wrong in terms of ethics.

Furthermore, I have long been intrigued by the fact that many of the major companies in Britain in the twentieth century—household names such as Cadburys, Unilever, Barclays, Wedgewood—started with a strong ethos based on religious faith; and that many major companies today in Japan, Korea and other parts of Asia, also have a strong ethos emanating from the traditional religions and philosophies of their countries.

Beyond that, the subject of values has become an important issue facing business today. Only a few decades ago, the major framework for management thinking was based on a scientific world view. It emphasized rationality, numbers, planning, optimization and management science. Structure, systems, and the performance of the key operating ratios became the day-to-day focus. During the last two decades, however, a new emphasis has emerged concerning the shared values of companies, corporate cultures, belief systems, the creation of meaning in work, the potential of leadership and the moral purpose of the organization. It is no longer possible to use the language of logical positivism to separate the world of facts from the world of values; to place facts, finance, technology, and scientific management firmly in one category, and the lives of people in terms of values, service and meaning equally firmly in another. Facts cannot be separated from values in this way. The ethos of a company has been discovered to be integral to the day-to-day running of a business itself.

I recognize, of course, that there is still a general reluctance to talk about values in business. Values are seen as intensely personal. Issues of values are perceived to be much more difficult to deal with than issues such as marketing, finance, production, systems or planning. Raising issues of values can often be seen as confrontational, disruptive and simplistic. Even when managers do discuss moral issues, these issues are frequently couched in terms of organizational goals and the bottom line. However, if values matter, then they deserve serious attention, regardless of how awkward the discussion may feel to some. In the final analysis, of course, the choice of values is a personal matter. But so are the choices of career, relationships and pension plans. Because a choice is personal does not mean that it cannot be discussed objectively. All of us, consciously or unconsciously, approach the issue of values with a viewpoint. But that is not the same as saying that we come with closed minds, unable to discuss the issues, or are not prepared to change our point of view on the basis of a good argument. The world of business is an open marketplace and the world in which business values are discussed should be just as open. It should be a forum of debate whose symbol is not the pulpit but the agora of ancient Greece.

WHY VALUES MATTER TO BUSINESS RIGHT NOW

The matter of values has been placed on the agenda facing business for a number of reasons. In the first place, values are perceived to affect the performance of companies, with different values producing different outcomes. The 1970s were a traumatic time for American business because of the success of Japanese companies in penetrating the U.S. market. When American business leaders analyzed the most successful U.S. companies, they found that while such traditional factors as structure and strategy were important, the most critical factor turned out to be the concept of shared values based on honesty, trust and employee satisfaction. As financial institutions over recent years have shown, honesty pays while dishonesty saps the vitality of the institution. If people in a company trust each other, then cooperation and teamwork become easier and the cost of doing business less. The Toyota system of lean manufacturing is possible only because of the high degree of trust among its employees. If service workers have a sense of dignity and fulfillment, customers will be better served. Two of the key costs of running a service business— turnover of staff and of customers—will go down. But shared values are more than this: they are the ethos of the company, its soul.

Subsequent research by James Heskett and John Kotter of Harvard Business School confirmed the importance of shared values and corporate culture in explaining business performance. More recently, a major five-year study of 20 large and successful European, Japanese and U.S. companies, including ABB, 3M, Canon, and Corning, concluded that the key to success for each of them was a fundamental change in the philosophy of top management. Instead of relying on the old model of strategy and control, senior managers spelled out the direction of the organization in fairly broad terms, made sure every employee was committed to it, then lessened top-down controls in favor of a more entrepreneurial culture. The companies invested in people and gave them more responsibility. By contrast, the study found that companies such as General Motors, IBM, Phillips,

Daimler-Benz, Matsushita and Hitachi, which did not follow the new model, ran into problems. All of this evidence confirms that when certain values are at the heart of a company's ethos, that company will have a significant competitive advantage.

LEADERS MUST BECOME TRUSTEES OF VALUES

Secondly, it has also become clear that if values are to raise performance, then leadership must articulate those values. Leadership is about vision, inspiration, and quality. It is about defining the nature of the business and accepting fiduciary responsibility. Leaders are the trustees for the values of the company. They establish the values, communicate the values and then take ownership of the values. The ethos of a company is defined and given substance by the example of its leaders, who have responsibility for passing on those values to the next generation. In this process, leaders must face up to their own values. Max De Pree, former Chairman and CEO of Herman Miller who has written extensively on leadership, says that an inescapable implication of fiduciary leadership is the enunciation of a clear moral purpose for the organization. For him, this includes a commitment to truth, acceptance of human authenticity, a sense of justice, and a vulnerability to followers. This theme is emphasized constantly by nearly all who write on this subject. James MacGregor Burns, one of the most prolific scholars in this area, stresses that the most powerful form of leadership is what he calls "transforming leadership." He argues that it raises both leaders and followers to a higher level of motivation, enabling them to fuse their interests in the pursuit of a common purpose. Writes Burns: "Transforming leadership ultimately becomes moral in that it raises the level of human conduct and ethical aspiration of both the leader and the led, and thus has a transforming effect on both."

Arguably, the highest form of leadership is servant leadership, which has been stressed by a number of writers in the United States. Heskett and Kotter conclude their analysis of corporate culture by emphasizing the importance of leadership, but they then state that unless leaders have the hearts of servants, there is a potential for tyranny. The same theme emerges strongly in Sam Walton's autobiography. He stresses no less than three times that servant leadership was the ideal he sought in running his business. Leadership cannot be separated from the needs and concerns of the followers. A major reason leadership needs to concern itself with the values and moral purpose of the organization arises from the demands and expectations of the people who work in the organization. A concern with values is a vital part of what it means to be human; people work for a cause and seek meaning in their work. People prefer to work in a company that is honest, fair and transparent. Because of concerns such as these, members of a company expect their leaders to be clear about their values.

VALUES IN A TIME OF RAPID UNSETTLING CHANGE

Third, values in business have become an important issue with the emergence of the post-capitalist, or post-industrial, society. Over recent decades, it has become clear that a fundamental restructuring is taking place in the world of business: the shift from manufacturing to services; the extraordinarily rapid pace of technological change; the information revolution; the growth of self-employment and part-time employment; the emergence of knowledge as a key resource; the replacement of the divide between worker and capitalist with that of knowledge worker and service worker; the "delayering" of middle management because of the application of information technology; the outsourcing of functions; and the emergence of the responsibility-based organization.

With increasing affluence, greater freedom and less dependence on traditional institutions, especially religious institutions, our society has become highly individualistic. Never has there been so much choice, not just of products and services but of where to work, when to work, what lifestyle to adopt and what kinds of relationships to make. This new individualism could produce a very unattractive society that elevates selfishness over responsibility. Charles Handy, one of the most thoughtful writers on the meaning of work, goes so far as to claim that these new freedoms will survive only if people take time to look over their shoulders and care for others beyond themselves, their families and their companies. "Proper selfishness is rooted in unselfishness," he writes, "we need a new religion to save us or at least a new fashion." He concludes: "Fraternity—the care for others as much as for oneself—must be our guiding ethic. It is a core value and it is established by the example of the people at the core, by the new elite, the fortunate ones."

An individualistic society carries the inherent threat of a fractured society. The new elite—the technocracy—is far from united. The different specializations of managers, intellectuals, scientists and professionals create fault lines in our society not only among them but also with the service workers who, though greater in number, lack the human capital of the 'knowledge' class. Modern societies therefore require a unifying force capable of binding the diverse values and beliefs of individuals into a pattern of common commitment.

One such unifying force is trust. But trust depends on people's ability to work together for common goals in groups and organizations, which in turn depends on shared norms and values within a group and the ability to put other interests before one's own. In his recent book on trust, Francis Fukuyama puts it this way: "Trust is the expectation that arises within a community of regular, honest and co-operative behavior, based on commonly shared norms with other members of that community." When we examine the roots of high-trust cultures, we find that they include religion, tradition and historical habit, or what Nietzsche called a people's "language of good and evil."

The emergence of the post-industrial society has occurred at the same time as a decline in religion. Although the age of faith is judged to have ended in the eighteenth century, faith reinforced by religious revivals has cast a long shadow across the Age of Reason. It is only in the last decade or two that large numbers of people have openly rejected the virtues of the Age of Faith—honor for its own sake, a commitment to service, the work ethic, the movement of self-help, self-restraint and so on—and embraced without apology a relativist moral code and philosophy.

Although Fukuyama, after analyzing trust as a foundation for society, does not attempt to promote religion in public life, he does quote approvingly the American historian William McNeil, who argues that perhaps moral communities of fellow believers are necessary for the social well-being of the contemporary, post-industrial society. The alternative could well be the growth of an elite technocracy without any transcendent ethic or rooted moral belief system to guide it and which as a result could easily become tyrannical. Whatever the future, the emergence of a post-industrial society coupled with the decline of religion will mean that the demands made on business to deliver what was formerly provided by other institutions will be a major new development.

IN SEARCH OF VALUES THAT REALLY WORK

Though values matter to business, are some values better than others? And on what basis can we make that decision? How, in practice, can we develop a strong sense of corporate values yet at the same time preserve the identity of the individual? How do business leaders as a practical matter articulate a moral purpose within the company, with its implication of truth and justice? How do they encourage servant leadership? Is a concern for others as much as for oneself a feasible ideal in a company?

I believe these questions boil down to three that must be answered.

- Are values subjective, varying from company to company and reflecting nothing more than the emotions and preferences of those choosing them, or do they reflect some objective reality about the way the world is and works?
- Are values relative, depending on the situation in which the company finds itself, without any foundation of right and wrong, or are there certain reference points on which these values are based?
- Are values merely utilitarian, chosen simply to raise productivity and performance, or do they embody human ideals believed in for their own sake, which most if not all, will find fulfilling.

These questions are so crucial because in most writing on this subject, a great deal is said about the importance of values, yet very little is said about the values themselves. One is left with the feeling that the whole area of values is a minefield through which writers and commentators pick their way with consummate skill hoping to avoid leaving any impression of affirming some values and rejecting others, or worse still of imposing certain of their own convictions on other people.

The area is in fact a minefield; and the mines were laid by some of the great names of the nineteenth and twentieth centuries, such as Darwin, Marx, Freud and Sartre. The reason the minefield exists is that since the late nineteenth century, a new world view has emerged in the West associated with the growth of science. As the scientific method has been extended from explaining the physical world to explaining the way human beings behave, starting with biologists and sociobiologists, psychoanalysts, and more recently neurophysiologists and geneticists, any basis for objective values, moral absolutes and an obligation to do what is right has been removed. Ultimately, it has to be said that this is a world view that denies the existence of God, the spiritual basis of reality and the lack of any moral purpose in the world.

The consequence of all this is that values have no real basis. For Sartre, they are merely the projections of our own desires on the external world. For Lorenz, they are a set of behavior patterns that inhibit certain behavior, lead to a degree of social cohesion and have been helpful to the survival of the species. For Freud, they are an infantile repressive mechanism. For Marx, they are the epiphenomenal expression of a social and economic structure. The point is simply this: in this post-modern world view, moral values have no objective validity. The only thing we can call truth is the objective scientific description of how the world works and the way human beings behave: any belief in absolutes has no place in this world.

Because of this we have to face up to a thorny issue in the world of business. We know that values are useful. We know that companies that espouse and live certain values are preferred employers, and over time, frequently superior performers. But we also know that in the modern scientific world view, there are no absolutes or reference points in terms of values. Managers therefore face a straightforward choice.

Either they can emphasize values, but recognize deep down that those values are subjective and relative, merely expressions of feelings and therefore without any logical or empirical foundation, or they can argue that values are not arbitrary, that there is a universal moral sense, and that these values make binding obligations on all of us, with the result that a business will be a better business to the extent that it identifies specific values as core to its existence.

If we adopt the first of these views we are really saying that the choice of values in business is no different than choosing one of the United Colors of Benetton or one of the flavors of Haagen-Daz ice cream. You have your own tastes and preferences and I have mine. And there is no way we can say that one is better or worse than the other. I find it difficult to accept this position for a number of reasons. In the first place, there are some businesses toward which there is overwhelming disapproval, even a sense of revulsion. I am thinking of such things as the slave trade, prostitution and drug trafficking. These, however, are the easy ones. Much more difficult are what Warren Buffett, in a report to the shareholders of Salomon soon after he took over the Chairmanship in 1991, defined as "activities that pass legal tests, but that we as citizens would find offensive." He suggested that in contemplating any business act, employees should ask themselves whether they would be willing to see it immediately described by an informed and critical person on the front page of the local newspaper, there to be read by spouse, children and friends. Any person who followed the logic of his or her convictions in arguing that values are purely subjective would not only be unable to speak out against the businesses mentioned above, but also would be a silent spectator in any debate about what is offensive.

Sartre started from just this position in attacking objective moral values. He claimed that intellectually it was not possible to condemn such practices. However, in later life, he came to see that this position was untenable. He recognized that if one put oneself in the position of the other person, it would not, for example, be possible to look a starving child in the face and kick it to death. Of course he would be free to do so. The problem with this position is that it depends on the empathy of the person looking at the starving child. In the early nineteenth century in Britain, the slave trade was not abolished earlier because upper class Englishmen did not empathize with Africans with whom they had no shared experience of life. It required a William Wilberforce, not just on grounds of empathy, but on a belief in the individual, regardless of color or class, to introduce a bill into parliament for eighteen consecutive years before it was finally passed and the slave trade abolished.

But because empathy is limited to personal experience, we cannot do without a belief in moral absolutes. Certainly in my own area of banking, the very titles chosen for books that describe certain aspects of the 1980s—*Barbarians at the Gate, Den of Thieves, Liar's Poker*—suggest that we should not. Second, there is a pragmatic test that should be applied to companies who view values as being subjective. Can such a company survive and make a profit? I have serious doubts that it can. If management concluded that values were irrational but useful, this would soon become obvious to everyone who worked in the company. They would realize immediately that there were double standards. The actions of managers would not match their words. The result would be to create a culture of deep skepticism, even cynicism, leading to an unmotivated workforce and a politicized and divided institution. People would put themselves, not the company, first and in a short time management would need to exercise greater authority and impose stricter controls to prevent drift and stop the process of fragmentation. Shared values that are not believed in for their own sake could well end up creating a worse state of affairs than no emphasis on shared values at all.

Third, the people working in such a company would become demoralized, lacking any idealism or challenge. They would be reduced to automatons. There would be no commitment to any purpose greater than their own survival. People would find no sense of fulfillment in service, in achievement, in excellence and there would be no sense of moral claim, that something needed to be done and that it was their job to do it. Our dignity means we are free and responsible. We can choose right or wrong. When we do the right thing, take the right action, we experience what it is to be a human. When we avoid that choice and refuse to make the decision, we become less than human. People need a goal towards which they work combined with a conviction that what they are doing is intrinsically worthwhile. This would be totally missing in such an institution.

Despite the fact that the philosophy behind subjectivism and relativism is an appeal to human freedom and dignity, I believe its consequences are precisely the opposite. Because of this, it is difficult to see how such a philosophy could be operational in business. I find it interesting in this context that business leaders rarely, if ever, articulate a relativist and subjectivist philosophy. This is left to the protected environment of academia, not the real world. The case against values as subjective and relative is strong. But of course, it is not possible to prove the alternative, namely that values do not have some sort of objective validity. I believe, however, that there are some strong pointers that managers must consider.

WE CAN LEARN FROM THE VALUES
COMPANIES CHOOSE

One piece of evidence is what companies actually do. An examination of the mission statements, corporate objectives and business principles of companies reveals that the values they choose are not arbitrary. A distinct pattern emerges. Time and again companies emphasize some or all of the following:

- A responsibility for profit
- A respect for people and their development
- Service to customers and clients
- Integrity and honesty
- Quality and excellence in products and services

- Trust and teamwork in building the firm as a community
- Responsibility to the communities in which the firm serves
- Concern for the physical environment in which the firm operates

Companies with values such as these do not turn a blind eye if there is a hint of dishonesty or applaud aggressively self-interested behavior. They do not locate a new facility without regard for the environment or sanction the abuse of corporate assets. Successful companies know that their values must be communicated with strength and clarity. Here are some examples:

- "We respect the rights and innate worth of the individual." (United Biscuits)
- "The goal of corporate communication is the truth—well and persuasively told." (Caterpillar Corporation)
- "Integrity and honesty are at the heart of our business. We expect our people to maintain high ethical standards in everything they do, both in their work for the firm and in their personal lives." (Goldman Sachs)
- "We are committed to quality and excellence in all that we do and the way in which we do it." (Herman Miller)

Of course, I realize that we cannot infer the validity of objective values from the values companies choose. These nevertheless are strong statements. The fact that different companies, in different sectors of the economy, in different countries and on different continents all emphasize similar values does suggest that there are certain recognizable universal values which are particularly relevant to business. Or if you wish to express it differently, that there exists a law of nature that describes the way the world is and to which good business, for whatever reason, will conform. As we examine the statements of companies, three themes emerge very strongly: they emphasize respect for the individual, stress the importance of truth, and make clear the responsibilities every employee should accept.

BORROWING FROM C. S. LEWIS:
THE TAO OF VALUES

These are similar themes to those that emerge from an altogether different and most unlikely source, namely The Tao in C. S. Lewis's *The Abolition of Man.* In that book, Lewis observes that whether one examines the great religions of the world, East and West, or writers such as Plato, Aristotle, the Stoics and Cicero, or whether one looks to the Babylonian Hymn to Samos, the laws of Manu or sources from Old Norse, Anglo-Saxon or Ancient Babylonia, all have in common a belief in "the doctrine of objective value, the belief that certain attitudes are really true and others really false, to the kind of thing the universe is and the kind of things we are." He calls it following the ancient Chinese, the Tao, the way the universe is, the law to which we must all conform, the Law of Nature. The Tao is not one among a number of possible value systems, it is the only source of all value judgments. Wrote Lewis: "The human mind has no more power of inventing a new value than of imagining a new primary color, or indeed, of creating a new sun and a new sky for it to move in."

There are, of course, differences of emphasis between the various approaches, as well as differences of defining exactly what is meant. But despite all these difficulties, and recognizing the different periods from which they are taken, and the cultures from which they emerge, they are all in substantial agreement on one point; that there is something in human nature that affirms the objective validity of value judgments in relation to behavior. People seem to know right from wrong, and to recognize fair play when they see it. All of the sources quoted by Lewis condemn murder, theft, bribery, dishonesty, injustice, disrespect from children and dishonor to parents. If we examine the Tao, I believe that it puts forward similar ideas to those we find embodied in the actual value statements of good businesses—respect for individuals, the importance of truth, and the moral obligations that all of us should accept. What we see in the various statements of business principles is a Tao of business values.

THE GREAT THEISTIC RELIGIONS
AS A SOURCE OF VALUES

As a third way of trying to get at these objective values, we could go deeper into three of the sources of the Tao, and look at the relevance of the teaching of the world's great theistic religions, Judaism, Christianity and Islam, which have had such an important influence on the development of business in Europe and America. They are unique in that they all derive from the Abrahamic covenant. Given this link, it is not surprising that they also share common moral, ethical and spiritual values. They start with God as creator of the world, with people made in God's image with the divine mandate to take responsibility for the earth and make it productive. The result is a respect for people and a moral basis for work and wealth creation. They are all revealed religions, with honesty, justice and equity being a part of a revealed law. If we had to summarize the implications of these religions for business, they would fit once again into the three categories we have already developed, namely respect for the individual, the importance of truth and our obligation to others.

So far we have looked at three kinds of evidence pointing to the objective world's three great theistic religions. All suggest that values are not simply subjective and certainly not relative. We now need to look in more depth at the recurring themes on values that emerge from these different sources, namely a respect for the individual, the importance of truth and binding obligations. At first sight, it might seem that these propositions are little different from motherhood and apple pie: sentiments with which everyone agree, and therefore so what? This, however, is to misunderstand their significance. As we examine these in more detail, I hope there will become clear a rational significance.

BEFORE ALL ELSE: RESPECT
FOR THE INDIVIDUAL

First of all, each of these sources has enormous respect for the individual. This starts with a recognition of the whole person, and not some abstract construction. One of the worst legacies economics ever gave management was the idea of "rational economic man," which reduced the behavior of individuals to nothing but material self-interest. Consumers, suppliers and employees, managers and shareholders were concerned with nothing but the least cost, values for money and the best price. It was not that other factors were unimportant. Economics readily affirm the validity of values in business—the shared values of companies, the Tao itself and acknowledge their importance. But because little could be said about non-economic factors, they were simply moved to one side under the rubric of *ceteris paribus* (all else being equal). Not surprisingly, such a one-dimensional view of the person led to a one-dimensional view of the company in which the objective of top managers, the one goal that described their total responsibility, was the maximization of shareholder value. This paradigm, linked to the definition of labor as a factor of production, a sort of inferior machine, has, I believe, done more to discredit the world of business than Karl Marx ever did. And the reason is simple. The idea of rational economic man made people less than human. It simply had no respect for the person.

I believe that most managers today would reject this point of view. They start from the innate dignity of people, who deserve respect for no other reason than that. They recognize that each person regardless of color, race or creed has unique talents and skills and personality. They know that people derive satisfaction from using their abilities and that each person has a unique motivation to do so. They know that employees have ideas of how to do things better. They recognize that compensation is important. But they also know that people will do certain things regardless of compensation, that at times people will sacrifice material reward to honor a commitment. These managers know that people have a sense of vocation about their work, that through their work they want to achieve other goals than making money. People want to excel. They want to be part of a winning team. They want to be accepted within the company. They need to be recognized for work done well. They want to do what is right and be treated fairly. They want to feel proud of their company. They want their job to help give meaning to their lives.

One implication of recognizing the whole person has been stated powerfully by Percy Barnevik, CEO and President of ABB, the European engineering and manufacturing conglomerate: "Our organizations are constructed so that most of our employees are asked to use only 5percent to 10percent of their capacity at work. It is only when the same individuals go home that they can engage the other 90 percent to 95 percent—to run their households, lead a Boy Scout group, or build a summer home. We have to be able to recognize and employ that untapped skill that each individual brings to work every day." The contrast between this view and the traditional view could not be more stark. Consider the famous, perhaps infamous, words of Henry Ford, "Why is it that I always get a whole person when what I really want is a pair of hands?"

Having respect for the individual has a number of clear implications. First is the important matter of compensation. A company that is stingy about basic pay, bonuses and long-term incentives can hardly be said to respect the individual. Sam Walton says that the single best thing he did in building Wal-Mart was not just to share his profits with his associates and treat them as partners, but to encourage them to take a stake in the company by offering stock at a discount and stock for retirement. Next there is the matter of investing in people. The second of the ServiceMaster objectives 'To help people develop' states this commitment very clearly. Peter Drucker, in answering the question "What is the business of ServiceMaster?" replied with his usual insight, "It is the training and developing of people." The company is in the business of delivering services. But these cannot be delivered without trained and motivated people. Hence, the passionate commitment by the firm to make training a top priority. Third, a respect for the individual will ensure that the individual has a voice in the business. Employee dissatisfaction is typically about relationships with immediate superiors. Respect for individuals will mean that line managers develop an early warning system to detect problems and then solve them. Empowering people in this way also turns out to have a very important consequence: such people are a crucial resource in terms of suggestions for improving quality. Finally, a respect for the individual will mean the company recognizes that it does not own the person. Individuals must continue to retain their independence, although committed to the company. Having respect for the individual in this way has important practical implications because the individual turns out to be a vital link in the profit chain of service companies. The driver of profitability and growth in the service sector is customer loyalty. This in turn comes from satisfied customers perceiving that the value they receive relative to the total cost of the service exceeds their expectations. This is so whether the service provided is cleaning floors, ticketing for airlines or financial brokerage. This value is created by productive, loyal and satisfied line service workers. In their analysis of the service profit chain, James Heskett and his associates of the Harvard Business School claim that this is the result of the internal quality of the working environment, which they define as the feelings that employees have towards their jobs, colleagues and companies. Writes Heskett: "Getting at the factors which influence internal quality is not easy but includes among others, the ability of members of the firm to provide a superior service for customers, their sense of dignity, and the infrastructure provided to enable them to achieve their objectives."

Appealing to the whole person in this way is far from easy. It demands integrity on the part of management, not slogans or platitudes. It also demands that management trust people to take responsibility, to take initiative and be enterprising, instead of simply giving loyalty to the corporation in return for compensation. As a consequence, members of the company will perceive themselves as taking advantage of opportunities that provide them with personal and professional development, and the result will be that they not only "own" their area of responsibility within the company, but also use it in such a way that the pursuit of their own interests and that of the firm converge.

When Max De Pree stepped down as a director of Herman Miller to accept emeritus status, he told the board that for him, Herman Miller had been not so much a company as a movement. I interpreted this as the greatest compliment he could pay to the company. In effect he was saying that the company, in pursuing its goals and interests on behalf of shareholders, had created for him an environment in which he could pursue a vocation to which he felt uniquely able to respond. Whenever there is such a convergence between the values and goals of the company and those of the individual, the result will be the total commitment of the person to his or her work and to the company.

THE IMPORTANCE OF TRUTH IN
ALL ASPECTS OF BUSINESS

The next characteristic of the Tao is truth. The values of judgments and moral rules that are part of the Tao have an objective validity. They are outside of us. They are over there. They do not depend on our personal feelings or thought. They have a permanence, and are unchanging. They are not relative to the different situations in which we find ourselves. It is because of this that truth is a fixed reference point. One of the immutable principles of ServiceMaster is that truth cannot be compromised. It is a principle that applies to all aspects of the business, but consider the most obvious area of application: the numbers that describe performance. Without reliable numbers, not only will a lack of trust develop between shareholders and management, but there will also be mistrust within the company. It is important that the accounting policy of a business is known by and acceptable to everyone concerned, that issues such as exceptional items, contingent liabilities and capitalization of cost do not come like a bolt from the blue, leaving people feeling deceived. It is important that changes in accounting policy are there for all to see. Similarly, the integrity of the audit process and the independence of the audit committee must be respected by management and the professional auditors involved. Nothing gives the lie to trust as much as a finance director or chief executive using creative accounting that produces unexpected numbers. Such numbers fail to give a true and fair view of the business and therefore turn out to be unsustainable.

Excellence is another area in which a commitment to truth is critical. It may be excellence in the product, excellence in the service provided, or excellence in the execution of a transaction. Excellence is about attention to detail, about thoroughness and about a commitment to the best possible outcome. The alternative to the pursuit of excellence is a philosophy of "it's good enough," "that should be sufficient," or "I can't be bothered to do anything more." A belief in excellence is based on a belief in truth, because without integrity it is impossible to produce excellence. It is not possible to believe in truth and accept the second best. The pursuit of quality demands total commitment from those providing it, which can only take place in an atmosphere of complete trust. Truth is also a personalized quality; hence in Judaism, God is described as truth. Truth in business does not start with a commitment to produce honest numbers, or a policy about not giving bribes for export contracts or about pursuing exceptionally high standards of performance. Truth is rooted in the quality of the people who form the company, including the caliber of its management. Reliability, sincerity, openness, firmness, trustworthiness: all of these and many more such words would describe the kind of person to whom the word truth applies. Perhaps the most powerful way to describe it is by the word *integrity*. If management has integrity then it will affect everything the company does.

Nemir Kirdar is the Iraq-born president and CEO of Investcorp, the London and New York based private investment firm that has had major stakes in high quality companies such as Gucci, Bulgari and Saks Fifth Avenue. After the firm's first decade of operations, he decided to set out what he saw as the 12 pillars of the company. The first is integrity. As an institution entrusted with the investment of other people's money, the statement goes, "nothing matters to us more than our integrity. It takes years to build, but one small slip and it's gone. An error of judgement can be forgiven—a lapse of integrity never." Within the company this rule is absolute. It permits no exceptions and applies to every action taken. The rule also applies to individuals. For an employee there is no quicker rout to dismissal than a lapse of integrity, whether it occurs at work or in personal dealings elsewhere.

If truth is to be meaningful in business, it must start with relationships, which are like covenants. We owe and are owed things by people. Being open to another person with the facts rather than hiding them, being prepared to disclose the facts about a new opportunity, reporting on the details of a visit, knowing that when you give your word you will be trusted: it is things such as these that are the basis of strong relationships. The trust that develops between people in a company is an important foundation for success. It takes time to build up and it can only be built on truth. It can be lost in a simple sentence, a wrong decision or a hasty action. And invariably it takes a long time to rebuild.

Jack Welch, the long-time, now retired CEO of General Electric, put it like this: "The only way I know to create trust is by laying out your values and then walking the talk. Trust is enormously powerful in a corporation. People want to do their best and believe they'll be treated fairly—then there's no cronyism and everybody has a real shot. You've got to do what you say you do, consistently over time. I think that any company that's trying to play in the 1990s has got to find a way to engage the mind of every employee. If you're not thinking all the time about making every person more valuable, you don't have a chance."

Another aspect of truth is fairness and justice. A sense of fair play or equity is at the heart of any community that is being built on trust. It may involve compensation, ownership, opportunity, promotion, selection, or recognition. If a company has at its core a sense of truth, then it will think carefully about these issues, communicate with everyone in the company and be prepared to defend its decisions as fair. In order to give substance to its belief in equity, a company on whose board I sit, has a rule that the CEO's cash compensation is limited to an amount twenty times the average annual compensation for a factory worker. Although there is no magic to the number twenty, it has worked well for many years and proved a credible basis for establishing relationships. Some more typical compensation packages in so many other companies in recent years would put that number at 100 or much higher.

One person who lived his commitment to truth was Ken Hansen, an early, formative leader of ServiceMaster. He was the first to admit that it was not always easy, in fact just the reverse. In writing about his career, he noticed that as he moved from selling and accounting into managing, he was primarily task-oriented even though he worked closely with others. But, he says, "I came to see that I was viewing people as a means to get work done. I viewed work as the end accomplished. It was painful to realize and then to acknowledge that this bent is sinful, harmful to others and to myself and dishonoring to God whom I seek to serve." The change for him proved difficult. But change he did, with a fresh commitment to using work to help people develop, rather than to using people to accomplish the work as the end.

OBLIGATIONS EVERYONE SHOULD ACCEPT

The Tao, however, is not simply a set of propositions about what is right and wrong, just and unjust, desirable and undesirable. The Tao makes demands on us. It requires that we do certain things and not others. It contains an imperative for action. It is a set of binding obligations about how we should live, what we should do, how we should behave, even though we may fail to do so. Human nature not only perceives the difference between right and wrong and good and bad, but also has a strong inclination to want to do what is good. In this there is in all of us an innate moral sense, a categorical imperative. Typically the objectives, mission statements and business principles of companies all contain obligations or responsibilities that each member of the organization is expected to carry out. For example, all are encouraged to help the company produce profit, to provide excellent service for clients, to accept responsibility within the community, to act as trustees for the environment and so on. Typically this list calls for a commitment to service, care and trusteeship from each member of the organization. All these obligations, either directly or indirectly, are responsibilities to people, and could easily be summed up by the precept "Do as you would be done by." Sir Thomas Armstrong would never ask his secretary, "When is my next appointment?" but "When is my next obligation?" It impressed me greatly as a commitment to others.

At first glance it might seem curious to put the responsibility for making a profit alongside service and trusteeship. But I believe it is correct because the responsibilities of business are a seamless robe. Making a profit is management's responsibility to the future. Without profit, a firm will ultimately go out of business. Making sure the company delivers a return on equity capital over a number of years is simply one of the costs of staying in business. It is as real a cost therefore as the accounting costs of wages, overheads and rent. Making a profit is a service provided by today's management to the next generation in order to ensure that the business survives.

Perhaps one final comment should be made on the Tao. I have stated the implications of the Tao in very general, almost unexceptional terms. The real challenge, however, comes in translating general statements into action. This either gives meaning or a lie to whatever statements companies make. And it is by these that a company's commitment to values should be judged.

PRACTICAL CHALLENGES OF MANAGING VALUES IN BUSINESS

So far we have seen that values matter for business and that the values of business have an objective validity of their own. Values are clearly important to business. But this does not mean that values are easy to manage. Far from it. I want to examine three particular challenges of managing values in business—the problem of how to prevent a strong culture from becoming a tyranny, the way in which it is possible to manage change within a strong culture and the accountability of management for values.

PREVENTING THE CULTURE FROM BECOMING A TYRANNY

Though I believe strongly that certain values should be at the heart of business, I have no doubt that strong values can sometimes create a tyrannical culture with little respect for the individual or for diversity. This first hit me in the mid-1970s when I was making a film for television on my view of trade unions. I had interviewed a well-known Scottish trade union leader on the banks of the Clyde and then went on to visit a manufacturing company that had a strong culture and no union. The trade union aspect of the company, which had originally prompted my visit, proved to be what I expected and made the point well. What I had not expected, and fortunately this was not the subject of the program, was that alongside the absence of unions, the company had created such an overwhelming culture that it seemed little short of cultic, religious or even brainwashing. Indeed in the middle of the program I felt compelled to leave the factory and take a walk because of the almost menacing effect of the environment. I realized then for the first time that any company with a strong culture, where the management is convinced of the importance of values to the company, risks creating just such an environment. The basic weakness in the company I visited was a lack of respect for the individual. Too great a value was placed on the institution and not enough on the individual. Individuals were expected to fit into the company, while the company paid insufficient attention to their needs. The result was that the company ended up "owning" the employees and therefore made unbalanced demands on their time, priorities and even their affections.

MANAGING CHANGE IN A COMPANY
WITH STRONG VALUES

Strong values at the heart of a company can produce extraordinary results. But strong values can also create a culture that is highly resistant to change. If strong values have been successful and the company has become number one in its industry with a good record of earnings and cash flow, the result can be hubris. Executives relax, lose focus, take their eye off the changing behavior of competitors and regulators and soon find, especially during a recession, that with over capacity and intense pressure on prices, the company is in the red.

Strong values, as we have seen, are built on equity, which is frequently presented by top managers as a covenant between themselves and members of the firm. Each person has certain de facto rights—the right to be needed, to be involved, to be informed, and to share in the rewards. Raising the expectations of employees in a period of continued top line and bottom line growth is one thing. But when the expectations remain high and conditions take a down turn, managing change becomes infinitely more difficult. In particular there is a resistance to change throughout the whole of the company. Sam Walton recognized this in building Wal-Mart: "When folks buy into a way of doing things, and really believe it's the best way, they develop a tendency to think that's exactly the way things should always be done." The result was that he made it his own personal mission to ensure that constant change—even change for change's sake—was a vital part of the Wal-Mart culture itself.

Possibly the most difficult issue in this area is distinguishing between the core values on which a company is built—which should never be changed—and those non-core values that may well need changing in response to a new environment. The example that must come to mind is the contrast between Thomas Watson Jr.'s statement about values of IBM and the subsequent experience of the company. Looking back on his career as the company's most significant leader, Watson wrote:

> I firmly believe that any organization, in order to survive and achieve success, must have a sound set of beliefs on which it premises all its policies and actions. Next I believe that the most important factor in corporate success is faithful adherence to those beliefs. And finally I believe that if an organization is to meet the challenges of a changing world, it must be prepared to change everything about itself except those beliefs as it moves through corporate life.

In other words the basic philosophy, spirit and drive of an organization have far more to do with its relative achievements than do technological or economic resources, organizational structure, innovation and timing. All these things weigh heavily in success. But are, I think, transcended by how strongly the people in the organization believe in its basic precepts and how faithfully they carry them out.

IBM achieved extraordinary performance under Watson and his immediate successors. It was universally applauded by employees, investors and the communities of which it was part. The values that made IBM great were real values—a passion for being right, rigorous method and procedures, first class training of employees, a focus on what customers wanted and a guarantee of lifetime employment. At its height, its financial success was staggering. But then came hubris, and these same values became transformed. Instead of being positive they were perceived as negative—as a fear of taking risk, a bureaucratic mentality, the brainwashing of employees, a failure to anticipate changing demands, an inability to adapt its workforce quickly enough to the needs of the industry. Hubris was soon followed by nemesis—$75 billion wiped off shares, 150,000 workers laid off, and a $20 billion write-off of assets. Even though the changes it faced were extraordinary by any standards, IBM had failed to respond to the changing environment.

Determining precisely the beliefs of the company by contrast with all else about the company is exceedingly difficult. It is easy to mistake a spectacular increase in profitability from a business cycle upturn as being the result of the beliefs of the company, so that when the profits slump in the down turn, the slump in morale can be devastating. It is just as easy to mistake a more sustained period of profitability, perhaps resulting from just one high margin product with the excellence emphasized in the values of the company, only to find that when for whatever reason the market demand for that one product has changed, the sense of excellence delivers a very mediocre return on capital. While there is no easy answer to this problem, there is a great deal of merit in Peter Drucker's principle of abandonment. Every three years a company should examine every aspect of its business—product range, production techniques, distribution channels—by posing the question, "Would we now go into this business if we were not already in it?" Such a question forces the company to test the assumptions on which it works.

ACCOUNTABILITY FOR VALUES

The very idea of values in business is treated with skepticism by many people. They are right to point out the potential dangers. Values can be empty words with little meaning. There will always be a problem of double standards and hypocrisy. Even the best companies will fall short of their values. For values to be credible and taken seriously, however, a number of conditions need to be fulfilled.

To start with, a belief in values must translate into action if they are to be taken seriously. Each of the values I have listed requires management to take concrete steps for implementation. The steps may well vary from company to company, but by taking such steps the relationship between values and action becomes obvious to everyone in the company. For example, a commitment to helping people realize their potential in a company must result in steps to provide first-class training; a belief in the quality of product or service must result in some sort of quality exercise; a belief in fairness and being part of a community must result in participation and ownership; a belief in responsibility for the environment must lead to specific actions; a belief in honesty means that bribes will not be offered by sales staff or accepted by buyers.

Another condition for values to be taken seriously is the example set by the leaders of the company. However fine the statement made by a company, the values contained in it will lack credibility unless they are lived by the leadership—the Chairman, the CEO, the executive committee, the Board, the heads of divisions and so on. Values in business are not disembodied ideas. They are seen in the behavior and the decisions of management. And once they are seen, so they are believed. But to be believed, they must be consistent. It is better not to have statements of belief, business principles and value statements if at the core of the firm there are double standards, because such inconsistency will breed skepticism that easily degenerates into cynicism.

The ultimate responsibility for values within the company rests with the CEO. The leader is the custodian of values of the company. Values are the one issue that can never be delegated. This brings enormous responsibility. It should also be seen as a responsibility of the Board. From time to time, maybe once a year, the Board should be given the opportunity to review the values of the company, the way they are perceived and the way they are interpreted. One particularly strong signal that management can communicate regarding values is when a clear and public breach occurs. The classic response to this must be the statement of Warren Buffett when he took over the chairmanship of Salomon Brothers in 1991 in the midst of a crisis of confidence. He made it very clear that compensation would relate to truth. "Last year," he declared, " the securities unit earned about 10 percent on equity capital—far under the average earned by American business—yet 106 individuals earned $1 million or more . . . Employees producing mediocre returns for owners should expect their pay to reflect this shortfall. In the past that has neither been the expectation at Salomon nor the practice." And he then went on to show how a profitable business could be built on certain values: "Salomon has the capacity amid favorable market conditions to earn substantial sums . . . I believe we can earn these superior returns playing aggressively in the center of the court, without resorting to close-to-the-line acrobatics. Good profits simply are not inconsistent with good behavior. Our goal is going to be that stated many decades ago by J.P. Morgan, who wished to see his bank transact 'first-class business . . . in a first class way'."

CONCLUSION: ETHOS IS ALL

The business of values is an important issue facing business leadership today. In an increasingly competitive and global marketplace, the values of a company can have a significant effect on performance. These values are not a superficial gimmick, but something that goes to the roots of our cultural heritage and of what it means to be human. Values are not a panacea in business and managing values is far from easy. But we have now entered a world in which companies simply must address this issue head on. The issue has added significance because the corporation has emerged as a dominant institution in the modern world. It has become widely accepted on all continents and in countries with very different ideologies that well-managed companies operating in competitive markets are the key to wealth creation, the growth of jobs, rapid innovation and the advance of knowledge.

More than that, business also has emerged across the globe as a significant social institution in all societies. The mission statements, business principles and objectives set out by companies are important statements of values in their own right. They set standards. They inspire. They provide a framework within which people seek meaning and fulfillment in their work, not just financial compensation. At a time when the traditional institutions that once were the source of values in our society—especially the family and religious institutions—have either been weakened or have abrogated their leadership, the corporation has become a significant source and carrier of values. This provides both a tremendous opportunity for the business community and an enormous responsibility. For any business to respond to this, it must face up to its own values and this is far from easy. It is a challenge not just to a corporation or an institution. Ultimately, it is a personal challenge.

RESPONSE BY PETER F. DRUCKER

Professor Drucker is a consultant in strategy and policy who has worked with many corporations, non-profits, universities, hospitals and agencies of the United States Government, as well governments around the world. He has written 28 books that have been translated into more than 20 languages. He has long been associated with the Peter F. Drucker Graduate Management Center at Claremont College in California.

The foregoing by Lord Griffiths is a text of rare eloquence and great power. It presents the case for business as ethics in action more forcefully, more cogently, more convincingly, than anyone else has done to my knowledge, and certainly more forcefully, more cogently, more convincingly than I have ever done or could do. It would thus be presumptuous of me to try to *comment* on Lord Griffiths's statement. But perhaps I can *reflect* on some of the things he says. Lord Griffiths repeatedly—and rightly—stresses that every business—indeed every organization—has a value system. The question is not whether to have values—every human being has them and every human group, however organized does too. The question is: Are they the right values or the wrong values? Are they values that give life or values that give death? And, as Lord Griffiths reminds us—and as all recent research validates—it is not the business whose values are pure opportunism, pure greed, pure selfishness and self-aggrandizement that does best, not even in the very short run. It is the business that has a set of values that enables it and the people who work for it to respect themselves, to have pride, to grow, that is the true winner in the market place. But there is one thing that perhaps can—and should—be added. It is also the business with these values, the business that believes that it exists to contribute rather than just to take, that will weather adversity. In good times, values may look like an ornament. They may be treated—and frequently are—as something we can indulge in as a "nice little extra." It is in times of adversity, in times "that try a man's soul," that values are a necessity. For if the right values are absent at such a time, there is no incentive for human beings to walk the extra mile, to make the extra commitment, to do the hard work of a rethinking strategy, of trying new things, of rebuilding. People won't do that just for the money. They will do it only if they believe that what their business does and can do matters. And it is this belief that is instilled by the right values.

Lord Griffiths repeatedly—and rightly—stresses that values are *commitments to action*. Preachments aren't values—they are good intentions, at best. And so let me ask the question: Which actions are the most important ones as validations of our values, and as *ethics in action*? This is one of the oldest questions of ethics, of course. But never before have we really had to ask it in respect to organizations, and especially in respect to business. Very few of us realize how very, very recent organizations are—not much more than a century ago practically no one, even in the then most highly developed country, worked in an organization or had anything much to do with it after having reached adulthood, that is after finishing school (and in the countries of Continental Europe and in Japan, military service). Today, practically everybody in developed countries makes his or her livelihood as member of an organization. And everybody, every day, is in intimate contact— often much too intimate for comfort—with all kinds of organizations, businesses, government agencies, community organizations. And then one has to ask: what is the one decisive, most unambiguous action that most expresses an organization's values? It is the *personnel decision*. In every organization—and not only in a business—the true and real values of its leaders are judged—especially within the organization—by who gets promoted and who gets fired, who gets rewarded and who gets punished. People decisions are highly visible. There is no way, even in the most secretive dictatorship, to hide them. At the height of Stalinism, Russian telephone numbers were considered a state secret. People were sent to concentration camps for treason because they had tried to get a hospital's telephone number. But even then, no factory in Russia, no Collective Farm, no Government Agency, not even the almighty and all-secret Politburo could keep secret who got promoted, who got kicked downstairs or got kicked out, who was becoming the boss and who was remaining the underling. But there is also a second reason why people decisions are the true test of values. People in an organization, even a very big one, are not abstractions. They are real. We have worked with the person who gets promoted and with the person who gets the boot. We *know* them both. And we know—it cannot be hidden—both what they have done and how they have done it. We know, in other words both their capacities and their character. Even in organizations that are only medium-size a good many people, including people pretty high up, often cannot judge the rationale, let alone the wisdom, of this or that *business* decision. But they always can—and do—judge the values underlying a people decision. And, no matter what the CEO says in his speech at the annual picnic, what he does in rewarding, placing or punishing people are the values the entire organization sees and takes seriously. And these are the values that inform and mold the actual behavior of the entire organization.

Many, many years ago, at the very beginning of my working life, I had the good fortune to work for a year for a man of rare integrity and great wisdom. I had tremendous respect for him; and so I was quite shocked when he did not promote an older colleague—let's call him Tom—who had clearly done an outstanding job. I was so troubled that I took my courage in my hands and went and asked the boss why he had so pointedly passed over our department's top performer. He looked at me with a smile and said: "I know you are too young to have a son—I was in my early twenties—but I understand you have a younger brother." Yes, I did. "Would you," he then asked, "want to have this younger brother work for two or three years under Tom and try to become like Tom?" He continued: "You are right, Tom has the performance; but does he have the character?" It is when an organization asks this question and takes it seriously that its values become action.

CHAPTER TWO

CORPORATE SOULCRAFT IN THE AGE OF BRUTAL MARKETS

By Elmer W. Johnson

Elmer W. Johnson, a corporate lawyer and former executive vice president of General Motors Corporation, has spoken and written on ethics-oriented issues of corporate capitalism for twenty years. His interest grew out of legal representation, during the 1970s, of major corporations and their boards concerning unethical business practices at home and abroad. This lecture was given in 1996 at the J. L. Kellogg Graduate School of Management at Northwestern University.

The economic and political arguments for the market principle over alternative forms of economic organization are to my mind irrefutable. It is on the moral level that the perplexing concerns about capitalism center, concerns that have been raised from the beginnings of the industrial era down to the present time. In this essay I will focus on one major aspect of the ongoing moral test of capitalism: the test of whether our major corporations can both succeed in their profit-making efforts and also serve as one of society's chief mediating structures that stand, like family, church and community, between the individual and the state. Should the corporation serve not only as a utilitarian arrangement for the efficient production of high quality goods and services, but also as a moral community that shapes human character and behavior?

James Q. Wilson, professor of management at UCLA, has no doubt about the answer. In a recent article he said: "The problem of imbuing large-scale enterprise with a decent moral life is fundamental." Corporations "are systems of human action that cannot for long command the loyalty of their members if their standards of collective action are materially lower than those of their individual members." Capitalists should recognize, he concluded, "that, while free markets will ruthlessly eliminate inefficient firms, the moral sentiments of man will only gradually and uncertainly penalize immoral ones. But, while the quick destruction of inefficient corporations threatens only individual firms, the slow anger at immoral ones threatens capitalism, and thus freedom itself."

For Wilson, then, the compelling reason for corporations and their leaders to behave morally is to evoke the trust and loyalty of their employees and the respect of the larger society, all to the end of ensuring the long-term viability of the enterprise and ultimately of capitalism and democracy. I agree that these prudential concerns are important, but my starting point is quite different. I start from a normative perspective that is embedded in both Judeo-Christian and classical Greek traditions. According to those traditions, morality imposes requirements that take precedence over all other modes of guiding conduct. These requirements are central to any conception of the good life and the good society. Thus, this world is about what I call soulcraft, and our economic and political arrangements should be judged by the qualities of character they tend to produce or help sustain.

The job of making a living and supporting a family constitutes the very matrix of the moral life. In an Encyclical Letter in 1981, Pope John Paul II wrote: "Man's life is built up every day from work, from work it derives its specific dignity." The workplace at its best is a school for education in virtue and community. In this light, the highest calling of the entrepreneurial steward of the enterprise is to create and sustain a workplace in which employees can flourish. They are enabled to flourish as they are guided by the end of providing the customer with top quality goods and services in a cost-effective manner, as each worker contributes to this end in cooperation with others and develops his or her skills and grows in responsibility, as they see how their respective parts relate to the whole process, as they come to value their friendships and conversations in the workplace, and as they share in the success of the enterprise.

It is from this normative perspective that I consider the question of whether the corporation should and can function as a moral community. I will do so in the context of two developments that have taken place, side by side, over the last 15 years or so. The first concerns the efforts of corporations, in both the manufacturing and service sectors, to bring about a participatory work place in which the dignity of the workers is more fully recognized.

CAN WE DEVELOP "NEW PATTERNS OF PARTNERSHIP?"

In the 1980s, a committee of United States Catholic Bishops issued a report entitled "Economic Justice for All: Catholic Social Teaching and the U.S. Economy." The report called for "imaginative new forms of cooperation and partnership among those whose daily work is the source of the prosperity and justice of the nation." It urged business leaders "to develop new patterns of partnership among those working in individual firms and industries." Much was made in the report of the obstacles in the way of such partnerships. For example, it noted the impact of advancing technology in downgrading and displacing workers; and the adverse effects on U.S. employees of imports of materials and products from foreign countries with low wage structures. Toward the end, the report referred to the legal dilemma of managers in being forced to give excessive weight to stockholder profits and inadequate weight to the stakes of employees and local communities.

At the time the report was issued, I was working at General Motors and was responsible for industrial relations and salaried personnel, among other things. It was sad to reflect on the long history of conflict between management and labor and the effects of the deeply held convictions of both sides that there is a basic conflict between success in the marketplace and human values in the workplace. As Karl Marx and others observed early on, when workers are reduced to the status of a means and their propensity toward purpose is denied except for the extrinsic goal of wage, no amount of material wage can redress this deep wrong to their personalities, and no amount of leisure in which to spend the wage can atone for the harm done them by their daily alienation.

In the twentieth century, the adversarial culture of management versus labor became embedded in a legalistic, rule-driven structure governing labor-management relations and collective bargaining. Any management attempts at cooperation by communicating with hourly workers outside union channels became suspect under the National Labor Relations Act as "unfair labor practices." For decades, elected union representatives maintained their power by demonstrating their confrontational skills in dealing with management, and the union leader who dared to work for a more cooperative kind of relationship ran high risks of political suicide. And so, over the years, the habitual dispositions of both managers and union representatives became fixed almost beyond redemption. Almost, but not quite.

THE TIDE BEGAN TO TURN WITH THE GM-TOYOTA JOINT VENTURE

The Bishop's Letter was issued at a time when it appeared the tide was beginning to turn. The GM-Toyota joint venture had been in operation for over a year. We had learned a lot about the Toyota production system. We learned, first of all, that a highly centralized autocratic management style undermines quality and productivity because the masses of employees rightly sense that their feelings, insights, and suggestions are not considered, even in respect to decisions of utmost relevance to their work lives, including the design of the production system and their particular work stations. Accordingly, managers tap only a fraction of the employees' potential for quality workmanship, innovation, and productivity.

In order to tap into much more of that potential, we learned that a radical change in management philosophy and style was required. Management began to solicit pertinent input from the persons most affected by its decisions. Management also began to delegate decision-making to the appropriate levels. The new style involved the concept of the team consisting of a half dozen or more members and a team leader. Each team was responsible for suggesting continuous improvements in both product and process. As these teams assumed more responsibility, unnecessary layers of middle management were eliminated. The new lean production system also meant that suppliers must deliver inventory just in time, that suppliers who fell below certain quality standards would lose out, and that the best suppliers would become strategic partners of the manufacturer in devising ways to improve the product. Finally, the Toyota system of empowering the workers was accompanied by a high degree of employment security.

It is ironic that we were forced by competitive considerations to learn from a non-Western culture some rather basic truths as they apply to the workplace. The ideas behind the Toyota system, translated into the language of the Western religious and ethical traditions, are simple and yet profound. First, each employee of the enterprise has complementary gifts and talents and resources. The wealth-creating power of the corporation depends on the recognition of that complementarity. Second, while there are necessarily different levels of authority and responsibility in the enterprise, we are all equal as human beings and our spiritual side far transcends the narrow commercial purposes of the corporation.

Accordingly, respect for all persons is fundamental. Third, while there may often be tension between these human values and our legitimate business purposes, there is no basic conflict. More often than not, the two are mutually reinforcing. The improvement in the competitiveness of American manufacturing during the 1980s was due in very large part to the widening application of these principles, and this development served to reaffirm the notion that the business corporation best serves its stockholders and customers by creating a moral community in which employees can develop their talents for individual achievement and team cooperation.

Despite this encouraging development, I have become less optimistic in recent years about the prospects for soulcraft in the workplace. The reasons for my concern arise out of a second development in the corporate world. Before I describe that development, though, I must paint the larger backdrop. Fred Hirsch, the late British economist, observed in the mid-1970s that the market's exaltation of self-interest and the invisible hand was undermining the moral and communal values that are its own essential underpinnings. "As individual behavior has been increasingly directed to individual advantage," he wrote, "habits and instincts based on communal attitudes and objectives have lost out. The weakening of traditional social values has made predominantly capitalist economies more difficult to manage."

WE ARE LOSING EDMUND BURKE'S "LITTLE PLATOONS OF SOCIETY"

Journalist-philosopher George Will wrote a column in the early 1990s urging us all to go out and join a bowling league. He was inspired to give this sermon after reading an article entitled "Bowling Alone: America's Declining Social Capital." It was written for a scholarly publication by Robert Putnam, professor of international affairs at Harvard University. The title certainly gets one's attention. The fact is that people bowl more than ever before, but they do it alone. Bowling leagues are much less common than they once were. This seemingly trivial statistic is symbolic of what has been happening to America. The networks of civic and social engagement, the little platoons of society as Edmund Burke called them, are in declining health. Yet they powerfully shape character by fostering sturdy norms of generalized reciprocity and by enhancing social trust. For much of this century, market societies were able to rely on the well-springs of what Adam Smith called our natural sympathy for our fellow human beings and on the impartial spectator that resides within our breasts and hold us in check. Did Adam Smith appreciate that these virtues of fellow feeling and self-restraint were the legacy of a pre-market age and that they require continuing nurture that can only be provided by non-market mediating institutions such as home, school, church and corporation? I don't know, but I do know that the character-forming power of these other institutions over the last few decades has been a poor match for the countervailing power of the market to privatize all life and exacerbate our most selfish tendencies.

How did this culture of self-interest get so out of hand? Some say that the primacy of technical, instrumental reason has eclipsed our higher ends. Others hold that the Western individualist tradition, dating back to Locke, is inherently unstable and that the notion of self-determining freedom, pushed to its logical limit, tips over into the most extreme forms of anthropocentrism. Still others would cite the movement of women into the labor force and their reduced time for community involvement; the uprooting effects of residential mobility; urban spatial patterns that entail the distancing of land uses and reduced opportunities for neighborliness; and the privatization of our leisure time as a result of television, the computer and other technologies. To this list I would add more generally the market's exaltation of "What is in it for me?"

MARKET-DRIVEN INCENTIVES HAVE HAD A
POWERFUL NEGATIVE EFFECT

What does the decline of social capital and the culture of self-interest have to do with the soulcraft perspective and the possibilities of the corporate manager as steward of a moral community? I must turn to the second development in order to make this link. Our society's current devotion to the motivational power of economic self-interest is so complete that we continually devise creative new ways for using market-like incentives to induce managers to do things for the stockholder that they could not be expected to do merely by virtue of their moral dispositions and convictions as fiduciaries.

One of these powerful devices in the 1980s was the junk bond-leveraged forcible takeover. In 1989, Michael Jensen, professor at Harvard Business School, wrote an article entitled "The Eclipse of the Public Corporation." He basically argued that the days of the public corporation were numbered. As he put it, "The idea that outside directors with little or no equity stake in the company could effectively monitor and discipline the managers who selected them has proven hollow at best." Only the junk bond leveraged buyout could provide the accountability and the strong incentives that were required.

The corporate governance movement was well under way by then, and over the next few years it led to greatly improved levels of board monitoring of executive performance, the very kind of board monitoring that Jensen thought impossible. Behind this movement was the newly demonstrated clout of some huge public pension funds that held large chunks of the voting stock of the major corporations and were demanding more accountability from boards of directors. Whether by takeover from outside the firm or by board-initiated shakeup from within, it was the dawning of a new era of the brutally efficient manager, driven by performance-based compensation programs.

CEOS GOT THE LOOT WHILE EMPLOYEES GOT THE BOOT

Actually, the rapid growth in such programs—cash and stock bonuses, stock options, stock appreciation rights, phantom stock options—had been under way for some time. In 1985, Arch Patton, retired director of McKinsey & Company, Inc. and a pioneer authority on executive compensation, wrote an article entitled, "Those million-dollar-a-year executives." In the article he expressed moral indignation over the excessive salaries, bonuses and stock options given to the CEOs of the top 100 companies. Thirty-two such persons had each received total income in 1983 in excess of $1 million, a three-fold increase from a decade earlier. His article appeared in 1984. Ten years later, a group of 292 executives of large corporations averaged $3.7 million in total income, 187 times as much as the average worker. In the mid 1970s that multiple was about 35. Think of it. CEO pay, as a multiple of average worker pay, increased by over five times in just 20 years. There has been much in the media about the growing gap between rich and poor. Suffice it to say that the radical increase in executive pay, together with the multiplier effects of that increase throughout the world of professional firms, has been a chief contributor to this larger societal concern.

Every proxy season the business press does its yearly exposes on executive greed. In the mid-1990s, the conjunction of harsh corporate downsizings and multi-million dollar bonuses and stock option gains has provided new grist for the journalistic mill. Many large corporations had shed tens of thousands of employees, closed numbers of plants, and disposed of losing operations, all to the worthy ends of regaining global competitiveness and enhancing stockholder value. This phenomenon, which got under way in the late 1980s, continued at an accelerating pace into the mid 1990s. *The New York Times* devoted a weeklong series of articles to the economic and psychological devastations that has been inflicted on "downsized" middle-class families across America.

The same Michael Jensen who scoffed in 1989 at the notion of public corporation that could face the tough issues, had to reverse his position. He wrote an

Op-Ed piece in which he extolled such leaders as Robert Allen, the CEO of AT&T, for their courage in laying off tens of thousands of employees. Admittedly, he said, "today's economic dislocations are wreaking havoc on the national psyche. But they are also the source of a wonderfully optimistic future . . . The Third Industrial Revolution that began in 1973 promises increased productivity, large reductions in the world-wide inequality of wealth, and substantial increases in world-wide living standards."

True, he wrote, there is some short-term pain for Western workers as a consequence of the world-wide move to market-oriented economic systems. "Their real wages are likely to continue their sluggish growth and some will fall dramatically over two or three decades, perhaps as much as 50 percent in some sectors. Wages will, however, reach a trough and recover as the cycle works its way through the system . . . There is no way to completely eliminate the private pain that comes from this adjustment. We all wish it were different, but without the private pain, most people will not change."

He conceded that inequality had risen, but not to worry. The same pattern manifested itself in the nineteenth century. Yet, after only a few decades real wages began to increase in the twentieth century. We have to be patient and avoid mushy talk about stakeholder capitalism or any concept of a kinder, gentler corporation taking increased social responsibility. We must not slow down the process of creative destruction even though these are dangerous times and even though the severe dislocations threaten to undermine the stability of societies and governments around the world. We must hang tough, he said.

SO MANY MANAGEMENTS BECAME FAT, DUMB AND HAPPY

There is good reason, as Jensen argued, to believe that much or most of this painful downsizing has been unavoidable. But I would submit it was mainly because so many managements became fat, dumb and happy over the 30 or 40 year period of post World War II stability and prosperity when American business reigned supreme around the globe. The increasing costs of bloated work forces and over-capacity could be passed on to the customer. Many if not most of the takeovers in the 1980s succeeded because managements and boards had been asleep at the switch. Bureaucratic cultures had undermined efficiency and management agility and had weakened management's focus on the customer. Length of service had become the primary criterion for promotion and pay increases, and the ranks of middle management had swollen under a philosophy of cradle-to-grave job security.

That was before the emergence of global markets, the explosion in computer and communications technology, and lean production systems. By reason of these developments, the large corporation was brought to a critical juncture in the 1980s. Could it provide an entrepreneurial environment, or was it the fate of the large corporation to witness the steady migration of the nation's best talent to private firms where the untrammeled market is allowed to carry out its distilling and refining process and where this talent need not live in goldfish bowls? If so, large corporations would become lifeless, leaderless bureaucracies, controlled by mediocre executives who must depend on outside consultants for the making of complex decisions.

In this context, it is not surprising that business and professional firms came to pay ever greater premiums for professionals who demonstrated high degrees of agility, resourcefulness and judgment. Investment bankers, management consultants and law firms greatly intensified their efforts over this period to recruit the best and the brightest, and at a mind-boggling rate of increase in starting salaries. Over the same period, we also witnessed a burgeoning of venture and capital firms that hold out to their executives the prospect of substantial capital gains. As a consequence, large corporations have faced formidable competition in recruiting, grooming, and retaining the most able people for top positions.

Does this mean that the explosion in CEO pay over the last two decades, and particularly the first years of the 1990s is fully justified, or at least explained by the market factors that I have just outlined? I don't think so. We have made the market something of a scapegoat. Graef Crystal, well-known compensation expert, likes to point out that inasmuch as the best CEOs in Japan and Europe make only a fraction of what top CEOs in America are paid, there cannot be a genuine market in CEOs as there is in the rest of the workforce. Why not? Very simple. The boards of directors of U.S. corporations select the top executives and set their pay, and those decisions are not based on some market pricing mechanism for CEOs.

IN CEO PAY, TOO MANY CARROTS AND TOO FEW STICKS

Arch Patton, whom I cited earlier, had a different explanation for the run-up in CEO pay, one that has nothing to do with the market. Patton saw a pervasive lack of integrity—too much coziness and mutual protectiveness—among directors, executives and outside consultants. He also argued that self-interest and personal greed had replaced the virtues of company loyalty and internal promotion. This trend had been greatly aided, he said, by recruiters and compensation consultants who knew the wisdom of deferring to management's wishes. It is only recently that compensation committees have begun to hire the outside compensation consultant and make it clear that it is the committee, not the CEO, to whom the consultant reports. Perhaps if there were less coziness, we might be able to develop real pay-for-performance packages for CEOs. We have been told that the point of stock option plans, under which most of the big money is made, is to provide the CEOs with strong incentives to maximize stockholder wealth. But if this is the purpose, and if we want CEOs to behave as if they were large stockholders, why don't we require them to be at risk as the stockholders are? Why don't we see more plans that facilitate and require a CEO's ownership of stock in his company in an amount that constitutes the major portion of his total assets? As Warren Buffett has said, the problem with CEO pay is that there are too many carrots and too few sticks.

That is one problem: the one-way street. Another problem with the use of stock options is that the CEO and other top executives can reap huge gains even when the stock of the company has increased in value only a fraction of the amount of increase in the S&P 500. The value of stock options often has much more to do with the vagaries of the stock market than with executive performance. We have not begun to see the kind of ingenuity that would truly induce corporate managers to think like large stockholders.

These problems pale by comparison to a third defect in so-called pay-for-performance programs. This is the short-term focus of these programs. And yet, as we well know, the most important decisions made by a CEO—those that will have the greatest long-term effect on stockholder wealth—are those pertaining, first of all, to strategies for building on the competitive strengths of the company and adjusting to changing conditions, and second, to the selection and orchestration of the key executives who will work with the CEO to mobilize the entire workforce to implement those strategies. This being the CEO's mission, the benefit or cost to stockholders cannot usually be known except over a period of years.

There are many ways this problem can be addressed. For one, top executives of a company might receive the bulk of their incentive compensation and stock awards as grants made every three years or so. None of the benefits, whether cash or stock, would vest until some years after the grants. Then, in the ensuing few years the amount of the payout would depend on how well the company performed in the interim in terms of return on capital or some similar measure, or how well its stock performed in relation to some relevant standard, such as the Standard & Poor's Index or some group of peer company stocks. In the closing years of the executive's career, the value of incentive awards would come to depend more on the company's performance in the few years after his or her retirement. Under such schemes, executives would be better motivated to take actions that create long-term wealth and to avoid the kind of short-term cost reduction and corporate dismemberment that improve current profits but could cripple the company's long-term generating powers.

Yet, even if we did all the right tinkering, there would remain the issue of whether CEO pay is so out of fair proportion to the pay of the average company employee as to undermine the possibilities of a productive, participative workplace and also whether that level is so out of proportion to what schoolteachers and others in the larger society earn as to undermine respect for the corporation and for the economic institutions of capitalism in general.

CEOS HAVE LET ECONOMIC INCENTIVES DRIVE OUT MORAL INCENTIVES

Let's pause for a moment. I said at the outset that I wished to inquire into the prospects of the corporation as a moral community and that I would address this question in the light of two developments. I first sketched the development of respecting notions of employee community and the resulting enhancement of worker productivity, product quality, and customer satisfaction. Before turning to the second development in the corporate world, I focused on some larger cultural forces that have tended to undermine the prospects for community of any kind. This was the necessary backdrop for the second development I then described: namely, the emergence of the market for corporate control, strong financial incentives for aligning the economic self-interest of management with the larger stockholder interest, and the evolution of corporate governance mechanisms for holding managers and boards of directors more accountable to stockholders.

These methods that we have employed to induce the stewards of our corporate enterprises to maximize stockholder value have provided the intended impetus for management to break up old bureaucratic cultures and eliminate waste. But what happens after that transitional mission has been largely accomplished? Will the same executives then be able to take on the enduring strategic challenges of anticipating emerging technologies and changing consumer demand? Will they be able to build a top team and an entire work-force of great talent and have an esprit de corps?

Or do corporate managers tend to change as they take on the role of "rationalizing" the corporate assets and slashing "headcount" (as the workforce has come to be referred to by the rationalizing manager) and as economic incentives drive out moral incentives? Do they tend to lose whatever virtues and strengths of character might have qualified them to serve as leaders of a community of employees and build an organization based on mutual trust?

To answer these questions, we must return to my theme about the soulcraft perspective, a perspective common to both the Greek tradition and the Judeo-Christian tradition. Aristotle said that virtue derives from the development of good habits. If he is right, and I think he is, then it should not be surprising that a corporate manager shaped for his or her entire career primarily by self-interest incentives would have little power to inspire a high level of social cooperation. Fifty years ago, the great economist and curmudgeon Joseph Schumpeter said, in effect, that corporate managers are anti-heroic and have no charisma; that their habits of life are not of the kind that develop personal fascination and sustain group feeling. They've been taught all their careers, as well as in business school, to keep their nose to the grindstone and their eye on current profits. Accordingly, said Schumpeter, outside the office the business executive is often unable to say *boo* to a goose.

IS A PROFESSIONAL MANAGER LIKE THE EXECUTIONER OF PARIS?

It would be sad indeed if we as a society have come to the point where the role of professional corporate managers is merely to maximize stockholder wealth and if this role provides them with an excuse for abdicating their other role as stewards of a moral community. Arthur Applebaum, professor at Harvard's Kennedy School of Government, has written an article entitled, "Professional Detachment: The Executioner of Paris." He uses as an extreme example of detached professionalism the imaginary defense of the actions, the attitudes, and behavior of the Executioner of Paris, Charles-Henri Sanson, who served with great skill and "professionalism" all the regimes from the monarchy to the most extreme elements of the Revolution in the years before, through, and after the French Revolution. The essence of Applebaum's theme is captured in the concluding words of his article:

> Left on our table are a number of claims Sanson has made in defense of his professional role that deserve closer attention . . . Sanson's arguments do not look all that different from the arguments offered by lawyers, business executives, politicians, bureaucrats, journalists, and soldiers to justify their commitments to their professional roles when these roles ask them to act in ways that, if not for the role, would be wrong. If versions of these arguments do indeed justify the moral permissions to harm others that are claimed by these professions, why do they not work for Sanson? And if we are sure they do not work for Sanson, should we not reconsider whether they work to justify less sanguinary professional roles?

Applebaum says that role is the moral concept central to a proper understanding of a profession. The unsettling question for professionals is whether they have permitted their role to be defined by the culture or the competition in such a way that excellent performance of that role is harmful to some larger public as well as to their own souls. This moral dilemma extends far beyond the modern business corporation. The corporate executive is a "professional" who views accountability to stockholders in much the same way as Sanson views his accountability to the social order or as lawyers view their responsibility for the zealous representation of the client.

I happen to be a lawyer, and I must confess that I am not very happy about what has happened to my own profession in recent decades. To quote Professor Barry Schwartz, a professor of psychology at Swarthmore College:

"The law and lawyers provide us with an inescapable model of how one lives a life. And it's a model from which notions of justice and responsibility are conspicuously absent. It's a model that tells us to seek and press every advantage we can over potential adversaries, and to assume that they are doing the same. As a result, it's a model for the disintegration of the person and the social fabric . . ."

The same could be said about business managers who make the maximization of stockholder wealth their sole reason for being. We have created a set of conditions in which employees' capacity for trust is at a very low ebb. They have been given a strong message over the last several years that their corporation competes in a harsh environment; that their jobs are insecure, and that they had better remain on the alert for ways to make themselves marketable outside the corporation in which they have honed their skills for twenty years or more.

WORKERS MUST BE ABLE TO THRIVE AS MORAL HUMAN BEINGS

And so I return to the question: whether the corporation ought to serve not merely as a profit-making enterprise for its stockholders but also as a moral community that shapes human character and behavior. The answer to this "ought" question from my perspective—what I have called the soulcraft perspective—is a resounding yes. Nothing else matters very much if the work environment is such that people cannot thrive as moral human beings and aspire toward their higher spiritual ends. We have created the greatest economic engine the world has ever known. But what will it profit a society if we all become highly prosperous and lose our souls? As one just-retired chief executive officer of a major corporation recently told me, "It used to be fun. It was deeply satisfying to be an agent for sustaining a community of highly motivated employees. Now, it's as if the CEO, so isolated by his pay packages and his 'rationalizing activity,' is himself Marx's ultimate alienated man. The cash nexus between the executive and his work appears to be all that is left."

We are at a crossroads in corporate America. We must rediscover the power of a turned-on community of employees led by a new kind of corporate manager who is motivated much less by money and much more by pride of product and by the joy of unleashing the employees' talents and energies and tapping their potential for personal growth and team cooperation.

"Ought" implies "can." One cannot be morally obligated to perform the impossible. How then do we begin to work our way out of the present dilemma? Part of the answer lies in refashioning economic incentives along the lines I earlier suggested so as to bring about a longer term perspective on the part of the manager. By reinforcing the long-term perspective, executives would tend to place much more emphasis on the need to build relationships of mutual trust with employees, customers, and suppliers. They would also begin to see the wisdom of building unity of purpose among employees at all levels of the company through aspirational programs to define the shared values that guide both management and the workforce, through common profit sharing plans, and by other means. These are among the preconditions to corporate-wide human productivity over the long term.

Second, boards of directors will have to rule out as candidates for top corporate positions those executives who are preoccupied with their own pay and who think of employees as 'headcount. Rather they will need to identify candidates who not only are highly competent but who also have a spiritual inner strength and set of convictions that preclude a narrow, egoistic view of the world. Without this kind of anchor, I don't think a top executive will have the vision and fidelity and caring to build a great organization.

SHOULD EXECUTIVE BONUSES BE PAID OUT DURING A DOWNSIZING?

Yes, economic incentives are important, but they are no substitute for character. Nor can they substitute for moral discernment. I wonder how many boards of directors, when considering a rich compensation package for the CEO, or a very sizable downsizing of the workforce, undertake a morally sensitive process of deliberation. Such a process might entail, for example, an inquiry into whether some or all of the employees should be offered a chance to stay on the job at reduced pay, perhaps combined with an opportunity for stock ownership, and whether large executive bonuses should be paid out simultaneously with a sharp downsizing of the work force. After all, the need for radical downsizing often arises as a result of many years of inattention to belt tightening and the failure to utilize attrition and selective pruning, year in and year out. And the board should consider whether current management was partly responsible for those years of neglect. Even if it was not, there are other considerations such as the likely consequences in terms of organizational morale and public reputation. I submit that this kind of process is not only right, it is also prudent. As employees come to understand that their board reaches decisions on executive compensation and corporate downsizings only after due consideration of the alternatives and after carefully weighing the economic and moral implications of these alternatives, they will be much more likely to accept the Board's decisions and respect the leadership of their corporation.

Will we find our way out of the present dilemma? I see some hopeful signs. One is that after all the downsizing and rationalizing efforts have been put mostly behind us and the dust has settled, competitive pressures will once again drive boards to choose managers who know how to build the greatest competitive advantage a company can have: a highly productive cadre of employees who care about the customer. Also, there are signs that public pension funds are becoming more interested in the corporation as an intergenerational partnership for the creation of jobs and wealth. They are strategically positioned to perform an important role once again by prodding boards of directors over matters that contribute to, or detract from, the building of such a competitive advantage.

FACING THE COSTLY CONSEQUENCES OF MISTRUST

Finally, there is evidence that many talented young adults, now in their 20s and early 30s, are profoundly distrustful, if not cynical, about our political and economic institutions and their leaders. These young people are the inheritors of an age of diminished expectations. This legacy was bequeathed to them by older generations who made out quite well, partly by mortgaging the future of their children and grandchildren.

These young people do not see the opportunities, on anything like the scale the baby-boomers saw, to work their way up a reliable corporate ladder. Many, out of distrust, are opting to own and operate their own firms where, as they put it, they will at least have some control over their future. Others, out of disillusionment, are looking for careers that are more purposeful, though less remunerative. So, in a strange way, this distrustful young generation may force the brutally efficient manager to face up to the costly consequences of mistrust. While there are these hopeful signs that the pendulum may swing, I am all too aware of how bad things usually have to get before a critical mass of leaders musters the courage to do anything. We are all so comfortable. Why get personally involved? Why speak out and stir the pot? The silence of the good people, said Augustine, was the reason for the calamities that had befallen the Rome of his time: "Where can we readily find a man who has the courage to hold accountable those persons on account of whose pride, luxury, and avarice God now smites the earth? For often we blind ourselves to occasions of teaching and admonishing, because we fear to lose good friendships, lest this should injure us in some worldly matter which either our covetous disposition desires to obtain or our weakness shrinks from losing."

Saddest of all is the thought, which I pray is not true, that any appeal to people's moral sense is likely to fall on deaf ears because our culture of economic individualism has already robbed them of that sense. That is the point of these lines from one of T.S. Eliot's Choruses from *"The Rock."*

> What life have you if you have not life together?
> There is no life that is not in community,
> And no community not lived in praise of God.
> And now you live dispersed on ribbon roads,
> And no man knows or cares who is his neighbor.
> Unless his neighbor makes too much disturbance. . . .
>
> And the wind shall say: "Here were decent godless people:
> Their only monument the asphalt road
> And a thousand lost golf balls."
>
> Can you keep the City that the Lord keeps not with you?
> A thousand policemen directing the traffic.
> Cannot tell you why you come or where you go.
>
> When the Stranger says: "What is the meaning of this City?
> Do you huddle close together because you love each other?"
> What will you answer? "We all dwell together
> To make money from each other?" or "this is a community?"
>
> And the Stranger will depart and return to the desert.
> O my soul, be prepared for the coming of the Stranger,
> Be prepared for him who knows how to ask questions.

RESPONSE BY PROFESSOR LAWRENCE G. LAVENGOOD

Professor Gene Lavengood's teaching and research at the Kellogg School of Business, Northwestern Universityhas focused on the study of ethics and moral conduct in business and business history. He was the editor of Moral Man and Economic Enterprise *and has written cases for classroom instruction in the social role of business corporations and business ethics.*

Elmer Johnson has reviewed some recent familiar chapters in American business history and has interpreted them in a disturbing and unfamiliar way. His interpretation is especially disturbing and unusual at the Kellogg school, which more usually is an environment for unhesitant celebration of the economic rational actor, the perfection of financial markets, and the primacy of stock market value among the measures of management success.

The disturbance is compounded and may even be made vexatious because Mr. Johnson's critical review does not dissociate itself from any of themes normally dominating this school. Rather, Mr. Johnson subjects economic rationally and profit maximization and the like, to a higher criticism than customarily they are asked to bear. And he does this by evoking some unusual standards—right on out to T.S. Eliot, who makes few appearances in management text books.

"ONCE YOU INTRODUCE THE WORD 'SOUL' YOU'RE ON A CURIOUS TRACK"

I find Mr. Johnson's essay fascinating and provoking. The title, "Soulcraft" appropriately echoes William Pollard's published account of the ethos of ServiceMaster, which he titles *"The Soul of the Firm."* Once you introduce the word *soul* with all its spiritual markings into an explication of business management, you know you're on a curious track. As Mr. Johnson follows this track, he soon is putting on view some old-fashioned and rather unacademic language. Words like *virtue, community, stewardship,* and *trust* abound in his text. They lend support to a bold, unfashionable assertion made early in the lecture, that, "The highest calling of the entrepreneurial steward of the enterprise is to create and sustain a workplace in which employees can flourish." This is not the accustomed language of business schools or of business conversations. Try using the word *virtue* around the water cooler and watch the uncomprehending response. (Try using "return on assets" or "market share" and all is back to normal.) I have sensed in the case of my own students, that the word *virtue* has scarcely squeezed past their lips in years. It isn't, I think, that these younger managers have no idea of the meaning of virtue. It's that professionally, at least, they've had no practice in seeing its relevance.

The lack of practice in discerning the relevance of moral reflection is, as I read it, the heart of Mr. Johnson's concern. I share this concern and thus have a particular interest in trying to understand Mr. Johnson's reasons for making it the point of his message.

A BUSINESS CORPORATION IS A SIGNIFICANT SOCIAL INSTITUTION

The first argument for the relevance of moral reasoning arises from Mr. Johnson's concept of the corporation as a mediator. The argument begins with a reminder that a business corporation is a significant social institution, not just a slave of customers' orders, but an engine of social influence and responsibility. He states that in the political economy of the United States, one of the corporation's public functions is to serve as a social mediator. Mr. Johnson describes the mediation as occurring between the individual person and the state, and surely this is true in the sense that the business organization provides occupation, material sustenance, and a significant measure of social education that otherwise in modern society might have to be arranged by the state.

But, I think we could add to Mr. Johnson's appreciation of the social function of the corporation by recognizing something that philosophers of market capitalism have often remarked on: in capitalistic market societies, there is an inescapable need to mediate between ego (with its own individual self-interest) and the public interest. Adam Smith taught us that one indispensable mediator between self-interest and the public interest is market competition. And here the business enterprise plays a stellar role, albeit a role that is largely unintended by the enterprise itself. Another mediator between ego and the public interest, though, is politics, including government—and Adam Smith recognized that. But a third, and so often unappreciated mediator, is moral conduct that constrains ego in regard to the range of interests of other humans. (Here, I think, Adam Smith's ideas are indistinct.)

Adding to Mr. Johnson's description of mediation, recognition of the need to manage relations between ego and the common good would, I think, buttress his beautifully posed claim that a corporation is a school for education in virtue and community. Consider:

- A well-managed corporation depends on trust for its performance. Where does trust come from? From the practice of virtue, a moral community that, as Mr. Johnson says, shapes human character and behavior.

- The corporation, furthermore, depends on the assumption that others out side the corporation will honor truth-telling, promise-keeping, and respect for persons.

- Therefore, the corporation must value community as a moral principle out side as well as inside its walls. No social institution can be that. All social institutions depend on a moral society. The rules of moral society thus have to be within the stewardship of business organizations. As a second argument for the relevance of moral reasoning in business management, Mr. Johnson presses the question of legitimacy: What makes business purposes socially legitimate? At one point, he defends their legitimacy in an interesting, backhanded way.

Between human values and business purposes there is tension, says Mr. Johnson, but no basic conflict. More often than not, he goes on to say, they are mutually reinforcing. The implication of that observation deserves, I think, to be stated sharply. If, indeed, business purposes do ever conflict with fundamental social values, then the business purposes are illegitimate. It is the public interest that consents to business purposes. It doesn't work the other way around.

The third reason Mr. Johnson gives for his concern about the relevance of moral reflection is linked directly to his interpretation of recent history. He puts the matter in the form of what I perceive to be his great didactic question: "What does the decline of social capital and the privatizing power of the market have to do with the soulcraft perspective and the possibilities of the corporate manager as steward of a moral community?"

His answer is summarized in a prophetic admonition worthy of the Old Testament's Ezekiel or Jeremiah: We have been brought to the brink of damnation. (He doesn't put it that way, but that's what he meant.) We are in danger, in his words, of letting "economic incentives drive out moral incentives." I take him to mean not that economic incentives represent evil, but that their overuse represents a deathly distrust of the relevance of moral incentives. Which brings us back to the beginning. The human society we value is morally based. All humans are moral agents—moral agency being one of the defining qualities of a *human* actor. Can, then, the business corporation as a social institution stand in the day of judgment if it is managed without consistent regard for this fact? Mr. Johnson's answer is clear and compelling, and I am grateful to him for it.

CHAPTER THREE

REFLECTIONS ON SOME PRESERVING PRINCIPLES OF CAPITALISM IN A DEMOCRACY

By Max De Pree

Max De Pree spent his business career at Herman Miller, Inc., a leading manufacturer of office furniture. During his tenure as CEO, the company's revenues tripled and its stock rose five-fold. Since his retirement, he has lectured widely on leadership. His books include the best seller Leadership is an Art, Leadership Jazz, *and* Leading Without Power, *aimed primarily at nonprofit organizations. This lecture was given at Harvard University in 1997.*

Some time ago, I got a note from a woman who works in the finishing department of one of Herman Miller's plants. She happened to be a friend of mine. She wrote a wonderful letter about a company program she had been through that had special meaning to her. Then came the important part of the letter. She invited the entire Board of Directors (I happened to be chairman at the time) to attend the next session of this program. She thought we would learn something. To me, her invitation revealed a strong sense of identity and the hope that she could improve her company. She was acting like a true citizen bent on expanding the potential community. She sensed the structure of human relationships and responsibilities that formed the corporation.

The combination of democracy and a free market creates a structure that holds tremendous potential not just for our country, but for the world. Both democracy

79

and the free market are imperfect, but there is nothing else quite like them available. Because they are imperfect, we have the opportunity to improve and enrich them. We must not lose the significance of our freedom and our economic system because of their success. I care deeply about realizing the potential of our system. Yet, as is true so often in life, we ourselves have become the largest threat to the very things we should protect. It seems to me that if anything is going to ruin capitalism in America, it will be our own failure to understand and express and honor the preserving principles of the system.

I'm sure there are many legitimate perceptions of what exactly are the preserving principles of the free market system. I suffer a good deal of anxiety over what I don't know about them. But let me start with dreams. Dreams have a wonderful legitimacy in a free society. Only in an environment of freedom do dreams regularly come true. Along with dreams, though, we must also take a hard-headed look at how Americans can think together about a future. My concern is rooted in years of direct involvement in both the free market system and American democracy. I have known both success and failure. I have some glimmerings of what makes the free market tick from a citizen's point of view. I am, for better of worse, an insider. One of the lessons I've learned over many years is that there are certain things a CEO may not delegate. As citizens, we are in the same boat. There are certain things that we may not delegate. One of them is the responsibility to consider what are the preserving principles we should honor.

I believe there are six principles that underlie our free market system: hope, common good, moral purpose, education, leadership accountability, and hospitality. In describing these six principles, I hope not to give the impression that these are the responsibility of distant leaders. I was once talking with a group of business executives who were bewailing the quality of our modern media. I asked them why they didn't do something about it? "What can we do?" they said. I asked them if their companies had the same standard for quality in raw materials and in advertising. They saw the connection. I think all citizens must begin to see the direct connection between what we say we believe in, and what we actually do.

HOPE: THE ABILITY TO CHOOSE AND TO BE INCLUDED

What is the function of hope in a free market system? It is not hard to understand why hope was one of the seven cardinal virtues of the medieval Catholic church. Without hope, it is difficult to explain existence and impossible to imagine a future. How, without hope, can we explain school to a child or the entailments of teenage pregnancy to a young woman? A lack of hope is utterly dismal, degrading and destructive to us personally and to us as a society. American society is rapidly aligning itself into the hopeful and the hopeless. Tragically, the number of hopeless is growing far more rapidly than the number of the hopeful. We often suffer under an enormous myth that because so many of us are doing so well, we are a healthy and hopeful society. I wish that were true, but of course it isn't. The belief that any of us can live without hope and still be healthy is a terrible deception. In a blind and single-minded defense of individual liberties, we are ignoring the simple fact that when a sizable minority of the members of a body is ill, the entire body is ill.

In a free market system, of what is hope composed? First, is the ability to make choices. To be without choices is a great tragedy, a tragedy leading to hopelessness and cynicism. The ability to choose leads in another direction—what do we choose? How do we choose? Our choices, after all, set us apart and shape our legacy. The words "volition" and "volunteer" are usually enthusiastic and leave behind some of the hope they themselves see. Volunteers have chosen to do something. In volunteers, we have a glimpse of the source of great hope for our system. Choices are part of personal and organizational accountability to ourselves and the people we serve. Choices are the stands we take, the friends and enemies we keep. Choices are part of the stewardship of life: What do we promise? What do we owe? What may we keep? What must we abandon? We all want choices, but we sometimes forget that meaningful choices are seldom easy.

Another element of hope is opportunity. Any hopeful person has the opportunity to work, to be involved, to be needed. Isn't it my right to have the opportunity to share in work, to move continually toward my potential, to have the opportunity to be an owner? To have hope is to have identity and to be included. If I know who I am, I know where home is. Identity means to know and be known. Identity means to be heard and taken seriously. Identity means both the chance to be chosen and the chance to choose. Hope includes equity—the right to be fairly treated, the right to access. For many years, we in the United States have talked about certain gifts: the gift of talent, the gift of wealth, the gift of health. Today, we realize that the access to those gifts may be as important as the gifts themselves. Access to health care, access to education, access to influence, access to justice, access to mentors who care about our future. The stewardship of access is truly a responsibility of all citizens.

Equity presupposes the authenticity of persons. All of us are authentic in our own right—not because we work in a certain company or hold a certain position. We're insiders in our great, cross-cultural society because we are God's mix. We are made in his image. Thus we are authentic before we acquire attributes like a job or an address or a title. Superficial and transitory characteristics like these are certainly important, but the fundamental truth is that we are all human beings—

from the beginning. For us to have equity and, therefore, hope, we must realize our undeniable presence as legitimate persons in a community or organization or nation. I see examples of hope builders every day, people and organizations working to maintain this preserving principle of capitalism in a democracy: people like Norman Lear and the Business Enterprise Trust, and groups like the Kellogg Foundation and Doctors Without Borders. They are fighting a serious dearth of hope in the United States these days. If we join them in our own ways, we will win the fight.

COMMON GOOD: THE DEVELOPMENT OF A SHARED VISION?

One of the great expressions of being a free people—citizens not subjects—is individual liberty. Nothing can replace it. But like so many precious things in life, individual liberty resembles a butterfly. Squeezing it too hard can be disastrous. Yet at the same time, both democracy and the free market system have the overriding requirement that they operate in the interest of the common good and not primarily only in the interest of the people who know best how to exploit the system. Reckless individualism often puts a common good at risk. Individual liberty, both in terms of the governing to which we submit and the economic laws we create and obey, has to be measured in terms of common good.

In considering a common good, let me quote a few people who have thought seriously about it. First—and how can we talk about democracy and capitalism without him—Alexis de Tocqueville. He says, "There is, indeed, a secret tendency in democratic institutions that makes the exertions of citizens subservient to the prosperity of the community in spite of their vices and mistakes." I think it's time that our institutions not be so secretive about their commitment to a common good. We've all witnessed how in this country the legal rights and privileges of individuals often become more important than communal rights. In his monumental book, *Habits of the Heart*, Robert Bellah gives testimony to the imbalance between individualism and communitarianism, and Bellah calls us to retrieve a communal ethic and commitment to a common good. Josiah Royce, who taught philosophy at Harvard for 34 years earlier the twentieth century, observed, "Man, the social being, naturally and, in a sense, helpless, depends on communities. Severed from them, he has neither worth nor wit but wanders in waste places, and when he returns, finds a lonely house of his individual life empty, swept, and isolated." There may be no smaller packages in this world than people wrapped up in themselves.

Yet how are we to distinguish between individual liberty and mere license? How are we to modulate our liberty in light of the common good? How are we to be faithful to our commitment to a common good? A poem by theologian Walter Wietzke *(Liberty and License Galatians 5:13)* interprets God's message to us in this regard: "I have not called you to license, for in that error, society and selfhood are lost. I have called you to liberty, for in its truthful tension, society and selfhood is found." Finally, I quote George Soros [in the *Atlantic Monthly* (February 1997)], who certainly understands how to use the system. He thinks that an open society may be threatened by "excessive individualism." "Too much competition," he goes on to say, "and intolerable inequities and instability . . . The doctrine of laissez faire capitalism holds that the common good is best served by the uninhibited pursuit of self-interest. Unless it is tempered by the recognition of a common interest that ought to take precedence over particular interests, our present system . . . is liable to break down."

To be serious about the common good as a preserving principle, let me ask some questions. Do we share a vision? With emphasis on the word *share*? Are we capable of shared, functional beliefs? If so, how do we express them and defend them in the public square? Can citizens begin to see the connections between their own prosperity and that of a community? Is it acceptable in our hard-nosed, free market system, to ask the question, "What would grace enable us to be?" Thankfully, there are many people and institutions and corporations asking and answering these questions.

MORAL PURPOSE: REMOVING EGO
FROM THE GAME

The next preserving principle, I believe, is moral purpose. Without moral purpose, competence has no measure and trust has no goal. This defining thought gives me a way to think about the place of moral purpose in our economic and social system. In every church and monastery in Celtic Britain and Ireland, a fire was kept burning as a sign of God's presence. This is the way I, as a Christian, see moral purpose—-as a sign of God's presence in our system. It's up to us as citizens to keep moral purpose burning in our system, to keep moral purpose alive and visible. In groups whose purposes have both pragmatic and moral dimensions, people reach outward to serve others and inward toward their own potential. Democratic capitalism must become the context for such human development. Diversity, creativity, and truth partly define a guiding ethical space in our system, giving us a leadership that replaces the ruthless pursuit of materialism and utilitarianism with a striving toward humanity and human potential. Moral purpose in organizations and individuals also leads to other signs of God's presence. Moral purpose allows leaders to make themselves vulnerable, which becomes a gift of all true leaders to their followers. Moral purpose enables leaders to be open—for the right reasons—to both the dazzling diversity of gifts and of persons that make up our society. Moral purpose changes the rules of measurement. It removes ego from the game. It injects the questions of what's right into strategy and tactics. More important, it makes us ask the question, "Who counts?" The answer, of course, is everybody—without qualification—male, female, black, white, old and young. Moral purpose enables us to deal realistically with an equitable and system-preserving distribution of results. I'm not talking here about redistributing wealth, but about distributing fairly the results of work in a capitalistic system. I am talking about the opportunity for challenging and rewarding work, for meaningful personal growth and for service to others. What is a just reward for persons from whom leaders demand a meaningful contribution? As the New Testament reminds us, "Who plants a vineyard without eating of its fruit? Who tends a flock without getting some of its milk?" Who, indeed! The equitable distribution of results may be the most convincing evidence of our commitment to open the free market system to all.

Another sign of moral purpose is personal restraint. More and more, we all work in public. More and more, many of us work under public scrutiny. I believe this is the way it should be, especially for leaders who function in public. Whether we like it or not, perceptions of leaders are crucial to their performance. How in the context of a world with limited resources are we to understand and practice simplicity? How often do we ask ourselves, "What may we keep?" Personal and organizational restraint, coupled with personal and organizational simplicity, are significant signals to a world that not only watches the United States as its model, but waits and urgently hopes to be invited into our system. For some sins of excess, forgiveness may be appropriate, but in terms of preserving our system, we must ponder whether forgiveness alone is sufficient.

Moral purpose manifested in the lives of leaders, visible in the actions of groups and signaled in the perceptions of all of us, becomes not only a preserving principle of our system, but a bright light of hope for much of the world.

EDUCATION: CREATING THE
ARCHITECTURE OF THE SOUL

Without question, one of our greatest strengths as a nation and surely a preserving principle over our first 200 years or so of history has been our educational system. To quote de Tocqueville again: "It cannot be doubted that in the United States the instruction of the people powerfully contributes to the support of the democratic republic, where the instruction which enlightens the understanding is not separated from the moral education which amends the heart." I think he chose the word *amend* for a good reason. Much of the moral fiber of America was spun from religious influences in our schools, which I contend is the education that amends the heart. It was a good thing that diversity moved the Protestant religion out of our state schools. Unfortunately, too many parents wonder what now "amends the hearts" of their children in school.

In a column in the *Wall Street Journal* (9/2/97), William Bennett said, "We should also talk about education as a way of conveying America's moral and political principles and nurturing the character of the young. We should speak about education in the context of human excellence, high standards, and national greatness. We must . . . articulate and defend the fundamental purpose of education, which is to engage in the architecture of the soul." So how can we "engage in the architecture of the soul?" How can we improve the results of American education and amend the heart and improve the system. Are the results of our current educational system adequate to the future demands of the society we wish to be and the preservation and enrichment of the free market system? Is forcing parents to send their children to government funded, aggressively secular schools appropriate? Is this not, after all, simply a new anti-religion religion? Having asked these questions—and I try to remember that the quality of answers depends on the quality of questions—I will tell you what I believe:

- All children have a right to a fully paid education from kindergarten through twelfth grade.
- State governments have a right and a duty to set appropriate standards in academic performance.
- The current system of public education will benefit greatly from becoming a part of the free market system. Deregulation has worked for AT&T, the Post Office and religion. Why not give education—teachers, administrators, parents and children—the benefits of the same freedom and competition?
- Parents have a primary right and responsibility to choose where to send their children to gain the moral underpinning that will guide their children's lives. They also have a responsibility to participate in that process.
- I believe education can be a preserving principle of our system only if over time some change is effected. Only through change can we become what we are not now.

LEADERSHIP ACCOUNTABILITY: WITHOUT IT, OUR FREE SOCIETY WILL FAIL

While I am a strong advocate of citizens as the primary workers in understanding and enriching, and in nurturing and changing the system, I'm also sure that the behavior of leaders must be understood as a preserving principle. Exactly what do I mean by "leadership?" It is not a position. Leadership, to borrow a phrase from John Henry Newman's *The Idea of a University*, is a "habit of mind." It is not an honor, but it is demanding, hard work. Leadership is not necessarily limited to appointed leaders, but devolves on all kinds of people at all kinds of times, from the people we elect to those who accumulate adulation, from the President of the United States to, say, Michael Jordan. There will always be dominant and influential leaders with stature and power. The key question in relation to preserving the system is whether or not these leaders will hold themselves accountable. Our system may help leaders become accountable, but this is insufficient. In the end, only leaders can hold themselves accountable on behalf of the people they serve and lead. In this sense, then, I believe that these leaders are:

- Those from whom we learn
- Those who influence the setting of society's agenda
- Those who have vision
- Those who acknowledge the authenticity of persons
- Those who create
- Those who set standards
- Those like Rosa Parks who endow us with surprising legacies
- Those who meet the needs of followers
- Those whose behavior and words positively reinforce the best in our society
- Those who trumpet the breaking up and the breaking down of civility
- Those who offer hope and those who say there is no hope
- Those who are the givers, those who are the takers
- Those who scrutinize
- Those who ask the painful and necessary questions
- Those like Mother Teresa who create trust
- Those who accept responsibility for their behavior

Leadership is a serious meddling in the lives of other people. Leaders should be able to stand alone, take the heat, bear the pain, tell the truth, and do what's right. Without accountable leaders, no matter how committed or how competent the rest of us are, our free society will fail.

HOSPITALITY: GIVING SUSTENANCE
TO PEOPLE WHO COME TO YOU

Finally, let's consider hospitality as a preserving principle. When I think about what it means to be hospitable, I think of giving sustenance. If you're truly hospitable, you give sustenance of some sort to people who come to you. What can democratic capitalism give to people, all people, in the way of sustenance: financially, spiritually, and emotionally? What does hospitality have to do with personal and family dignity and with a sense of achievement and with reaching one's potential? Are elements such as these essential to the renewal and preservation of the system? I think so. If capitalism is to survive into the future, it seems to me that hospitality—not inhospitality—will be one of its chief characteristics. Think of all the inhospitable cultures and economies—China, Albania, Russia, Rwanda. These cultures are especially afraid of essential concepts like trust, meaning in work, personal commitment and hopeful opportunity. One of the current inhospitalities in the United States is our inability to deal constructively and, I must say, lovingly, with our diversity. Organizationally and culturally, capitalism has traditionally been both hospitable and inhospitable at the same time. We have always welcomed entrepreneurs, but competitors have fought tooth and nail to keep them out. It is an interesting paradox, a kind of "tough hospitality" to test newcomers for their stamina to stay in the game.

One the positive side, I see marks of hospitality in organizations every day: civility, human scale, beauty, appropriate availability of choice, openness, a system that sheds old baggage (remember how forgiveness has helped each of us become who we are), good manners and leaving no one on the fringe. Above all, hospitable organizations and culture are never indifferent. I think of hospitality personally and locally when I consider what it means for a leader to be a safe place. Outside my family, David Hubbard, President of Fuller Theological Seminary for 30 years, was my best friend. A year and a half ago, a heart attack ended his life. A few days after he died, several good friends were gathered and talking about David. Dr. Richard Mouw, his successor, said that, for him, David was always a safe place. This is an apt hospitality in today's society. If our society is to be preserved, we have to be the safe place for the creative person, for the person with contrary opinion, for the truth-telling person, for the person who believes differently.

One part of David's hospitality was to be an ethical space, a space defined by what he believed. An ethical space in capitalism would surely make our system more hospitable to new ideas and new people and fresh energy. Though I don't understand all the implications of such a space, I believe we need to consider this a responsibility of leaders. If our system can, through its leaders, provide an ethical space for newcomers—or even for oldcomers like me—would we have all the problems we do with greed and exploitation of the system? I don't think so.

A final thought about hospitality. One of the ways we express our freedom is by disagreeing with each other. Often this escalates into polarized positions and gridlock. If we are to keep hospitality as a preserving principle of our free market system, I believe that all citizens—but especially leaders—must take responsibility for reconciliation. I don't mean by that a kind of organizational philanthropy. Reconciliation for me is essential to a system like ours, which is so dependent on human relationships; therefore reconciliation is required initiative for leaders. It is not a choice. Reconciliation packs enormous organizational energy, but it must be intentionally released. By its nature, reconciliation cannot be hierarchical.

CONCLUSION: A ROCK-SOLID BELIEF IN THE FUTURE

Is our system vulnerable to change? Are we as citizens vulnerable to change? Are we as vulnerable to change as the staff of the Hermitage Museum in St. Petersburg? Let me end with a story. In the seemingly hopeless summer of 1941, as the German Army approached what was then called Leningrad, the staff of the Hermitage Museum packed up tens of thousands of paintings and sculptures, antiquities and treasure, to be shipped east, away from the Germans and the upcoming siege. It was a tragic time. The staff left the empty frames and pedestals in their proper places in the museum. They were convinced that someday they would be able to restore the Hermitage and its priceless collection of art. Though they were losing their art, they were determined not to lose hope. The Germans surrounded Leningrad for more than two years, and the Russians endured that long and arduous time with little to eat, often under attack. The staff of the Hermitage and their families moved into the basement of the museum, resolved to preserve the building. Russian soldiers and citizens came regularly to help clean up the damage done by the German artillery and to patch up as best they could the broken windows to keep out the snow. As a way of saying thank you, the staff conducted tours of the museum for them. But of course the art wasn't there. Photographs show the Hermitage curators conducting the tours, avoiding piles of snow on the beautiful parquet floors, with the groups of soldiers standing in front of empty picture frames and forlorn pedestals. The curators described from memory and in great detail the Renoirs and Rembrandts to the soldiers, filling in the blank spaces in their wonderful museum with their own dedication, commitment, and love. These people had a rock-solid belief that there was a future and they and their system were going to be part of it. So can we.

RESPONSE BY RONALD F. THIEMANN

Ronald F. Thiemann is Dean and John Lord O'Brian Professor of Divinity at Harvard Divinity School and Director of the Center for the Study of Values in Public Life. His most recent book is Religion in Public Life: A Dilemma for Democracy.

Max De Pree's essay bespeaks an uncommon wisdom—about capitalism, democracy and their common governing principles. Knowledge in our information-saturated age is in great supply; wisdom is far rarer. All the more remarkable is that these sentiments have been offered in simple, commonsensical prose that may mask the degree to which these recommendations are genuinely uncommon. Perhaps most striking of all is the degree to which Mr. De Pree has developed his proposals by drawing explicitly on religious and theological commitments. He has taken the risk of speaking as a man of faith that gives him a distinctive understanding of the principles of both democracy and capitalism. The Divinity School's Center for the Study of Values in Public Life is devoted to the task of exploring the religious values embedded in the language and practices of business, politics, voluntary associations, and the like. Thus, in response, I want to lift up some of the most important *theological* insights of Mr. De Pree's essay, and then raise a few critical questions.

Responsibility and accountability: His suggestion that we are accountable and responsible both to ourselves and to one another emerges from his conviction that we are governed and evaluated by a power higher than ourselves, that is, we bear primary and ultimate responsibility to God. This insight is fundamental to the Christian ethical tradition and particularly to the Reformed tradition within which Mr. De Pree stands. He is suggesting that an ethic of responsibility grows out of the recognition that there is a transcendent dimension to all that we do. I share that conviction, but I always recognize—as he does—that in a secular and pluralistic world, not everyone will agree with that insight. How do we encourage responsibility and accountability in a pluralistic workplace in which persons hold a wide variety of views on the transcendent dimension of life? And how does one build an organizational culture in which common principles might be shared among persons who hold vastly different belief systems?

Hope: Mr. De Pree has identified five dimensions or implications of hope—freedom, opportunity, identity, equity, and authenticity of persons. He has struck a welcome balance between emphasis upon the individual and upon the community. He said, "In a blind and single-minded defense of individual liberties, we are ignoring the simple fact that when a sizable minority of the members of the body is ill, the entire body is ill." Those of us raised in communities suffused with biblical images recognize immediately his allusion to St. Paul's image of the Body of Christ in 1 Corinthians 12: "If one member suffers, all suffer together with it; if one member is honored, all rejoice together with it." So perhaps here we have relevance to those who are not members of that religion. So, also, his reference to the theological notion that we all created in the image of God yields the quite general observation of the "fundamental truth that we are all human beings—from the beginning. For us to have equity and, therefore, hope, we must realize our eternal legitimacy in a community or organization or nation." One last comment that I believe is compatible with Mr. De Pree's analysis of hope. Hopelessness or despair is not only the plight of those who have few financial resources. We are, I believe, in the midst of a crisis of hope among those who have many resources signaled by the form of despair known as apathy.

Common good and moral purpose: Here his essay is less fully developed, and, I believe, somewhat more controversial. He asserts that democracy and the free market system both need to "operate in the interest of the common good and not primarily only in the interest of the people who know best how to exploit the system." The question remains, however, how to discern the common good and, once it is identified how to pursue it. Surely one of the most difficult challenges to democratic societies today is to define a common good that embraces the full diversity of our cultures and yet identifies some principles and values that we share in common. The sociologist James Davison Hunter has written a book entitled *Culture Wars* which argues that contemporary societies are unable to reach agreement on such common principles and thus we can only wage cultural war over issues like abortion, gay and lesbian rights, welfare, and the like. Can a religiously based vision like Mr. De Pree's help us to discern common principles in the midst of such diversity? Can principles derived from Christianity still have relevance for Jews, Muslims, or even atheists?

Education: Education, particularly public education, is one of the hard tests for contemporary democracy, and it raises hard questions to Mr. De Pree's essay as well. He asserts two principles: "All children have a right to a fully paid education from kindergarten through twelfth grade" and "The current system of public education will benefit greatly from becoming a part of the free market system." Rights, even if they are ultimately grounded in divine authority, must be guaranteed in the body politic by governments. I do not get a clear sense in his essay about the proper place of government in the maintenance and renewal of democratic and free market principles. And given the emergence in recent years of new partnerships among business, government, and faithbased social service agencies, I would be particularly interested in hearing his reflections on the viability of these new partnerships among public, private, and voluntary institutions.

Leadership and Hospitality: The obligation to offer hospitality to the stranger is one of the most universal principles of all religious traditions. Deuteronomy 10:17-19 reads "For the Lord your God is God of gods and Lord of lords, the great God, mighty and awesome, who is not partial and takes no bribe, who executes justice for the orphan and the widow, and who loves the strangers, providing them food and clothing. You shall also love the stranger, for you were strangers in the land of Egypt." At a time when many have argued that issues of immigration, race, and class division have made us as a nation less hospitable than ever before, how can this biblical injunction take root again in our common democratic life? What kind of moral renewal is needed for us, once again, to "love the stranger" in our midst?

By way of conclusion, then, let me summarize three questions I have tried to ask.

1. How can a religiously based vision be shared by those who do not believe the transcendent principles that underlie it?
2. What are the various responsibilities of government, business, and civil society (particularly communities of faith) in the moral renewal of democracy and free market systems?
3. How might the renewal that Mr. De Pree so powerfully recommends be brought about in an increasingly diverse and fragmenting society?

RESPONSE BY PROFESSOR LYNN SHARP PAINE

Lynn Sharp Paine's current research at the Harvard Business School focuses on leadership and organizational value systems, with special emphasis on business values in different cultures. She is the author of Leadership, Ethics, and Organizational Integrity, *a text and casebook.*

Max De Pree has put before us a compelling message—one that is both sobering and inspiring. Pointing to the perils of success, he reminds us that democratic capitalism is not merely an abstract theory about governments and markets. It is the day-to-day process of living and working together. It is a process that functions best when citizens are willing to embrace the ideas he calls the "preserving principles of capitalism." His implicit message is that we are not giving these principles their due. As a result, he suggests, we are missing opportunities to improve and strengthen our system of democratic capitalism. We may even, he warns, be putting ourselves and the system at risk.

Like all engaging essays, this one prompts a host of questions: What is democratic capitalism? Why is it worth preserving and improving? Are the principles Mr. De Pree discusses really essential? What other principles are important? Rather than addressing these issues, however, I want simply to underscore his central thesis and offer some observations on two issues: why it is critical that we heed Mr. De Pree's warning and, at the same time, why it is easier said than done.

First, though, a comment on the nature of the principles Mr. De Pree discusses. It is very important to note what he did *not* say. He did not, for example, tell us that preserving democratic capitalism requires that we pay more attention to discounted cash flows. Nor did he urge us to enforce our antitrust laws more vigorously. He did not tell us to embrace direct marketing, to change the rules of international trade, to adopt performance-based incentives, or to increase the efficiency of our work processes. Nowhere did he offer even a small dose of the usual nostrums dispensed in business schools to future leaders of capitalism around the world. Instead of focusing on structural and technical aspects of democratic capitalism, Mr. De Pree draws our attention to the moral dimension. Every principle he discusses relates to the domain of ethics or morality—the domain of human well-being, broadly conceived. Some might question whether all this attention to ethics is really necessary. Of course, people who have thought deeply about this matter have long understood that an ethical framework is essential for social and economic development. Let me quote a well-known passage from the *Leviathan* by Thomas Hobbes, the seventeenth century English philosopher. Hobbes describes what life would be like in a world of hostile individuals, reliant solely on themselves and lacking a shared conception of justice:

"In such condition there is no place for Industry: because the fruit thereof is uncertain; and consequently no Culture of the Earth; no Navigation, nor use of the commodities that may be imported by Sea; no commodious Building; no Instruments of moving, and removing such things as require much force; no Knowledge of the face of the Earth; no account of Time; no Arts; no Letters; no Society; and which is worst of all, continual fear and danger of violent death . . ."

Hobbes and De Pree aside, many people today consider ethics to be something that is perhaps nice, but hardly necessary. Until faced with a vexing dilemma or a shocking lapse, they simply take for granted the principles Mr. De Pree discusses. At best, the principles raise issues for someone else to worry about. Nevertheless, history and experience teach us that ignoring the ethical dimension—in business or any other sector—is dangerous. As legal historian James Willard Hurst has argued convincingly, both social responsibility and economic efficiency have been critical to corporate legitimacy in the U.S. In this regard we should note the results of a 1994 Harris poll which surveyed Americans' confidence in the U.S. corporate system. Only 26 percent of those surveyed had "a great deal or quite a lot of confidence in business." The same poll found that only

19 percent had "a great deal of confidence in the people running major companies," compared to 55 percent in 1996. Moreover, only 22 percent of those surveyed in 1994 rated the ethical standards of executives as "high" or "very high." About the same number rated them as "low" or "very low."

DEMOCRATIC CAPITALISM AS A MORAL ENTERPRISE

As we look abroad at the fragile experiments in capitalism being conducted in many regions of the world, we already see threats to legitimacy and public acceptance emerging from high levels of corruption, widespread social dislocation, insufficient transparency of information, and gross inequalities of opportunity. Today's euphoria over the triumph of capitalism seems exceedingly premature. Unless adequate regard is paid to the principles Mr. De Pree talks about, the triumph is likely to be short-lived. Democratic capitalism is not just an economic enterprise. It is also a moral enterprise. Ethical principles are as essential to its effective functioning as economic principles. If the system is to realize its purpose, if it is to provide a context for developing and releasing our potential as human beings, then it must do more than generate the kind of value we measure in economic terms. It must nurture a wide range of other values essential to our well-being—values like hope, dignity, trust, mastery, understanding, justice, and community. The system's legitimacy depends not just on the sheer quantity of wealth it creates, which is surely impressive, but also on its openness, its inclusiveness, and the promise that every individual can find a way to contribute and at the same time earn a livelihood.

Nevertheless, what Mr. De Pree is proposing—enlarging the space for ethics within democratic capitalism—is easier said than done. We have some troubling habits that stand in the way. One is the tendency to see economics and ethics— money and morals—as antagonists, occupying separate and more or less self-contained realms. This schizophrenia is often laid at the doorstep of the economists and business people who talk about commerce as a value-free domain of rational self-interest. But we see it every day in our own behavior. How often, as consumers, do we consider the working conditions of the people who produce the goods we buy? As shareholders and pension fund beneficiaries, how much attention do we pay to the business practices of the companies in which we invest? This disconnect is reinforced by philosophers, theologians, and ethicists who speak as if ethics were only about altruism and self-sacrifice, having nothing to do with economics and personal interest. This disconnect is very problematic. Maybe it was once true that we could separate society into the self-contained spheres of business, religion, government, and so on—each governed by its own internal logic. Such a separation is not possible today. For better of worse, we live in a world where ethics and economics are intertwined at every juncture. Most of the serious issues we face—from health care to social disintegration—have both ethical and economic dimensions.

THE NEED FOR A NEW KIND OF LEADER

To address these problems effectively we are going to need more leaders who are what I call "multi-logical." Multi-logical leaders are as comfortable in the realm of ethics as the realm of economics. They are people who can discern and reason in both ethical and economic terms. Of course, we already have some leaders like this. In business, we have examples like Max De Pree and William Pollard, former chairman of ServiceMaster, who viewed their companies as having both economic and ethical purposes. They saw their organizations not just as instruments for creating economic value, but also as communities for developing people through service to customers and society more broadly. This infusion of moral purpose, social awareness, and principled commitment into business has broad implications for organizations and management. As Mr. De Pree noted in his essay, this infusion "injects the question of what's right into strategy and tactics." That may sound like a minor adjustment, but the implications are profound. It would mean, for example, that in making investment decisions, managers would consider the impact on key stakeholders as well as the economic returns. In evaluating employees, they would look for principled behavior as well as financial performance. In the search for opportunities, they would seek socially positive ways to enhance the bottom line. In other words, managers would hold themselves accountable to both economic and ethical standards.

Let me conclude with a story. It's about a man named Jacques Zwahlen, the CEO of a small privately-held Swiss mail order company. One morning in 1994, Mr. Zwahlen was reading the newspaper and having a cup of coffee when a report on the radio in the background caught his attention. An international children's rights group was accusing IKEA, the well-known Swedish retailer, of selling hand-woven carpets made in South Asia by children working under appalling and inhuman conditions. The report gave Zwahlen cause for great concern. Only three months earlier, his company had added a line of hand woven carpets from South Asia to its selection of home furnishings, and Zwahlen had no idea whether his suppliers were sourcing from producers that used child labor. Zwahlen immediately contacted the company's carpet buyer and asked him to find out whether children were involved in making the carpets. When three of the company's four suppliers declined to provide information about their sources, Zwahlen decided to sever their relationship and search for alternative suppliers. Zwahlen didn't stop there. Recognizing that simply boycotting goods produced by child labor might ultimately make children worse off, he also sought guidance from a child welfare organization. His aim: to see if there were constructive ways his business could contribute to improving the lot of child workers and other forced laborers. Eventually, the company settled on a program of supplier monitoring, coupled with support for an experimental program to combine work and education for children in the carpet industry.

News of Zwahlen's actions spread quickly. He was asked to appear on a well-known news and talk show on French television. After a rather lengthy discussion in which Zwahlen, and others, spoke about the child labor issue, the host turned to Zwahlen with his concluding questions: "Very quickly, M. Zwahlen, two questions. First, what motivates you? Is it, so to speak, a feeling of world citizenship, a humanitarian instinct, or is it also a necessary business precaution to work like this because if anyone ever found out, you would be ruined?" The host's question reflects the dichotomy I talked about earlier between ethics and economics. Yet Zwahlen refuses to be forced into a choice between one or the other. He replies, "It's both, I think." When the host then suggests "that we take the cynical position for a moment," Zwahlen again refuses. "No," he replies, going on to elaborate: "First, it's intolerable from a humanist point of view to imagine participating in a destructive economic practice, leading nowhere, which does nothing for the communities which practice it, nor for their countries, nor for the consumer country. So the humanitarian aspect is there, but behind it, one must realize that . . . a company caught participating in this type of commerce risks losing its reputation."

This story shows how difficult it is to break through the intellectual and emotional wall that separates our thinking about ethical and economic matters, particularly in the business context. Somehow in business, it isn't quite acceptable to speak in such direct humanitarian terms. Such concerns have to be packaged and presented as reputational or legal issues in order to command attention. Zwahlen, however, resists this framing. He speaks with conviction in both ethical and economic terms. In order to move in the direction Mr. De Pree has laid out, we must develop more leaders who have this capacity. Only then will we realize the full potential of democratic capitalism.

UNIVERSITY OF
NOTRE DAME

CHAPTER FOUR

THE INTERNATIONAL VOCATION OF AMERICAN BUSINESS

By Michael Novak

Theologian, author, and former U.S. ambassador, Michael Novak holds the George Frederick Jewett Chair in Religion and Public Policy at the American Enterprise Institute in Washington, D.C., where he also serves as Director of Social and Political Studies. Dr. Novak has written some 25 books on the philosophy and theology of culture. He has received numerous awards including the 24th Templeton Prize for Progress in Religion. This lecture was given at Notre Dame University in 1998.

Not long ago, the business school of the Jesuit University of Wheeling printed up a T-shirt for its annual gathering, inscribed as follows:

The Calling of Business is to Support the Reality and Reputation of Capitalism, Democracy, and Moral Purpose Everywhere and Not in any way to Undermine Them

Permit me to borrow that quotation from a T-shirt as a starting place. Behind that quotation lie six presuppositions, which I would like to make as clear as the snowy peak of Mont Blanc against a cold blue sky.

1. A life committed to business is a noble vocation.

2. The moral structure of the corporation is propelled by important moral

ideals (creativity, community, and practical wisdom) and nurtures many virtues (such as teamwork, honesty, a willingness to serve others, disciplined work, sacrifice, vision, and strength in confronting hard decisions).

3. Without specific moral virtues and respect for moral law, neither democracy nor capitalism can long endure.

4. A person in business works in a form of human community that at its best exemplifies a relation between person and association that Christian teaching has always tried to inspire.

5. Business firms operate within a system that is usefully named "capitalism" (from *caput*, L., head) because it is law-governed, mind-centered, creativity-driven, rather than merely being named a "free enterprise" or "market" system. For an inventive, creative capitalism is a necessary (but not sufficient) precondition for the emergence and healthy development of democracy.

6. Business is also the primary support (on the material side) of the associations and organizations of civil society.

Until a few years ago, these six solid premises were being widely ignored under the spell of unreality cast on many social thinkers by the dream of socialism. Those of you still undecided about one or more of these premises may consult an array of studies. Few today believe that socialist economics is the wave of the future. But most nations still find it difficult to root themselves in capitalism, democracy, and moral purpose. Most have little experience under the rule of law. Most of the countries of the former Soviet Union, most of Asia (emphatically including China), much of the Middle East, and most of Africa lack many of the cultural and political habits (and institutions) required for a successful capitalist system. What, then, is the proper conduct for U.S. businesses with respect to such countries? Let us invent a composite, fictional nation called Xandu, and do a case study.

A TEST CASE: XANDU

Suppose that a graduate from the Notre Dame business school went to work for Kavon (a fictional, new electronics firm), and suppose that Kavon was scouting out the possibility of launching an operation in Xandu. The general rationale for these projects is that "constructive engagement" is the only way in which Xandu will be brought into the circle of democratic, capitalist, and law-governed nations. No doubt, that rationale has merit. But will its premises be realized? What must be done to make sure that they are? The political system in Xandu is still a narrow, closed, paranoia-feeding system, whose elites remain in power only by maintaining total political and psychological control over the population. These elites are intelligent and have come to see that capitalist methods deliver abundance where socialist methods deliver scarcity.

But the Xandunese leaders have studied recent history and found that many societies that first pursued economic growth also then awakened demands for political democracy. That was the sequence in Greece, Portugal, Spain, South Korea, and the Philippines; from Chile and Argentina in South America's southern cone northward throughout Latin America; and in Kenya. They can see that a system of economic liberties generates a desire for political liberties. The social mechanism seems to be as follows: Successful entrepreneurs learn by experience that they are smarter and in closer touch with some realities than political commissars. They begin to demand republican institutions—that is, institutions of representative government. Thumbnail sketch: In the year 1900, there were only four democratic regimes on earth, but by the year 1998 there were at least 70. All are characterized by capitalist economies, and many followed the path from economic to political liberty.

In the Xandunese diagnosis, therefore, the business corporation is the camel's nose under the totalitarian tent. The country's leaders know that they need Western corporations, at least for the next 20 years. But they discern the essential moral character of business, and its subversive effect, since the corporation embodies principles of limited government, the rule of law, and high internal ideals of person and community. Through the practices of business corporations, these ideas spread like a "disease," which Xandu wants to keep in quarantine. The Xandunese need the technical and moral *culture* of the corporation—the technology, the skills, the methods, the training. They do *not* want the *political* culture to which it gives rise. They hope that by redoubling their efforts at control, they can quarantine liberty within the economic sphere. They want at all costs to prevent the principle of liberty from gradually seeping into the political life of Xandu.

By seven or eight favorite devices, the Xandunese leaders attempt to control the efforts of Kavon and all the other foreign companies now bringing their factories, know-how, and new technologies to Xandu. First, the Xandunese insist that all employees of new foreign firms be selected and "prepared" by a Xandunese personnel company. This company will be run by the Xandunese National Party, and this Party will insist on having an office on the site of the foreign firm to mediate any labor problems. From that office, it will also maintain strict political control over the workforce. Second, to the extent that labor unions will be represented within the foreign firm, these will be limited to official Xandunese National unions and will also be used as instruments of political control. Third, some foreign firms will be required to provide information about the behavior of their employees. For instance, signs of religious practice or having children beyond the mandated minimum or reading certain political materials are matters about which the labor monitors want to be informed. Fourth, foreign entrepreneurs who own small firms will be obliged to enter into "partnerships" with Xandunese firms—firms owned either by the government or by freelancing officials. From time to time, in fact, a recalcitrant foreign entrepreneur has been arrested and thrown in jail, his assets seized and communication with the outside world entirely cut off. One such imprisonment has already been know to last six years. Larger foreign firms will be expected to turn a blind eye.

Concerning the government, there is no rule of law. Even one or two large firms have been bilked out of large sums—$50 million in one deal, $100 million in another—when Xandunese partners (government officials or their proxies) walked away from losses caused by their own behavior. Fifth, foreign firms are sometimes expected to accept suppliers assigned to them. Factories in Xandu, unhappily, are very often staffed with slave labor maintained in appalling conditions and forced to toil for years for the sole benefit of the ruling party elite. To say that standards of nutrition, sanitation, and living quarters in the Xandunese labor camps are primitive is too weak. They are intended to humiliate and to intimidate. Details have been confirmed in texts smuggled out by survivors. Sixth, Kavon and other high-tech companies will be requested, cajoled, and compelled to share with their counterparts in government firms important secrets of U.S. satellite, missile, metallurgic, or computer technology. (Obviously, they will also have to share these secrets with their own Xandunese work force, put in place by the party.) Xandunese engineers, scientists, and technicians learned enormous amounts from their American counterparts, particularly when their own rockets, hired to carry aloft U.S. satellites, blew up and when, to avoid more such heavy expenses, U.S. technicians coached the Xandunese in the details of more advanced rocket technology. The latest Xandunese rockets are now being sold to at least three sworn enemies of the United States. Seventh, the government of Xandu regards religions of the Creator (such as Judaism, Christianity, and Islam) as threats to its own total power. Because the leadership is obscurely aware that respect for the individual arises from belief in a Creator Who transcends the power of governments, the government of Xandu regards personal acts of religious piety as dangers to the regime. It discreetly watches over Xandunese employees of international firms for signs of religious deviation. It especially persecutes Christians.

Under conditions such as these, the mere presence of American firms in Xandu will not necessarily lead to social change for the better. "Constructive engagement" that is complicit in the practices described above can be a delusion. If American businesses blindly, unintelligently, and uncritically collaborate with leaders who implicate them in barbarous practices, they will destroy the reputation of capitalism, democracy, and their own declared moral purposes. A handful of American firms, for instance, are led by evangelical Christians with strong commitment to following the practice of Jesus by taking their efforts to the whole world, no matter how unsavory the reputation of the regime. Even such firms will need to have procedures in place to protect themselves against complicity and scandal, lest they be taken advantage of. So also will other firms whose interests are predominantly economic. There may be some firms whose leaders are so cynical that they make it a practice not to raise moral or political questions against the sort of abuses listed above, lest large sums be lost in crooked dealings. Corrupt government officials are found all around the world. Some firms know better than others how to draw a bright line around the edges of their own dealings and to instruct their agents clearly to live by U.S. company standards. They do not enter negotiations expecting Sunday school, but they are prepared to spot and to avoid abuses in advance.

No doubt, few are the governments that *in the full range* of their attitudes and practices manifest all the behaviors ascribed above to this fictional country of Xandu. Yet even within countries whose record on the whole is good, there are rogue operations that need to be checked. Thus, in planning their operations in Xandu, the executives of Kavon might wish to consult a checklist of all the abuses of sound business ethics that have been reported in various countries. They should certainly prepare defensive tactics. They will need an ongoing capacity to gather accurate information about their business contacts. They will also need to be on guard against contractual provisions for any practices about which they would not wish the world to know. They also need a set of positive proposals to suggest *in the place of* those they find objectionable. Having looked briefly at a concrete (albeit fictional) case, let us now return to some of the underlying substantive issues.

THE MORAL AMBIGUITY OF HUMAN FREEDOM

As a set of practices, business is an inherently moral occupation—rooted in free creativity, dependent on and nourishing an important form of cooperative association, and inculcating humble realism. But if business is an inherently moral occupation, then in the very practice of its craft, practitioners are capable both of moral and immoral acts. Again and again, every day, they must choose whether to fufill their own firm's moral ideals, presuppositions, and tendencies—or to betray them. Since the practice in which they are engaged is inherently moral, they are held to high standards. Should they betray those standards, they injure not only their firms and themselves, but the reputation of the entire business system. Those three betrayals—of their firms, themselves, and the business system—inflict an enormous loss on a great many human beings, especially the poor, whose economic welfare depends upon a successful business system.

Moreover, betrayals by business are certain to be noticed. Many members of the literary class—journalists and moviemakers as well as novelists, poets, cultural critics, and historians—have inherited a literary culture steeped in anti-business sentiment. Such sentiments flow abundantly from two reservoirs—one socialist, the other aristocratic. Both Tories and Socialists teach that "economic liberalism" is a sin—in Spanish, *Libleralismo es pecado*. Both are inclined to hold that business is immoral; even worse, that it is amoral (i.e., nonhuman). Business, in the view of socialists and aristocrats alike, is irretrievably *vulgar*. It is concerned with the cash nexus, the *almighty dollar, filthy lucre, greed*. It overlooks such noble things, such end-in-themselves, as beauty, truth, and compassion. This view is wrong, of course, but it is deeply entrenched in literary culture and among historians. Hence, it is that we often meet in literary productions the figure of the humanly misshapen businessman, whose callous misdeeds (those of Scrooge, for instance) are employed as an indictment of an entire profession, even an entire economic system. I ask you point-blank: Can you think of a novel, play, poem, or essay in literary criticism that does not portray business in terms of moral inferiority?

For such reasons, people in business must anticipate that every moral failing of theirs will not be discounted merely as a personal lapse. It will be magnified as evidence of the moral corruption of the entire system in which they spend their lives. Really good people, it is sometimes suggested even in serious universities, even Christian universities, would not go to business school. Serious Christians, in particular, called to lives of compassion for the poor, and service to a Divine Master who lived in such poverty that he had not whereon to rest his head, should not work merely to make a buck. Going to business school, hoping to make a lot of money, expecting to live well and constantly to better one's position—such things are held to sit uncomfortably with the Gospel of Jesus Christ. We know from the history of Christian reflection on business that such derogations from the vocation of business represent neither moral reality nor true Christian belief. If you remember that in fine textiles, design, fashion and other fields, northern Italy has for centuries been one of the most entrepreneurial regions of the world, it should not surprise you that popes from northern Italy have often envisioned a large and creative social role for entrepreneurs, as in this text from Pius XII in 1956:

Every exchange of products, in fact, quite apart from satisfying definite needs and desires, makes it possible to put new means into operation, arouses latent and sometimes unexpected energies, and stimulates the spirit of enterprise and invention.

Almost ten years later, told men and women in business that he saw in them reflections of the divine:

> You represent a splendid development of the faculties of man, which, as used by the, have given proof of vast and superb capabilities. Indeed, they have further revealed the divine reflection of the face of man and displayed still more the traces of a transcendent and dominant thought in the cosmos that has been opened by scholars for new explorations and by yourselves for new conquests.

Thus there should be no doubt in our minds that the vocation of business is inherently noble. An historical example from the early economic development of the West may deepen our insight. From the fourth century onward, Benedictine monasteries were the first outposts of civilization. Around their walls, and taught by their learning, the wandering barbarian tribes of Europe learned for the first time how to live above the level of subsistence and how to establish towns for many new civilizing pursuits around the monastery libraries and centers for the arts. Invention and discovery flourished. The monasteries also became the first multinational business corporations. By organizing long-term economic systems for efficient, lawlike, and rational production, the monks were able to invest in the construction of institutions of higher civilization and take some of their own profits in the form of leisure for prayer and contemplation.

Today, the high hopes of the poor depend on a widespread fulfillment of the business vocation. When national economies are in freefall, in recession, or in decline, it is difficult even to imagine raising up the poor from poverty; the creation of new jobs, new wealth, and open opportunity; the strengthening of civil society and its nonprofit sector; the economic growth that inspires confidence in democracy; and leisure for contemplation and the pursuits of civilized living. Under conditions of scarcity, depression, or economic stagnation, such goods are threatened. Social well being depends upon at least some measure of creative business activity. Yet none of these potential contributions removes from business endeavors the fateful ambiguity that inheres in all human freedom. None of these good fruits of business activity flows automatically, ineluctably, necessarily. Being in business is a morally serious vocation, freighted with grave consequences for nations and civilizations. An index of this ambiguity is found in the opinions of the American founding fathers. The problem of the international vocation of American business is not, at the end of the day, much different from the burning question posed for the founders of our republican experiment in the beginning—whether to foster an ethos of active commerce.

We should not forget that North America was the original "underdeveloped country." By comparison, South America was awash with gold and silver and blessed by abundant and easily plucked supplies of food. The decision whether to promote commerce and invention in North America was a fateful decision.

THE COMMERCIAL REPUBLIC OF THE FOUNDING FATHERS

The American founders held that each type of political regime influences the habits of its people, but each in a different way. Aristotle had noted much earlier that, under occupation by a foreign power, some people become sycophantic and corrupt, while others resist corruption heroically. In other words, the individual does not mature in isolation, but in a particular city. Each individual is a child of his *polis*: Man is a political animal. Ethics, properly understood, is a branch of politics: The character of the *polis* shapes the *ethos*. This *ethos*, in turn, impresses the sentiments and habits of individuals. This insight was familiar to the founders; it was part of their own world view. A republican form of government, they believed, would form a better type of citizen than a monarchy. A monarchy forms *subjects*; a republic would form *citizens*. As the character of the *polis* is different, so also the *ethos*.

For instance, in a letter written to Mercy Warren six months before the Declaration of Independence, John Adams took up the fundamental Aristotelian principle: "It is the Form of Government which gives the decisive Color to the Manners of the People, more than any other Thing." Since Adams believed a republic demands a high ethical standard from its citizens, he at first believed a republic would *not work* in America:

> Virtue and simplicity of manners are indispensably necessary in arepublic among all orders and degrees of men. But there is so much rascality, so much venality and corruption, so much avarice and ambition, such a rage for profit and commerce among all ranks and degrees of men even in America, that I sometimes doubt whether there is public virtue enough to support a republic.

Nonetheless, Adams had no doubts about the comparative effects of a republic and a monarchy upon moral character:

> But a Republic, altho it will infallibly beggar me and my Children, will produce Strength, Hardiness, Activity, Courage, Fortitude and Enterprise; the

manly noble and Sublime Qualities in human Nature, in Abundance. A Monarchy would probably, somehow or other make me rich, but it would produce so much Taste and Politeness, so much Elegance in Dress, Furniture, Equipage, so much Musick and Dancing, so much Fencing and Skaiting, so much Cards and Backgammon; so much Horse Racing and Cockfighting, so many Galls and Assemblies, so many Plays and Concerts that the very Imagination of them makes me feel vain, light, frivolous and insignificant.

Yet even after Adams became convinced that republican self-government was morally better, he was deeply worried that the *commercial* spirit would undercut republican virtue.

I sometimes tremble to think that, altho We are engaged in the best Cause that ever employed the Human Heart yet the Prospect of successes is doubtful not for Want of Power or of Wisdom but of Virtue. The Spirit of Commerce, Madam, which even insinuates itself into Families, and influences holy Matrimony, and thereby corrupts the morals of families as well as destroys their Happiness, is much to be feared and is incompatible with the purity of Heart and Greatness of soul which is necessary for an happy Republic.

Thomas Jefferson, Adams' lifelong friend and correspondent, shared similar fears: "Our greediness for wealth, and fantastical expense has degraded and will degrade the minds of our maritime citizens. These are the peculiar vices of commerce."

The spiritual strength of a nation, Jefferson held, lies in the *proportion* of its citizens who husband the soil, and he believed (like many of the ancient poets such as Horace and Virgil) that manufacture and commerce introduce rot into the body politic. For Jefferson, the corruption of morals that arises from commerce is:

The mark set on those, who not looking up to heaven, to their own soil and industry, as does the husbandman, for their subsistence, depend for it on the casualties and caprice of customers. Dependence begets subservience and venality, suffocates the germ of virtue, and prepares fit tools for the designs of ambition.

Some of these are powerful arguments. Even today, we see some evidence on their behalf. Montesquieu, whose *The Spirit of the Laws* was well known to the American founders, is usually regarded as the progenitor of the new American ideal of the "commercial republic." His basic insight was that every regime is centrally constructed around one social class: the royal family and its aristocracy; the military; the clergy; men of manufacturing and commerce; or the lower classes (hunters or cultivators). In Montesquieu's time, the freest country in the world and the most mildly governed was Britain, and Britain was manifestly a "nation of shopkeepers." In this, Montesquieu saw an important connection: "Commerce is a cure for the most destructive prejudices; for it is almost a general rule, that wherever we find agreeable manners, there commerce flourishes; and that wherever there is commerce, there we meet with agreeable manners."

Is Montesquieu right about this? We may test his thesis against contemporary examples. Under communism, shops in Eastern Europe were run by state bureaucrats; customers expected to be ignored and insulted. In the same shops a few years later, under the spirit of commerce, agreeable manners slowly returned. In Washington, D.C., to go to city hall for a driver's license and to shop in a private store are two quite different experiences. Commerce *does* seem to encourage agreeable manners, more so at least than government agencies.

Next, Montesquieu adds another testable observation about building democracy on commerce:

> True it is that when a democracy is founded on commerce, private people may acquire vast riches without a corruption of morals. This is because the spirit of commerce is naturally attended with that of frugality, economy, moderation, labor, prudence, tranquillity, order, and rule. So long as this spirit subsists, the riches it produces have no bad effect. The mischief is, when excessive wealth destroys the spirit of commerce, then it is that the inconveniences of inequality begin to be felt.

In America, Tom Paine used an even stronger argument against the fears about commerce expressed by Adams and Jefferson:

> I have been an advocate for commerce, because I am a friend to its effects. It is a pacific system, operating to unite mankind by rendering nations, as well as individuals, useful to each other . . . if commerce were permitted to act to the universal extent it is capable of, it would extirpate the system of war.

Alexander Hamilton's observations from his own upbringing in Jamaica also brought him to lessons almost opposite to those of Jefferson. Hamilton argues that men do not work well in uncongenial fields; in nations, therefore, the larger the variety of occupations, the more abundant the flowering of human talent. To cherish and stimulate the activity of the human mind by multiplying the objects of enterprise is not among the least considerable of the expedients by which the wealth of a nation may be promoted. Even things in themselves not positively advantageous sometimes become so by their tendency to provoke exertion. Every new scene that causes the busy nature of man to rouse and exert itself adds a new energy to the general stock of effort. In direct opposition to Jefferson, Hamilton adds that the spirit of enterprise "must be less in a nation of mere cultivators, than in a nation of cultivators and merchants; less in a nation of cultivators and merchants, than in a nation of cultivators, artificers [manufacturers] and merchants." In a nation in which enterprise multiplies the fields of activity, the tyranny of a majority is less likely.

Finally, Alexis de Tocqueville also praises the spirit of commerce in America; he sees both its dangers and its positive advantages. At first, he seems to give a sharp rebuke to Jefferson: "Democracy not only multiplies the number of workers . . . It gives them a distaste for agriculture and directs them into trade and industry."

Still, Tocqueville makes only modest claims for commerce. It does not produce high virtue, but it prepares the soul for it:

> The doctrine of self-interest properly understood does not inspire great sacrifices, but every day it prompts some small ones; by itself it cannot make a man virtuous, but its discipline shapes a lot of orderly, temperate, moderate, careful, and self-controlled citizens. If it does not lead the will directly to virtue, it establishes habits which unconsciously turn it that way.

The inner structure of commerce, in fact, encourages many garden-variety virtues:

> . . . in democracies the taste for physical pleasures takes special forms which are not opposed by their nature to good order; indeed they often require good order for their satisfaction. Nor is it hostile to moral regularity, for sound morals are good for public tranquillity and encouraging industry.

A little later, though, Toqueville sees an opposite danger:

> Carried to excess, however, the taste for pleasure destroys the vigilant protection of rights. When the taste for physical pleasures has grown more rapidly than either education or experience of free institutions, the time comes when men are carried away and lose control of themselves at sight of the new good things they are ready to snatch. Intent only on getting rich, they do not notice the close connection between private fortunes and general prosperity. There

is no need to drag their rights away from citizens of this type; they themselves voluntarily let them go.

Yet, while success in commerce may breed moral laxity:

There is a closer connection than is supposed between the soul's improvement and the betterment of physical conditions. A man can treat the two things as distinct and pay attention to each in turn. But he cannot entirely separate them without in the end losing sight of both.

The human being is an embodied spirit. Concern for one's own body cannot be entirely separated from care for the interior life of one's soul. Each without the other lacks an essential side of one's being. This seems to me a sound Christian point.

But here is a third argument for commerce: To invest in the future is to give up consumption in the present. Parents or even an entire generation must sacrifice their pleasure for the benefit of those to come into the future. It is a condition of business that people are able to transcend their own immediate gratification. That is why religious nations [Toqueville observed] have often accomplished such lasting achievements.

For thinking of the other world, they had found out the great secret of success in this . . . As soon as they have lost the way of relying chiefly on distance hopes, they are naturally led to want to satisfy their least desires at once; and it would seem that as soon as they despair of living forever, they are inclined to act as if they could not live for more than a day.

The font and origin of business, in other words, lie in the human spirit. But a total preoccupation with commerce-or with physical pleasures-dries out the soul; the cistern cracks, and there is no living water. In short, the life of commerce is more closely related to the life of the spirit than its critics often suppose. To summarize this section: Despite the ambiguities inherent in founding a republic upon commerce, the founders soberly considered commerce the best of available foundations. Commerce increases diversity, the diffusion of power and wealth and talent, and the healthy multiplication of interests, in such fashion that no one faction can become tyrannous. And yet a man of solely commercial interests and commercial purposes may lose sight of larger purposes. He may stultify his soul. He may lose his taste for eternal life and, thus, his sense of the immortal dignity of every human being, the very ground of human rights. This ambiguity, inherent in the commercial republic, is a fact of human life. It is not an ambiguity unknown to other types of regime. Yet, in the commercial republic, facing it squarely is even more important than in other regimes. For the commercial republic depends on a doctrine of the incomparable worth of the human person.

THE BUSINESS CORPORATION IN XANDU

Let us now return to our main theme. Earlier, we noted seven or eight ways in which Xandunese authorities have asked Western firms to carry out certain political activities on behalf of the government. Some major American corporations have refused to go along with these demands, and in those cases, the Xandunese authorities have let the matter drop. One can imagine the surprise and contempt that the Xandunese authorities must feel toward those companies who, without any sign of resistance, simply comply with their demands. The chief justification for encouraging American businesses to invest in foreign societies such as Xandu is to help to build up an international civil society. If and when business corporations indulge in activities that injure or destroy civil society, then they commit a fourfold evil: (1) They do things *evil in themselves*; (2) they distort and damage the *internal moral structure* of the corporation; (3) they injure the moral *reputation* of their firm; and (4) they defile the model of the *free society* to which they swear allegiance, and in whose name they justify constructive engagement in the first place.

By such practices, some companies *have* injured the moral reputation of capitalism around the world. They have acted as if all they were interested in was their own financial gain. They have allowed observers to infer that they were indifferent to the plight of human beings and to the immoral and oppressive structures of the lawless nations in which they operate. It is *because* business organizations are economic organizations, rather than political or moral organizations, that they are allowed to function in totalitarian countries, while moral and political institutions are not. Nonetheless, business corporations are not *merely* economic institutions, for they develop to normal growth and in normal ways only within certain kinds of political regimes, and only in certain kinds of cultural ecology. In this sense, corporations are fragile plants; they grow only in certain kinds of soil. Corporations, therefore, cannot shed their commitment to law, liberty, and moral purpose as snakes shed their skin. (Unless, of course, some *are* snakes.) Commitments to law, liberty, and moral purpose are part of their inner constitution.

What should corporations do in countries like Xandu? Let us suppose that in recent years a number of prison labor camps have been identified in Xandu. Suppose that these camps were built both for political and religious dissidents. In these labor camps, torture is a frequent practice. Punishment is meted out daily, and indoctrination and "moral reeducation" are daily aims. In these labor camps, goods are produced that are offered for sale to Western and other corporations. Some American corporations may already have participated unknowingly in buying goods from slave labor camps. This would be evil stuff. First, if such happenings became known, such purchases would be impossible to justify before the world. Trade in goods made by the sweat of blood of slaves is an abomination. Second, Western companies themselves have a stake in the rule of law. Some foreign authorities have already treated Western companies capriciously, seizing their assets and changing unilaterally the terms of contracts signed earlier. The abrogation of the rule of law, in short, imposes heavy costs. Third, absent an active civil society, there will be no associations or groups within Xandunese society to protest against abuses. Naked authority will rule nakedly. This would not be a long-term environment for productive commercial activities. In such circumstances, it is crucial for American and other Western firms to maintain their moral self-respect. They must become acutely conscious of their own moral and political identity, determined not to sell themselves as less than they are. Business corporations truly are the *avant-garde* of free societies. They represent the first wedge of the development of healthy civil societies, the rule of law, and the new birth of activities, associations, and organizations independent of government.

NEW RULES OF ENGAGEMENT: PRACTICAL STEPS

The first practical step for Kavon and other companies is to recognize that some rare nations may, for a time, under a certain regime, be so bad that it would be a blunder for any self-respecting firm to collaborate with them. Such decisions are easier when international sanctions (or even national laws) prohibit trade and investment. They are more difficult when companies must reach decisions in hard cases without political guidance. Today, of course, sanctions are too profligately and unsystematically used: the U.S. currently exercises sanctions against some 70 countries. This renders long-range investment planning useless. Still, the long-range good of the human race depends on bringing all nations, even rogues nations, back within the circle of law-abiding and tolerable moral behavior. The leaders of nations are not choirboys, and the morality of nations is in some ways more gross and less observant than the morality of individuals (although in some ways it can also be nobler and higher). Still, there are four powerful reasons why the executives of Kavon and other companies must support the rule of law and sound moral codes:

- Trade, investment, and commerce depend on the rule of law and on clear standards of morality.
- Companies have a long-term interest in promoting international moral and legal standards and in making sure that these standards are framed with economic development in view.
- Misguided standards set by antibusiness elites both at home and abroad could do a lot of harm, and careless behavior by companies strengthens such elites.
- Internally, business corporations need high standards themselves, in order to gain moral authority to take the lead in international activities.

The second practical step is for some enterprising business school to launch a major research project outlining new "rules of engagement" for our new international era. This project would consist of two closely related surveys. The first would develop a list of 50 or so of the most common abuses of ethics or human rights by governments or firms around the world—a kind of checklist of pitfalls that managers ought to have in hand. Such a list should include the seven or eight abuses enumerated in this paper, plus others such as bribes, secret fees, kickbacks, hidden shares in profits, and sweetheart deals, whether demanded by local officials or offered by competitors.

The second survey would generate a parallel list of practical strategies and tactics for successfully defeating all attempted abuses. A corporation whose field officers are fully trained and amply armed with the relevant authority to foil anticipated abuses would have in hand, as it were, clearly stated "rules of engagement," by which to report and to repel outside attempts to compromise the home company.

Internal rules of behavior (it goes without saying), including conditions of immediate dismissal for specified acts of wrongdoing, would guide internal corporate initiatives and practices. The cleaner the ethical principles within the company, the easier decisions are for executives in the field. They know in advance which sorts of behavior will receive moral support from the home office and which will end in reprimand or dismissal. In business as in football and other contact sports, energy is more swiftly channeled when the rule book is clear. *Negatively*, then, businesses must avoid those activities that injure or destroy the moral structure of civil society. *Positively*, they must proactively seek out ways— quiet ways—to nurture the political and moral soil that the universal growth of commerce requires. For instance, using due prudence, modestly and without fanfare, they might instruct employees in the rule of law and the corporate code and teach them the elementary history of liberal political and economic institutions, so that employees might understand the ethos of the firm. Obviously, companies should avoid proselytizing for a particular political party or engaging in domestic politics, local or national. Nonetheless, they should import reading materials and introduce the literature of liberty to their own executives and employees, as well as into schools and libraries in the host country. For practical reasons, they need to regard themselves as teachers. They should be forthright in recounting the history of their firm, telling the stories of its heroes, explaining its corporate ethos, and defending the cultural and political presuppositions on which it depends. They should always conduct themselves as full-fledged carriers of the thinking and morals of the free society. To do less would be to lack self-respect. If they fail these responsibilities, they will win disdain from the very foreign tyrants who will welcome them like prostitutes bought and paid for. And they will not deserve to be honored by their fellow citizens back home.

By contrast, when firms fulfill their responsibilities to their own full identity, they strengthen commerce, and commerce is the foundation of a free polity.

Commerce is the "commercial" half of "the commercial republic" envisioned by our founders. Commerce multiplies human opportunity and generates economic growth and thus opens upward pathways for the poor. Commerce promotes inventions and discovery. As new talents rise, and obsolete technologies die, commerce constantly stirs the circulation of elites. Commerce helps to establish a complex system of checks and balances. Further, commerce makes resources available for projects outside the orbit of state activities and thickens social life while subtracting from the power of the central state. It gives incentives to enterprise and character and inculcates an important range (but not the full range) of moral virtue, especially the virtues necessary for prudent living and the rule of law.

Let me summarize: The success of many new businesses from the bottom upward is crucial to economic growth. The success of these businesses is crucial to the success of democracy, especially where large majorities are poor. All these goods belong not solely to Americans but to all people on earth. To help set in place the preconditions for the achievement of these great social goods—to help break the chains of worldwide poverty—is the international vocation of American business. Being a business leader today, then, is a highly moral profession. The bad news is that one can fail. The good news is that one can succeed. That is the human drama. That is the suspense.

RESPONSE BY NATHAN HATCH

Nathan Hatch was the former provost of the University of Notre Dame and is currently President of Wake Forest College. He is regularly cited as one of the most influential scholars in the study of history of religion in America. His book

The Democratization of American Christianity, *published by Yale University Press in 1989, has garnered three awards and was chosen in a survey of 2,000 historians and sociologists as one of the two most important books in the study of American religion.*

Michael Novak has addressed important themes about the international vocation of American business. The framework and presupposition of his essay is that business has a deep moral purpose. It is a noble and worthy vocation. In a world rife with tyranny and sundry forms of corruption, he suggests that business has the opportunity and responsibility for serving as moral and democratic leaven to the world. He has chosen a surprising set of terms to talk about business: He talks about calling and vocation. In the history of Catholicism, pursuing a vocation traditionally has meant becoming a priest or a woman religious. Protestants like Luther and Calvin expanded the term of vocation to mean all kinds of work. In Calvin's words, "No task would be sordid and base provided you obey your calling in it." It is also interesting that in choosing to link vocation and business, he seems to erase the long-held distinctions between commerce and the professions.

Professions such as law, medicine, higher education or the clergy were typically assumed to involve a moral commitment of service to the public that went beyond the test of the market or of personal profit. The ideal of the professions is that the accepted measure of success is not merely financial gain but some larger purpose, whether it be advancement of science, the case of the infirm or the maintaining of justice. For instance, Jeremiah Gridley, the leading lawyer in early Boston, said to the young John Adams, "Pursue the study of law rather than the gain of it." The professional person, it has been said, does not work in order to be paid, but is paid in order to work.

Michael Novak's analysis detects the same deep moral current coursing through business activity. And he remains a vigilant advocate for the inherently moral purposes of business against those who would attack commerce, whether they be socialists, aristocrats, literary critics or serious Christians who might advise their colleagues not to soil their hands in commerce. Here at Notre Dame, that doesn't seem to be the problem. In fact, students are flooding into the College of Business Administration. Dr. Novak staunchly defends the virtue of business against these culture despisers.

My central question about the essay is whether it too readily accepts the binary categories of those who dismiss any moral potential in the business corporation. Dr. Novak's temptation is simply to invert them. Instead of seeing the business person as a callous Scrooge, we see him or her as a moral exemplar, a corporate missionary. Viewing business historically, I would prefer to suggest that business, like any of the professions, has the potential for being moral or immoral and sometimes in complicated and contradictory ways.

Recently I had the pleasure of reading the book *Titan*, Ron Chernow's marvelous biography of John D. Rockefeller. The striking thing about Rockefeller, patron saint of American business if ever there was one, was how excruciatingly complicated were his motives and his behavior. Throughout his life he was deeply religious, refusing to give up his Sunday school class in Cleveland even after he had moved to New York. He was also deeply generous, tithing his profits from the time he began earning money as a young lad. At the same time, Rockefeller could not have been more acquisitive and ruthless in executing designs to crush the competitors of Standard Oil. Rockefeller viewed his behavior as a moral crusade to impose order upon a fragmented and chaotic petroleum market. He saw no reason to interrupt the forces of the market, no matter what its effect on other companies or his own workers. In the most celebrated case, Rockefeller's inaction led to the inadvertent massacre of men, women, and children who dared to strike one of his Colorado mines, an incident for which he was embarrassed about for the rest of his life.

My point is, to alter a phrase that C.S. Lewis said about humankind, that sometimes nothing too good or too bad could be said about the businessman John D. Rockefeller. He was a complicated enigma of devout principle and scheming manipulation. His passion about his work as a religious calling was matched only by the lengths to which he justified his actions to himself and often insulated himself from the means by which his subordinates achieved his ends. I use Rockefeller as a metaphor of the complicated nature of issues of morality and work. This is particularly true as American industry assumes a more international focus. Business at its best does build a foundation in the rule of law, of accountability and cooperative association. Yet American business and the relentless advertising by which markets are often built also can breed a deep consumerism that can be morally corrosive. As John Paul II warns in his 1991 cyclical *Cente Simus Annos*, "It is not wrong to want to live better. What is wrong is a style of life presumed to be better when it is directed towards having rather than being."

I recently had the occasion to visit Dublin, where Notre Dame has established a new academic center. The positive effects of the market economy in Ireland are quite astounding. I had the occasion to visit with Joe Mulholland, who heads RTE, the Irish state television. Amidst all of the positives of features associated with the so-called Celtic Titan, Joe paused to note the rampant secularization that is consuming Irish youth. He was most concerned about the introduction of independent television, American style. Jerry Springer and the like had just hit the airwaves of Dublin. The intoxicating profits produced by such fare threatened the viability of traditional television in Ireland, television that has tried to come to terms with the common good and in the moral development of youth. In his view, the free market of television, one of America's major exports, had very deep and very negative moral consequences. If business as a moral enterprise is in danger, it is not principally from external foes. The danger is from within, from an acquisitiveness which refuses to give place to any moral compass other than the market itself.

My question is whether the structures of modern society and the assumptions of modern culture make it increasingly difficult for business people, as for other professionals, to act as moral agents. How ample are the wellsprings of self-restraint and prudential judgment among those of us who are middle class, on whose judgment so much of public life depends? In an unregulated environment, are our corporate people and other professionals prepared to use their influence for the common good? Are we training managers and other professionals who are committed, at some level, to the common good?

In conclusion, as I think about young people starting to climb the corporate ladder, I worry about at least three things. First, the unintended consequence of size and scale in business organizations. In a world of larger banks, larger telephone and computer companies, larger oil companies, I worry about the lack of local rootedness, a taproot of corporate civic responsibility. From my local experience in the United Way, I recall all too often the diminishing commitment of a company and its people whose headquarters have left the region. Much philanthropy and corporate responsibility is local and will be difficult to sustain in a world of megacorporations.

I also worry about the trend for work to function as free agency. Most corporations are not yet at the level of the National Basketball Association [where players can sign ever more lucrative contracts with the highest bidding competing teams], but there is a clear withering of long-term corporate communities, cultures in which important human and moral factors can be weighed so that people take care of each other, hold each other accountable, and give place to the priority of family and community.

Third, I worry about the danger of rhetorical veneer. All modern institutions—universities, government agencies, business corporations—are effective in depicting our mission in our work in moral terms. Organizations need customers to think they care, whether or not they really do. And a caring, high-tough work environment helps to recruit and motivate talented employees. The danger for business corporations, as for any of us, is profuse moral rhetoric unconnected to where real decisions are made, those affecting the bottom line.

In sum, I agree with Michael Novak that business can be a highly moral profession. Where I may disagree is a matter of emphasis. I think the road may be more straight and narrow than he conceives, and fewer will have the necessary community and set of mentors to sort through the difference between a life of self-interest and one of principle and integrity.

RESPONSE BY RALPH CHAMI

Ralph Chami is assistant professor of Business Economics at the University of Notre Dame College of Business. His specialties include the economics of informa- tion, risk and uncertainty, and development economics. He has published in jour- nals such as Economic Inquiry, Economic Letters, *and the* Journal of Economics *and has been involved in analyzing the value of trust of altruism in business.*

Mr. Novak presents us with a number of thought-provoking issues, but I would like to focus my comments on one issue in particular, and that is the role of ethics is business. I will caution you, though, that I bring in my own biases and views as an economist, and also as one who believes in the market mechanism

SKEPTICISM ABOUT ROLE OF MORALS IN BUSINESS: THE REAL MESSAGE

Mr. Novak states that the members of the literary class are quick to point out the "amoral" nature of business. Unfortunately, I would add that even those who por- tend to be friends of the market mechanism, including many market practitioners, seem to share that same view, but for different reasons. It is the view that the objective of profit maximization is somehow independent or even inconsistent with the ethical considerations that may be involved in achieving such an objec- tive. We often hear phrases like "Let the market decide," "Business is business," and other comments, that somehow give the impression that either we worry about ethical implications of conducting businesses, or we shut our moral senses and go for the buck.

However, I would argue that such statements and sentiments are not only mis- placed but more importantly do not reflect the thoughts and concerns of those economists who are credited with developing and advocating the "efficacy and efficiency of the price mechanism." Kenneth Arrow, one of the pillars of modern economics and a Nobel laureate whose path-breaking work on the "efficiency of the market system" is mandatory reading for all graduate students in economics and finance, recognized situations where the price mechanism may fail. In his essay on the relationship between gifts and the efficiency, he states:

> It strikes me that the essential point is the great importance of such a virtue as truthfulness in widely prevalent circumstances of economic life . . . Virtually every commercial transaction has within itself an element of trust, certainly any transaction conducted over a period of time.

Further on in the same essay, Arrow states: "The price system is not, and perhaps in some basic sense cannot be, universal. To the extent that it is incomplete, it must be supplemented by an implicit or explicit social contract."

What is it about such moral characteristics such as trust, altruism, forgiveness, truthfulness, that makes them essential to the economic life, and in particular to the business endeavor. Simply, when these traits exist and are shared equally, they are valuable in situations where legally enforced property rights and contingent contracts cannot be written, and in other situations where there is quality uncertainty and a difference in the degrees of knowledge possessed by buyers and sellers. Well, how do they work? As Proffessor Oded Stark puts it, they work by transforming the state of "self-interest" into "enlightened self-interest" and by "reinforcing self-enforcing agreements." Economic agents who possess such noble traits internalize the cost of their own actions on other members of the society and thus refrain from those actions which would harm others. For by harming others, they are really harming themselves. Thus, there is no need for other forms of incentive schemes, monetary or otherwise, or monitoring devices to ensure the proper behavior by such ethical individuals.

IMPERFECT MARKET ALTERNATIVES

But, why is it, then, that businesses use other forms of costly persuasion to try to induce individuals to behave in the proper manner? For example, we have all heard of the use of incentive schemes by businesses, such as bonus systems, stock-option plans, where owners attempt to induce managers to do the job for which they were hired. Or, employers concerned about the rising health-care costs, and worried about the behavior of doctors, employ managed-care companies to monitor their behavior. Or, insurance companies concerned with frivolous suits and fraudulent behavior opt out of covering certain activities and raise their premiums and limit their payouts on others.

In short, why is the level of trust or mutual confidence in the society so low? Perhaps the answer lies in the fact that for these worthy traits such as trust, altruism, truthfulness and others to operate for the betterment of the society as a whole, their level must be high; they must be shared among all members of the society and must be shared equally. Otherwise, they invite exploitation and inefficiency. But his requirement is very difficult to ensure. Perhaps this is one reason many societies consist of individuals who are largely selfish. And here, this verse from *The Bible* comes to my mind: Leviticus 19, verse 18: "You shall love your neighbor as yourself." The prescribed dosage of love is "exactly as yourself." No more. No less. This is not an easy task by any means.

THERE IS NO SUBSTITUTE FOR TRUST AND ETHICS, BUT WHERE DO WE LEARN THEM?

But has the market's attempt to fix the problem succeeded? Have these incentive schemes implemented by businesses, or the use of managed-care companies, and other monitoring devices worked? The answer is "no," and is splashed all over the media and newspapers. Bonus systems turn out to have their loopholes and pitfalls, and they foster an environment of lack of trust, which is self-fulfilling. Managed-care companies that are supposed to monitor doctors' behavior are now suffering from their own problems, including fraud and quality deterioration. Moreover, the number of frivolous suits and other types of insurance fraud have not diminished but continue to rise and cost us billions of dollars a year. Perhaps the greatest casualty is the social contract—the implicit understanding among members of the society that specifies each member's rights and responsibilities. Thus, there is no real substitute for fostering an environment of trust and ethical behavior.

There is a dire need for an individual who possesses all these moral characteristics that I mentioned earlier: trust, altruism and truthfulness. Where do we find such an individual? How and who can instill and nourish such noble and worthy traits in individuals? The answer is simple: the family unit.

In work with my colleague Connie Fullenkamp at Notre Dame, we have been engaged in studying these issues for quite a while. The family unit, through its allocation of time and resources, imports to its members virtues and a value system. These family members are the ones who in turn enter the market as sellers and buyers, owners, managers, doctors, lawyers, and public officials. Thus, there is a direct link between the family and the business environment. When the family is healthy, the business is healthy. When the family is characterized by virtuous behavior, so will the market experience its positive effect, and will reward it accordingly. Thus, ethical behavior learned within the family unit is translated to moral behavior in conducting business.

As a result, there will be no need for costly monitoring devices and the presumption of "guilty until proven innocent." Businesses also will profit from the high level of trust, where individuals perform their tasks fully and on their own, and as a result, firms will reward them by compensating them fully for their efforts, without having to resort to these costly devices and incentives that I mentioned earlier. This is a win-win situation. The family and the business work together and complement each other.

One important lesson here also is that businesses should pay close attention to the needs of the family. Day-care centers and family leave are just early signs that maybe the business sector is developing an awareness of the need for a healthy family environment. That is how I understand the message in the six presumptions stated by the guest speaker that the "moral corporation is very much linked to the community," and the assertion made that "business is an inherently moral occupation, dependent on, and nourishing, an important form of cooperative association."

WHERE IS THE GOVERNMENT IN ALL OF THIS?

Finally, one must ask whether all the players have been accounted for. Obviously not. The clue is in the fictitious scenario of the country (Xandu), presented by Dr. Novak. The government is the third and very important player. The government, through its actions, can either help or hinder the working of the business market. But, also more importantly, it can adversely affect the family. We need all three players to understand each other's motives and incentives, so as to enhance the welfare of the society. For even when the government has the best of intentions, it can inadvertently harm the same individuals it is trying to help. Milton Friedman in 1980 made a very interesting observation that the introduction of social security has led to a decline in the level of attentiveness of children to their parents. Is it that such programs, by reducing the need to rely on other members of the family for help in old age, unintentionally adversely affect family relationships? What should the government do, and how should it design its programs so as to help the family and not usurp its values? These questions and others have yet to be answered seriously and are the focus of current research.

Obviously, in the case of Xandu we can see an extreme form of a government that abuses its power. That cannot give rise to a healthy environment of trust. Not only are business and democracy under siege in that country, but the family unit is also suffering. And when the family suffers, the rest of the economy will surely feel it, and the general welfare of the society as a whole will decline.

As Arrow puts it is his essay on "Gift and Exchange:" "It can be plausibly argued that much of the economic backwardness in the world can be explained by the lack of mutual confidence."

In work with my colleagues here, Scott Baier and Connie Fullenkamp, we are exploring this issue further, tracing how higher levels of trust can lead to higher economic growth. But one thing should be clear: that all three entities—business, family, and government—need to understand each other's objective and incentives. No one entity can operate alone in a manner that would ensure the higher welfare of the society as a whole.

So, I hope I have been able to dispel a myth that neoclassical or market economists do not see the need for morals in business. We may differ from others who also advocate the need for ethical behavior in the business environment, only in that we would like to induce the business to see its own need for moral behavior, rather than impose our presumptions on the market. We may use a different framework to make our point, but our verdict, and mine in particular, tend to fall on the side of the argument made by Michael Novak that, indeed, "business is a noble and moral vocation."

CHAPTER FIVE

THE ROLE OF THE BUSINESS CORPORATION AS A MORAL COMMUNITY

By Lord Griffiths of Fforestfach

This lecture was given by Lord Griffiths at Saïd Business School, University of Oxford in 1999.

The significance of values to the way that corporations work is a relatively recent emphasis in management thinking. It came to prominence in the United States in the 1970s, which was a traumatic decade for American business because of the inroads made by Japanese automobile and electronic companies. This prompted a good deal of soul-searching by the American business community, which in turn led to extensive research on the performance of U.S. companies.

The conclusion was that one significant factor in the superior performance of certain companies was the shared values of the corporation: namely a set of beliefs and values championed throughout the organization that became the basis of its corporate culture. Further research at Harvard Business School confirmed the importance of values in influencing performance. This led to a major shift in management thinking, with less emphasis on management science, corporate planning and economies of scale and much greater focus on the customer, the contribution of the individual employee and the creation of a corporate culture. Since then, the issue of the values companies choose has remained a major item on the agenda of American corporations and, increasingly, corporations in other countries as well.

Within this ongoing debate, consider four questions. Can a corporation function without a moral standard? From where does the business corporation gain its moral standard? How does the corporation function and implement the standard in a pluralistic society? How significant is the corporation as a bearer of a moral standard? These questions should be of concern to the senior managers of all public companies.

First, what does the term "moral standard" mean? By a moral standard in business, I mean a set of values, norms or ethical principles that are accepted as a benchmark, reference point or criterion for all who work within the company and that as a consequence will guide and influence behavior. By this I mean not just that certain kinds of behavior are deemed acceptable or unacceptable, but something stronger: namely that these kinds of behaviors can also be categorized as good or bad, right or wrong. A moral standard will be the basis of ethical rules for everyone employed by the company. It will be the foundation on which a company will be able to build its distinct ethos and culture. Typically such standards are set out in the business principles or mission statements of companies and reinforced by statements from the chief executive officer. It is because of the emphasis companies give to establishing and maintaining standards and values that the modern business corporation can and should be conceived of as a moral community.

The issue of what should be included in a company's moral standard and the way in which it is expressed will vary from company to company. But in examining the statements of a variety of companies, I find recurring themes: the need for integrity, transparency and telling the truth; a respect for individuals because of their innate dignity as fellow human beings; a sense of fairness in the way people are treated; the ideal of service especially in relation to customers but also in the style of leadership shown by executives; the responsibility of the corporation to respect the environment; and a commitment to play an active role in those communities in which the company operates. In fact, so common are these themes across different sectors, different countries and different cultures that they are more than particular values chosen by companies: they begin to acquire the character of a set of universals.

A moral standard goes beyond the requirements of the law. It sets more demanding standards of behavior. It may require that a company turns down a potentially profitable business. It may require a commitment of resources to sort out problems in the environment or in a local community. As a result, the adoption of a moral standard may adversely affect profit in the short term. In other words, when a company chairman stands up and says that the company has a moral standard, it will make a difference in the way that company does business.

Now consider the questions.

CAN A CORPORATION FUNCTION WITHOUT A MORAL STANDARD?

In principle the answer must be yes: a company could operate with a moral standard, with an amoral standard or with an immoral standard.

Of course, a company that covertly carried on its activities according to an immoral standard would quickly find itself in conflict with the law. One example might be organized crime, another might be a company that set out to evade (not avoid) the tax authorities, and another company that knowingly traded in services or products classified as prohibited, such as certain kinds of drug dealing, the sale of human embryos and the sale and purchase of children. These companies would not only produce products or results that would be widely described as immoral. They would also engage in immoral practice, which would inevitably result in extortion, violence and fraud. Executives found to be running such companies would face financial penalties, criminal prosecution and possible imprisonment. A company with an immoral standard could function in the short term, but it is difficult to see, regardless of any consideration of the desirability of such an outcome, how it could be viable in the longer term.

A company that operated on an amoral standard is more interesting. Such a company would operate within the law, but would not be concerned with moral principles. It would have a standard of honesty based purely on expediency. Personal integrity would not be important. Individuals would be valued only as they made a contribution to the bottom line. Cardinal virtues such as prudence, temperance, justice and fortitude would be irrelevant. The sole responsibility of management would be to create shareholder value. Responsibility for the environment or for the communities in which the corporation operated would be the concern of the government, not the corporation or its people. Its fundamental operating assumption would be that all shareholders connected with the company were interested in maximizing their own short-term material advantage.

A company with an amoral standard would be a cold, bleak and insecure environment in which to work. Loyalty would not exist. A person's commitment to honor any promise would forever remain in doubt. There would be no trust. The drawing up of contracts would be lengthy, tiresome and complex. Negotiating executive compensation plans would become a headache. A joint venture would be a nightmare to negotiate because one could never be sure if the other side were telling the truth. The internal audit function would need strengthening. Due diligence would become a long and tedious affair and a significant obstacle to acquisitions. There would be a constant stream of disputes, conflict and litigation. The commitment made by members of the executive team to the future of the company would be uncertain. One would never know whether a colleague had declared his or her true interest in matters affecting the business. Because of the company's reputation, recruitment of staff would be difficult. One major consequence of an amoral culture is that the cost of doing business, what economists term "transactions cost," would be that much greater, so that the firm would find itself at a competitive disadvantage.

"RELIGION IS ONE THING, AND TRADE IS ANOTHER"

Perhaps the person who has come closest to recognizing the value of this kind of approach is Bernard Mandeville in his satire *The Fable of the Bees*, which he subtitled "Private Vices, Public Benefit." In describing the flourishing beehive, a metaphor of a successful commercial trading nation such as the England of his day, he recognized that the most distinctive characteristic of the beehive was its devotion to vice. Distinguishing commerce from virtue ("Religion is one thing and Trade is another") he argued that a permissive attitude to the vices and self-interest of the bees in commerce would lead to an extension of the division of labor, the widening of the market and a consequent growth in trade that would be to everyone's benefit. His conclusion on the beehive was that "Every part was full of vice/ Yet the whole mass an earthly paradise." By contrast, the practice of a Christian ethic of self-restraint and charity would have the perverse effect of resulting in impoverishment of everyone.

Not even Milton Friedman in his well-known essay, *The Social Responsibility of Business is to Increase Its Profits,* suggests that the sole objective of business should be to increase its profits. His argument is that business executives should "conduct business in accordance with their desires, which generally will be to make as much money as possible while conforming to the basic rules of society;" but then, and this is very important, he qualifies the 'basic rules of society' to include "both those embodied in law and those embodied in ethical custom." Thus Friedman makes clear that the assumption of profit maximizing need not be inconsistent with respect for cultural norms or a moral standard.

The third alternative is a company that operates with a moral standard. The leaders of the company would establish and cultivate a set of values. These would typically include virtues such as honesty, reliability and service; a regard for the importance of persons and their development; the ability to play in a team and put the interest of the team first; and responsibility to others, both within and outside the organization. These values may be proposed for a variety of reasons. But if executives are convinced of their intrinsic worth, then one of the consequences of this approach will be to create a high degree of trust within the company.

Within such company there will be less need for lengthy and complex contracts. Rules and regulations will not have to be spelled out in detail. The compliance, internal audit and supervisory functions need not be so extensive. People will name companies such as these as preferred employers, making recruitment of new quality staff that much easier. These benefits result from trust; and trust is an example of what an economist would term "an externality." Externalities are goods that have tangible economic value and that increase the productivity of the company's operation, but they are not commodities that can be bought and sold in any meaningful sense.

A corporation with an effective moral standard will not only have lower transactions costs but also a strong culture based on trust, so that the adoption of a moral standard may well become a source of competitive advantage to the corporation.

The answer, therefore, to the first question, "Can a company function without a moral standard?" is in principle yes, but in practice not very likely, especially if it wishes to survive as a significant player in its industry.

WHERE DOES THIS MORAL STANDARD COME FROM?

Three alternatives are worth exploring: the self-interest of the corporation itself; a global ethic based on a rational humanistic foundation; and a revealed religion such as Judaism, Islam or Christianity.

The idea that the corporation can supply its own ethic based on self interest is an intriguing one. Francis Fukuyama in his recent book *The Great Disruption* states that "the assertion that a virtue like honesty necessary for commerce must depend on religion for its survival is, in the end, absurd. The self-interest of businessmen is sufficient to ensure that honesty (or at least the appearance of honesty) will continue to exist" and

> The corporation that requires a high degree of honesty and civility in its customer service or the firm that immediately takes a defective product off the store shelves, or the CEO who takes a pay cut to show solidarity with his workers during a recession are not acting altruistically: each has a long-term interest in a reputation for honesty, reliability, quality and fairness or for simply being a great benefactor. These virtues become economic assets and as such are sought after by individuals and firms interested only in the bottom line.

This argument recognizes that honesty, like trust and cooperation, is one of those social virtues that builds up the social capital of an organization. But social capital should not be thought of as a public good, which will be underprovided through the free market. It is something that private markets will provide because it is in the interest of executives to supply it, with individual companies typically investing in building up their social capital through education and training programs.

This approach is very much in the tradition of economists such as Hayek and Friedman who claim that the market economy is but one example of what Hayek termed a spontaneous order: namely a system developed not through the central direction or patronage of one or a few individuals, but through the unintended consequences of the decisions of myriad individuals, each pursuing their own interests through voluntary exchange, cooperation and trial and error. This process of spontaneous evolution is not confined to explaining the economic order, but can also account for the development of language, culture, social conventions and even values. The values which companies will choose to invest in will be those which enhance their own prospects of survival and so raise shareholder value. In other words there is a remarkable parallel between economic and social evolution on the one hand and biological evolution on the other.

IS PURSUIT OF SELF-INTEREST ENOUGH?

The issue that the idea of self-interest as the basis of a moral standard raises is how dependable and robust such a standard will be. Fukuyama argues that self-interest can be relied on to ensure that honesty, or at least the appearance of honesty, will continue to exist. But it is precisely this distinction that provides a weak foundation for his case. C. S. Lewis posed the question as follows: "Is there a difference between a man who thinks honesty is the best policy from an honest man?"

The answer must surely be yes.

The pursuit of self-interest may well result in a company wishing to secure a reputation for honesty, but pursuit of self-interest by itself will never produce a commitment to a belief in integrity or truth as an absolute in itself, which everyone in the company should acknowledge and be judged by. The reason is that there will be situations in which honesty is not in the best interests of the firm; and if the probability is very high that no one will be found out, dishonesty will pay and the reputation of the company need not suffer.

The consequence of pursuing the appearance of honesty rather than honesty itself will be a lack of integrity at the heart of management and the acceptance of double standards. The more dishonesty is condoned and practiced the greater the likelihood that it becomes a habit, leading inevitably in time to some form of scandal. Without corporate leaders convinced that an absolute standard has a validity independent of their own self-interest and to which they must submit, it is difficult to see how a company could continue to include honesty among its core values. The crooked timber of humanity in which self-interest resides is too insecure a foundation on which to build lasting moral absolutes. Unfortunately more than the self-interest of business executives is needed.

An alternative to the self-interest of business as the basis of a moral standard might be some form of global ethic based on common human values and incorporating the view of the world's religions and ethical traditions. Such an approach would recognize that religion remains a powerful force in the world, but at the same time it would also accept that the process of secularization has meant emancipation from religion for many in the West. Even though individuals perceive of themselves as autonomous with opinions on every subject under the sun, true heirs to the Enlightenment, nevertheless, there still exists a strong drive for a basic moral orientation and a binding value system based on common human values, which would be a standard for behavior. The concern, therefore, within this approach is to construct a global ethic that draws on the great religious traditions but that can also be supported by non-religious people.

Professor Hans Kung, who has spent a good deal of time and energy seeking to develop a new global ethic as the foundation for a global society, sees it as "the necessary minimum of common human values, criteria and basic attitudes." The Council of the Parliament of the World's Religions, which met in Chicago in 1993 and was the first such gathering in history, commissioned a declaration towards a global ethic. This ethic was based on the twin principles that every human being should be treated humanely and that you should do to others as you would wish yourself done by. It covers all aspects of life, including business, and involves key commitments such as a respect for life, a just economic order and solidarity, truthfulness, tolerance and equal rights. Although it does not develop a business ethic specifically, its approach is in the tradition of the Code of Ethics presented at the Davos management forum in the 1970s, the Principle for Business which emerged from the Round Table (1980) and the Interfaith Declaration on a Code for Ethics for International Business (1988), though the last of these was confined to a statement by Jews, Christians and Muslims. All these approaches in business emphasize responsibility not only to shareholders but also to stakeholders, especially employees. They emphasize the basic values of human dignity, truth, fairness, mutual respect, service and a sense of moderation and modesty, while the global ethic of Kung emphasizes in addition the need for a new social consensus that draws up a new social contract between labor, capital and the state.

THE DAVOS CODE: PLURALISM AND SECULARISM

The strength of this approach is that it accepts pluralism and secularism, and rejects moralism and fundamentalism. It is inclusive and contemporary and carries no baggage from the past. The problem with it has to do with motivation. Why should someone practice a global ethic? We may construct a comprehensive, humane and challenging ethic for business that is accepted by believers and non-believers alike. But the Declaration recognizes that the planet, including business, cannot be changed for the better "unless the consciousness of individuals is changed." Hence the pledge that accompanies it: *"to work for such transformation in individual and collective consciousness, for the awakening of our spiritual powers through reflection, meditation, prayer or positive thinking, for a conversion of the heart. Together we can move mountains!"* But a global ethic, which is of necessity the lowest common denominator of values between the religious and the non-religious, can never give an ultimate answer to the meaning of life or provide unconditional absolutes or values, norms and ideals as a standard of behavior or hold out a sense of hope grounded in history or emulate the call for commitment made by an all-powerful but all-loving God whose service is perfect freedom. Living a global ethic requires a transformation of consciousness, but without religion from where will it come?

The third alternative as a source for a moral standard is a revealed monotheistic religion such as Judaism, Islam or Christianity. In these religions the standard was literally written on tablets of stone and recorded in a Book.

While there are major issues in moving from the Ten Commandments to a standard for a modern corporation, the commandments nevertheless embody an objective set of moral absolutes with an obligation to obey moral law. As a matter of history, the Judeo-Christian heritage has been an important influence on the values of business, especially in Britain and the United States. This approach shares a number of insights with other approaches to ethics such as the recognition of an innate sense of moral obligation, the intuitive awareness of moral distinctions, the conception of a perfect world and the importance of striving towards a moral goal. But the distinctiveness of this approach is that its ethics are grounded in religion.

In the Old Testament, the world is a created order and the motivation for an ethical life is obedience to the revealed law of God by a people who are in a covenant relationship with Him. In the New Testament, the religious experience of salvation, baptism and the inner presence of the Holy Spirit is the basis on which the individual responds to the ethical claims of God.

The Code of Ethics argues that the three faiths have a common basis of moral and religious teaching, with key recurring concepts that are critical to business.

Four are singled out: one is the principle of justice or fairness; another is mutual respect or reciprocal regard, "love thy neighbor as thyself;" a third is stewardship or trusteeship that is a delegated responsibility by man for God's creation; and finally there is honesty or integrity, which incorporates truthfulness and reliability.

The strength of this approach is its emphasis on absolutes embodied in the law and the Ten Commandments with the clear injunctions "thou shalt" and "thou shalt not." Its rules are specific and they provide a sanction on people's behavior. It is also remarkably adaptable. Despite the many changes in the development of language, culture and economic systems, the revealed religions have shown an extraordinary ability to adapt to new circumstances without changing core beliefs.

A MORAL STANDARD MUST BE CONCRETE AND PRACTICAL

The weakness of the Code is that in a modern or postmodern world, it embodies an essentially pre-modern view of the world. It should be pointed out, however, that despite secularization, the moral capital of the Judeo-Christian heritage, remains strong and has been renewed in public life through the significance of various publications and statements. For example, since the early 1960s there have been no less than fourteen papal encyclicals dealing with business and economic issues, as well as the publication of influential statements by the Catholic bishops in America. In Britain, there has been a lively debate on the justice of a social market economy and the corresponding responsibilities of the business community. Despite secularization and the growth of post-modernism, religion remains a force in the West.

In grappling with the second question therefore, "From where does the corporation gain its moral standard?" there is clearly more than one answer. For a moral standard to be meaningful, it must be concrete and practical, not vague and made up of mere abstractions. It must be robust; it must stand the test of time and be seen to embody wisdom; and it must ultimately affect behavior—it must be a sanction on behavior.

Judged by these criteria, I am very doubtful whether self-interest as a source of a moral standard is sufficiently robust to be able to affect behavior. There will always exist the temptation to trim. A humanistic global ethic is again open to question on the grounds of motivation and the need to transform the consciences of people. From this point of view, religion is powerful. I believe that any religion in which business is seen as a vocation or calling, so that a career in business is a life of service before God, is the most powerful source from which to establish, derive and support absolute moral standards in business life.

For a moral standard to function in a corporation it is vital that it be set out explicitly. There is a difference, however, between making the standard itself explicit and making explicit in detail its source, which will in all probability be complex. Because it is set out explicitly, everyone should know on joining the corporation exactly what kind of company they are joining and what is expected of them. A standard can be set out in the mission statement or objectives of the corporation, in its business principles, through various training programs and speeches, in the annual report, and through activities which the firm chooses to sponsor.

HOW DOES A MORAL STANDARD FUNCTION IN A PLURALISTIC SOCIETY?

It is important in implementing a moral standard in a pluralistic society that the standard is accepted by those who work for the company. A corporation is not a democracy, but you cannot establish standards without the tacit consent of those who make up the corporation. People must own the standard for themselves. If they do not, there will effectively be more than one standard, which will create confusion. More than that, if they reject the standard, they can walk away and join another company whose approach they prefer. If the shareholders do not own the standard, then they can campaign against it; investors can cause trouble at shareholders meetings; customers can protest and take their business elsewhere and the communities of which this corporation is part can protest via the political process.

If people are to own the standards, then the standards themselves must be seen to have a purpose, to provide better service to customers, improve the quality of sourcing, treat employees with dignity, help employees face change, offer opportunity and improve the quality of life within the company. If, on the other hand, people are dissatisfied with the standard and unhappy in such a working environment, they will act in a negative way—complain, protest and ultimately leave to work for another company.

The leadership of a company has a special role to play in maintaining a standard. The example set by leadership will speak powerfully about the importance the corporation attaches to its values. Above everything else, leaders must live the standard.

Setting out the standard in a cognitive way and making clear the various principles involved and the different dimensions of the standard will lend coherence and clarification. But it is only a part of the story. Aristotle in his Ethics made a distinction between intellectual virtue and ethical virtue: "Ethical virtue is for the most part the product of habit (ethos) and has indeed derived its name, with a slight variation of form, from that word." He then developed this theme: "Our moral dispositions are formed as a result of the corresponding activities . . . It is therefore of no small moment whether we are trained from childhood in one set of habits or another: on the contrary it is of very great or rather supreme importance." This insight, that the formation of habit is of supreme importance in ethical behavior, has great implications for the implementation of a moral standard within a company.

CONSISTENCY: THE INDISPENSABLE INGREDIENT

The everyday practices by which a company does business, the way relationships develop between people within the corporation, the way leaders relate to employees, the way the conscientious and the shirkers are treated are the daily routines that everyone in the company observes. If consistent practice of people in the company reflect its values, then those values become a habit and have the power to strengthen the company's standard. If, on the other hand, there is a lack of consistency, with difficult issues not being faced up to and some individuals exempted from the standard because of their star quality, this too will be quickly observed, and new habits will be formed that in time will detract from the standard the company has set itself.

In implementing the standard, the leadership of a company should never focus on a single individual, or make one leader its embodiment. If a standard is to be established successfully there must be a core of committed leaders at the highest level who are prepared to champion it. In addition, leaders throughout all levels of the organization must be prepared to make it a priority. This has a major implication for recruitment and staffing. One criterion in recruitment policy should be that people hired should accept the explicit values of the corporation: those who cannot or will not should be rejected. This should also be an important criterion in promoting people. Those who embody the company's culture should be placed in positions from which they can have a major impact on the organization. But I must add one caveat. Nothing is more debilitating to team spirit than if people are promoted based primarily on conformity to cultural norms but without the management skills to carry out their new responsibilities.

While it is impossible to prove conclusively, I believe that over time an independent moral standard is not only good in itself, but is also in the interest of shareholders and employees. Such a standard is never a substitute for strategy, systems, infrastructures or talented executives. But over time, honesty will be seen to build up trust, people will respond differently when treated with dignity, a better quality of service will build up customer loyalty, and there will be reduced turnover of customers and staff. A company that adheres to a standard will find it is put to the test every working day, and every working day can make a difference one way or another.

A CORPORATION WITH A MORAL STANDARD CAN MAKE A DIFFERENCE

Although it is rarely given sufficient credit, the corporation has become an important standard bearer of values in our society. The reason it does not get much credit is because people identify the corporation with the attempt to maximize profit. This in turn is perceived to lead to the restriction of competition, high executive compensation, financial scandals and environmental risks, all of which are against the public interest. This is a complex subject that cannot be dealt with here, but the following points are significant:

- Most modern corporations have an explicit set of standards that make strong moral judgements. These publicly-stated standards are demanding in terms of the behavior of all who work for the corporation.
- With the decline of the church and the breakdown in family life in the West, the corporation has become an increasingly important community in its own right in which people spend a great deal of time and typically form significant friendships.
- The corporation is increasingly a vehicle through which people contribute in cash and in kind to charitable causes.
- Because of their track record of efficiency in managing resources, private sector corporations have been called on to run under-performing schools and play a more significant role in the provision of welfare and health-care services.
- Individuals see their own personal development linked to the training and responsibility they are provided within the corporation.
- In the area of training, the public sector is looking more and more to the private sector to form a partnership to implement programs of training and life-long learning.
- And finally, increasing emphasis on good corporate governance in many Western countries, linked to regulatory requirements to increase the transparency of their activities, makes the corporation an important institution in raising standards of accountability, especially in post-communist countries.

SO WHAT DOES IT ALL MEAN?

The concept of the corporation as a moral community is only one facet of business life. It is rarely high on the agenda because its impact is difficult to measure as is its long-term influence. But managed properly the establishment of a moral standard can bring significant benefits to everyone associated with the company.

RESPONSE BY RAM GIDOOMAL

Ram Gidoomal, a successful entrepreneur and corporate executive, is Chairman of the South Asian Development Partnership. He is an honorary member of the Faculty of Divinity at Cambridge University.

THE ROLE OF GOVERNMENT IN CORPORATE MORAL STANDARDS

Government should encourage ethical and moral behavior by business. Of course it should. But what are the practical implications? That was an issue I faced as Chairman of the Anti-Discrimination Legislation Sub-Group of the Better Regulation Task Force in Britain, which highlighted the classic tension of pressure groups: conflicts of interest. There were those who wanted more legislation/intervention the better to enforce their mandates, and those who wanted less legislation/intervention on the grounds that it reduced competitiveness, profitability and long-term survivability. These conflicts of interest inevitably involved moral issues.

Most business exists to create profit. But that does not mean business cannot act morally. Some businesses (for example, those run by a charity or a religious organization) are morally or ethically committed by definition. But current pressure on all businesses to rise above vested interest is coming from many directions besides government. A senior Shell executive acknowledged that increasing pressure on Shell with regard to human rights and environmental issues was coming from public relations and corporate complaints departments—groups whose authority was increasing.

Nonetheless government, too, is increasingly morally prescriptive. Consider, for example, the current debate over whether directors' legal duties should embrace ethical requirements. In Britain, the Department of Trade and Industry, in reviewing Company Law, suggested that directors should take into account the needs of the community as well as of shareholders. My own recent appointment to a National Health Service Trust Board required assent to codes of conduct and accountability that were essentially moral statements (an even more welcome development if it occurred throughout private and public sectors). Government is pushing, too, for greater transparency and openness from corporations–again, a moral directive, because it impinges on social justice.

Two strands emerge:

A pragmatic incentive to business morality. This is the Vested Interest argument that holds that a workforce dealt with fairly and decently is better than one immorally exploited; clients dealt with morally create a stronger client base; in the very competitive hiring market for senior executives the most desirable candidates are increasingly drawn to companies where moral values and accountability to the larger community are seen as important.

Greater expectation has been put upon the business community by today's stakeholder economy. Businesses are expected to adopt policies for the greater common good even if, and especially if, they bring no financial or other direct benefit to the company.

These two strains are not necessarily mutually exclusive. The Tomorrow's Company report in Britain envisages a "license to operate"—a morally reverberant issue. The license could be revoked by government if it felt a company had violated moral standards. Loss of such a license would hurt shareholders' profits. So moral behavior, though apparently unprofitable in the short term, may well turn out to be very good business indeed!

Certainly much (probably most) business is driven by vested interest. Few businesses are charities and fewer still are missionary societies. Even if there are few direct casualties of wealth creation, the wealth is hardly distributed according to need. But there is often indirect harm—*environmental harm* (profit above ecological considerations); *community harm* (disregarding local needs and amenities); *personal harm* (conflict between profit and safety); *economic harm* (to whole communities, due to profit-driven decisions such as closing of a major plant); and so on.

There is also a conflict of rights: between those of investors who have a stake in the profits, and those who have a moral entitlement on the company's profitability (to give one simple example, the right to compensation). Abstract and unfocused principles are involved because those who benefit have often contributed nothing to the business. A morally responsible environmental policy, for example, may increase the value of neighboring properties, where a less responsible policy might lead to blight.

So to whom should a business corporation consider itself morally accountable? And how is it to be compelled to be responsible?

The Better Regulation Task Force, mentioned above, found that the most effective way of implementing good practice is by the use of non-legislative levers rather than more legislation. Far preferable is the classic carrot-and-stick approach—rebates, exemptions, and so on—rather than the threat of further legislation.

GOVERNMENT AS MORAL AGENT

If government is to be involved in what one might call advocating righteousness, how far can it go? We don't live in a theocracy. Our legislators are not priests. Governments are not elected just to cater for the interests of moral minorities.

This is particularly important because of the government's role in defining moral and ethical behavior. In an increasingly secular age, it does so single-handedly for most of the community. But Alexander Hill, in *Just Business*, points out the limitations of "positivism," the prevailing legal philosophy. Governments—not priests, moralists or philosophers—decide what is right and what is wrong. Law defines "What you must not do," resulting in a legalism defined by "The least that you can get away with." For example, it is perfectly legal to acquire a company with the sole purpose of destroying it as a competitor, with an inevitable cost in jobs and personal security.

But doing so fails entirely to satisfy the moral necessity of loving one's neighbor and not causing him or her avoidable harm. In this sense "law" sets the boundaries of permissibility; within them business can go where it wishes.

Morality is more than law. Morality sets a direction and a goal towards which to strive. In an important speech, British Prime Minister Tony Blair repeated Harold Wilson's vision of the Labour Party in government as a "moral crusade" but also defined the "moral purpose" of his government: the happiness and personal fulfillment of all the British. A government with such a moral purpose cannot leave it outside the door when dealing with business.

Yet there are limits to this high view. Democratic governments are consensual, elected by and implementing the will of the majority (at least in the sense of "majority" in a multi-party, first-past-the-post electoral system). Morality is often, by contrast, a minority view: moralists are often lone voices. But it provides a necessary breadth. Laws often lack an absolute dimension, that over-arching context within which laws have categories and relationships to some concept of absolute truth. Religion calls it a "higher law." Law defines what is "right" and "wrong;" morality and ethics define what "right" and "wrong" mean. And although the sphere of government and that of law and of morals are not interchangeable, government, as moderator and implementer of constraints towards right behavior and away from wrong behavior, must legislate under a higher law.

SUPPORTING MORAL BUSINESS STANCES

A key role for government must surely be to create and maintain a level playing field, a climate of "fair play," even if some or many businesses then go on to behave unethically and immorally. This task, as we have seen, involves issues only very obliquely related to maximizing shareholders' profits. Government has a duty to take a moral stance in all sorts of areas, and to support business corporations when they adopt moral stances and standards.

This can include small cases—ensuring that maternity and sick leave, for example, and injury compensation, do not unfairly penalize the company—or very large ones, such as ensuring that the government does not negate the moral compassion of the nation by imposing a VAT burden on the donations of a large part of British business, a decision widely regarded as a moral failure.

There are, however, situations where it is desirable for government to limit the extent to which it supports businesses in taking a moral stance. The fact that democratic government is elected, and rules by consent, brings with it a quite different type of accountability to that expected of business. And bearing in mind what we have already said about vested interests and the conflicts of interest that are common in business, it can be highly dangerous when businesses engage in defining morality. Bishop Lesslie Newbiggin has pointed out that the quest for values is often the quest for power in sheep's clothing. Moreover, businesses have neither clean hands nor pure motives. Though it would be naïve to suggest that the hands of governments are never grubby and their motives never murky, government is held morally accountable in a way that business traditionally has not been. Until, perhaps, in our own day when business is being scrutinized much more comprehensively so far as its obligations (moral, ethical and practical) as members of the global village.

GLOBALIZATION COMPLICATES THE ISSUES

Today no business, the poet Donne might have observed had he been alive today, is an island. Let me give you some examples.

A Geneva-based American multinational many years ago decided to hold its conferences with representatives of developing countries in Paris, given that its French associates had a competitive edge that London did not possess. The reason was that Paris prostitution was legalized. British business was being disadvantaged, but it could be argued that the British government was applying a higher code of morality by refusing to legalize brothels, thus limiting the ability of the businesses in question to make business policy out of a morally suspect agenda.

Similarly, Britain's decision to abolish slavery clearly put British businesses at a competitive disadvantage over those countries that did not abolish slavery. It was clearly the right action in the context of higher law, though painful for business in the short term. But the long-term opportunities afforded to businesses in the global context are today immeasurable.

Though the markets were not as global in the time of William Wilberforce, the abolition of slavery is a good example of a case where there was a clear need for the governments of individual countries to cooperate. Here are three cases where governments have failed in this respect:

- The Russian/IMF scandal in which the Bank of New York was used to launder billions of dollars of fraudulently obtained funds.
- The need to help developing countries with their debt payments—another example of the responsibility to achieve social justice.
- The global implications of environmental issues, such as the ozone layer, and also the problem of polluting the Danube as it traverses Europe.

The last two illustrate a developing view of company law away from a duty merely to maximize shareholder value, to that of a duty to balance the triple bottom line: monetary value, environmental impact and social justice.

So government has a responsibility for the moral standards of business corporations. It has a responsibility to apply criteria and yardsticks of higher standards than those of which business and commerce are usually capable. And government has a responsibility to support (or limit) the activities of business firms and corporations where those businesses are operating with that higher standard. Thirdly, for good measure, it has a responsibility to do all this in a global context.

FINDING VALUES IN THE 21ST CENTURY

A central question of moralists and philosophers lurks behind our discussion. Where do moral values come from? As a Hindu follower of Christ, I might be suspected of having a religious agenda of my own here. But I would not argue that the only moral government that pluralist Britain could and should have in the twenty-first century is one exclusively based on the Christian gospel. There is a "good practice" that is almost universally recognized by all societies that claim moral concerns. I find moral concerns not just in the Ten Commandments but also in the Indian scriptures, in the Koran, in the holy books and wise sayings of many world religions. In my own British Asian community, Islam and Hinduism foster concern for the weak, respect for the elderly, moral purity in relationships, obedience to parental and other authority, and much more. Even thoughtful secularists often hold high ethical and moral standards and seek to apply them in every area of life.

This is not the stuff of legalism. You cannot frame company law by saying "Love your grandmother" or "Don't be promiscuous." But good practice *can* incorporate values like "You must site new factories with regard to local quality of life," or "Your company health and safety code must include promoting your workers mental and spiritual well-being." For example, maximizing sales by keeping stores open on Sundays is considered by many people as compromising the spiritual and mental needs of staff, customers and the community.

A government, moreover, that draws its values and frames its legislation in the light of a "Higher Law" will be making law from a unified perspective, not simply creating ad-hoc legislation. Human imperfection notwithstanding, the result will be a recognizable application of a core moral philosophy.

Government not only implements morality but also prescribes it by the public perception that "What is permitted/legal is therefore moral," and if governments are to define morality, it is preferable they do so out of the broad "higher law" overview, than out of a series of disparate legal rulings.

We've seen that the modern social climate itself is tending to force company law in that direction. Individual companies are taking the initiative, and they are not crank organizations on the business lunatic fringe.

THE OFFICE AND THE OFFICE-HOLDER

As I have already noted, business activity *can* create a moral quagmire. Self-interest, situationalism and short-termism tend to dictate decisions and policies that are barely, if at all, to be called moral. Even when merely telling people what they must not do, government may succeed in controlling and limiting the tendency of business to operate without reference to, or sometimes in opposition to, the moral good of society. But if that is as far as it goes, government will remain capable only of applying Band-Aid remedies. Yet in a pluralist society with many moralizing voices, how can government go beyond mere expediency? I would suggest that that is precisely what it must do: it is its role, almost by default. Working within the "higher law" will come almost naturally to democratically elected governments.

The reason is not because democracy has some high moral character, but because electorates tend to share commonly held moral views. As we have seen, certain broad values are common to most of humanity. Few societies condone murder; most respect the elderly and the very young; some societies hold to a commonwealth of property, others (like the Kalahari bushmen) have few possessions, but few societies glorify theft. Even in societies like our own with an increasingly secular view of marriage, we do not as a nation consider adultery admirable.

British Prime Minister Tony Blair was elected by only 42 percent of the population, but the other 58 percent of Britons hold to the same broad moral consensus as that 42 percent do. And if government in office reflects that broad moral consensus (what Christians call the 'image of God') its decisions will, and should, reflect that over-arching perspective to which the parts relate and from which they derive their point and direction. And that is a built-in corrective to piece-meal, knee-jerk legislation.

That may all seem remarkably optimistic—a view highly vulnerable to the first adulterous cabinet minister or careless politician. But I am not suggesting that to implement a morally coherent, focused government one has to be a remarkably moral person oneself. In a democracy, the offices of state have their own moral value over and above the incumbent. President Bill Clinton confessed to good old-fashioned [sexual] "sin," but the office of the presidency survived any short- or long-term effects of his disgrace. The office is better than its holder. If the office-holder has behaved inappropriately, or fallen from grace in some way, then if it is the office that is the source of the legislation (with all the checks and balances that that implies) there should, in theory at least, be no problem.

WHO, FINALLY, IS ACCOUNTABLE?

The Roman satirist Juvenal asked a great question: *Quis custodiet ipsos custodes?* "Who will watch the watchers?"

I've suggested that democratic government partakes of the electorate's common stack of moral awareness, and is capable of legislating in its light. When it does so, it applies a moral perspective, and thereby has the right and duty to assist and, where necessary, limit the moral standards framed by the business corporations operating within its sphere of authority.

But such a system works best when society itself monitors the legislators and the people hold their government to account. In modern Britain, does moral failure by government or politicians result in a popular moral outcry? The people do not, it must be said, take to the streets in protest.

As a society we rarely do hold our legislators to moral account; usually, only when our own interests are threatened. Indeed, government is often unpopular when it makes a moral stand: U. S. President Jimmy Carter's Panama Canal policy was, he estimated, unpopular with 85 percent of Americans. He proceeded, nevertheless, believing it to be a matter of plain right and wrong.

When such matters arise and the question of moral accountability begins to appear, we acknowledge the limitations of government as moral supporter or restrainer, while not denying the practical opportunity, and even need, for government to exercise moral intervention of many kinds.

CONCLUSION

Some final thoughts.

Workforces are today a rapidly changing ethnic mix. The Judeo-Christian heritage and cultural identities are no longer distinctive of many democracies. Will we ever reach a national consensus on what values are required for a common culture? We will now forever be a multi-cultural society. That does not mean we cannot reach national agreement on core values, but the range of these values will continue to constrict as we recognize and accept increasing diversity. So the range of consensus values at national level will continuously decrease.

This would suggest a decreasing contractual basis for government for influencing the moral standards of business corporations in the future. So is it perhaps time to broaden our vision beyond the role of government—perhaps, even, to redefine government?

Secondly, Jerry and Larry Jensen in their seminal book, *Families: The Key to a Prosperous and Compassionate Society for the 21st Century*, argue that the family—not the individual or the government—is the foundation of healthy national life. They expose the failed attempts of government to substitute for the family, as the provider of security and care, and argue that the widening of the rich/poor gap in society is a reflection of the failure of governments to implement the true national agenda: "to equalize the economic inequalities that result from the capitalist system."

In this new millennium, clarifying or even agreeing on what the role of government should be in supporting or limiting the promotion of a moral standard for business is going to become more and more challenging. But whatever position we adopt, I am convinced that in the future governments will be judged not by how much wealth they have made it possible for a few people to accumulate, but on whether they have the ability to create the best possible quality of life for as many people as possible.

RESPONSE BY JOHN KAY

Educated at Edinburgh University and Nuffield College, Oxford, John Kay was formerly Professor of Management and Peter Moores Director of the Saïd Business School at Oxford University, and Professor of Economics at the London Business School.

THE ROLE OF BUSINESS IN SOCIETY

Since the time of Aristotle, and perhaps before, business has been disparaged by people of culture and refinement. The critics of business have argued that the people who engage in it are selfish in their motivation, narrow in their interests, and instrumental in their behavior. In the last twenty years or so, something very odd has happened. This unattractive characterization of business, previously put forward only by those who were hostile to it, has been enthusiastically adopted by business people themselves. Here are some quotations:

> While business has relations with customers, employees, etc. its responsibilities are to its shareholders.

This statement comes from the Confederation of British Industry's evidence to the recent Hampel Committee on Corporate Governance and was reproduced, approvingly, by the Committee.

> The social responsibility of business is to maximize its profits.

This well-known, widely quoted, assertion comes from Milton Friedman of the University of Chicago.

> The most ridiculous word you hear in boardrooms these days is 'stakeholders.' A stakeholder is anyone with a stake in a company's well-being. That includes its employees, suppliers, the communities in which it operates, and so on. The current theory is that a CEO has to take all these people into account in making decisions. Stakeholders! Whenever I hear the word, I ask 'How much did they pay for their stake?' Stakeholders don't pay for their stake. Shareholders do.

This comes from a recent book by Al Dunlap, former Chief Executive of Scott Paper, variously nicknamed "Chainsaw Al" and "Rambo in Pinstripes" for his stewardship of that and other companies. In business, and perhaps in life, the only form of relationship he can conceive of is a commercial, contractual one: the only source of obligation to another human being is that they paid you. And there is no doubt that that is what Dunlap genuinely believes. He goes on to say: "If you want a friend, get a dog. I'm taking no chances, I've got two."

It was easy to find those examples. It was much harder to find justifications for their assertions. Part of the problem is that the claim that business is only about profits has in the past been contrasted with two unconvincing alternatives. One is that the purpose of business is to do good. Those who are in business should shed material preoccupations and we should all work for the benefit of the community. Another is that profit is immoral and, in consequence, all the assets of corporations should be transferred to the state. Since neither of these approaches appears to work very well, Al Dunlap has a relatively easy ride.

But I prefer to treat these assertions against a much more powerful contrary position: that successful business is not in reality selfish, narrow and instrumental. Think about other walks of life. What makes one a good parent, a fine teacher, a great sportsman? The answer is a combination of talent relevant to those activities and a passion and commitment for them. Similarly, the motives that make for success in business, both for individuals and for corporations, are commitment to, passion for, business—and this is not at all the same as love of money. What we mean by a good business is as multi-dimensional and complex as what we mean by good parenthood, good education, or good sport. But nevertheless, there is widespread agreement on which are indeed good businesses. They are characterized by satisfied customers, motivated employees, well-rewarded investors, and high reputations within their communities. They are admired by everyone: their customers, governments, the financial community, the people who work for them, and other businesses.

There is a similarity between the way I have described parenthood, education and sport—and would wish to describe business—and what the philosopher Alasdair MacIntyre has called a practice. What gives MacIntyre's view particular interest is that MacIntyre was recently challenged to explain how his concept of a practice related to commercial activities that appear to have external criteria of success, such as profitability.

Here is what MacIntyre said in response:

A fishing crew may be organized and understood as a purely technical and economic means to a productive end, whose aim is only or overridingly to satisfy as profitably as possible some market's demand for fish. Just as those managing its organization aim at a high level of profits, so also the individual crew members aim at a high level of reward . . .

MacIntyre describes by contrast:

> . . . a crew whose members may well have initially joined for the sake of their wage or other share of the catch, but who have acquired from the rest of the crew an understanding of and devotion to excellence in fishing and to excellence in playing one's part as a member of such a crew. Excellence of the requisite kind is a matter of skills and qualities of character required both for the fishing and for achievement of the goods of the common life of such a crew. The dependence of each member on the qualities of character and skills of others will be accompanied by a recognition that from time to time one's own life will be in danger and that whether one drowns or not may depend upon someone else's courage.

Now MacIntyre is a moral philosopher, and there is no reason why he should ask the question which would concern Al Dunlap, or me: which of these crews catches more fish? Indeed I think that one thing on which Al Dunlap and Al MacIntyre would agree is that they would expect the first crew—whose aim is only or overridingly to satisfy as profitably as possible some market's demand for fish—would be more successful commercially.

But would either of them be right? As so often, we have a Harvard Business School case to help us. It is the case of the Prelude Corporation (Harvard Business School, 1972), once the largest lobster producer in North America, which sought to bring the techniques of modern management to the fishing industry. Listen to its President, Joseph S. Gaziano:

> . . . The fishing industry now is just like the automobile industry was 60 years ago: One hundred companies are going to come and go, but we'll be the General Motors...The technology and money required to fish offshore are so great that the little guy can't make out.

If you wonder why the Prelude Corporation is not now grouped with General Motors in the *Financial Times* and *Wall Street Journal*, it is not because I have made the story up. The Prelude Corporation did indeed exist, but not long after the Harvard case was written, it become insolvent. It did so, moreover, for entirely explicable reasons—reasons which are clear enough from MacIntyre's account. You don't make fish, you hunt it. Your success depends on the flair, skills and initiative of people who cannot be effectively supervised. The product of people who feel genuine commitment, who "have acquired from the rest of the crew an understanding of and devotion to excellence in fishing" exceeds that achieved when the "only aim is overridingly to satisfy as profitably as possible some market's desire for fish." And that is why MacIntyre's second crew is still fishing while his first is not.

There is something paradoxical here. How can it be that a fishing crew organized on rational lines to maximize its catch and its profits would be less successful in achieving even those ends than one that was less selfish in motivation, less narrow in its objective, less instrumental in its motivation?

The issue has been noted before. I first came to it in my research on characteristics of exceptionally successful companies. Others have made similar comments. A recent study assessed eighteen paired comparisons of successful and less successful companies in the same industry. Their judgement: "The visionary companies have generally been more ideologically driven and less purely profit driven than the comparisons in seventeen out of eighteen cases."

Individual illustrations abound. The founding prospectus of the Sony Corporation, for example, declares: "We shall eliminate untoward profit-seeking." The most profitable large American companies today are Merck and Microsoft. George Merck set out the company's approach in explicit terms: "We try never to forget that medicine is for the people. It is not for the profits. The profits follow, and if we have remembered that, they have never failed to appear." And the profits appeared, and appeared, and they kept on appearing.

As for Microsoft, the contrast between Bill Gates and Al Dunlap is striking. Gates is enthused by what businesses he might set up, Dunlap by those he might close down. Above all, while Dunlap's primary concern is money, Gates is basically interested in computers. Yet it is Gates, not Dunlap, who is the richest man in America.

I call this paradox the principle of obliquity. It says that some objectives are best pursued indirectly. I owe the phrase to Sir James Black, the chemist, whose career illustrates the principle in action.

Black made more money for British companies than anyone else in the history of British business, by inventing beta-blockers and medicine to treat ulcers. The first he discovered in the laboratories of ICI, the second in those of Smith Kline French after he had decided that ICI was more interested in profits than in chemistry.

We are all familiar with one application of the principle of obliquity. While Americans, characteristically, talk of the pursuit of happiness, happiness is rarely best achieved when it is pursued. Instinctively, we understand why.

My principal theme is that business is, and ought to be, a practice, a profession like any other. It requires the same sort of acceptance and dedication to its values, the same sort of breadth of understanding of the complexities of society and individuals, the same sort of sensitive understanding of people and the problems that they face, as parenthood, education, sport, or any other complex human activity.

Successful businesses are organizations that serve the needs of their customers, provide a rewarding environment for those who work in them, which satisfy the requirements of those who finance them, and support the development of the communities within which they operate.

CHAPTER SIX

THE NATURE OF THE
EXERCISE OF AUTHORITY

By David R. Young

David Young is the founder and president of Oxford Analytica, an Oxford, England-based firm that draws on the scholarship of Oxford University to provide business and government leaders with analysis of world events. He practiced law in New York City and was on President Nixon's White House staff in the years leading up to the Watergate scandal and Nixon's resignation. He has lived in Oxford since 1975. This lecture was given at Yale University in 2000.

My focus is not the marketplace but a political place. Even so, I believe my reflections apply to both in the matter of how people behave in the pursuit and exercise of power. I give these reflections not as a professional politician, academic, theologian or lawyer, but as someone sharing reflections on one of the most lasting and profound memories of my years in the White House and its impact on my life since then. That memory was and is of a sense of "battle"—not between armed forces in Vietnam or hard negotiations over strategic arms deployments with the Russians, or of conventional wars elsewhere, or even of conflict between economic blocs—but of a sense of a spiritual battle between Good and Evil. By Good and Evil, I mean the spiritual forces of good and evil at work in the highest places as well as those in each individual human heart. To quote from Alexander Solzhenitsyn's classic work, *Gulag Archipelago*:

> Gradually it was disclosed to me that the line separating good and evil passes not through states, not between classes, not between political parties either— but right through every human heart and through all human hearts. This line

shifts. Inside us it oscillates with the years. And even within hearts overwhelmed by evil, one small bridgehead of good is retained. And even in the
best of hearts there remains an uprooted small corner of evil . . . It is *impossible* to expel evil from the world in its entirety, but it is possible to constrict
it within each person.

To this I would only add that the line that passes through every human heart
also passes through the history of human behavior on a grand scale. And as discouraging as that history may seem, my underlying assumption is that God is nevertheless the God of History and that in the end—in the "Last Battle"—Good will
prevail over Evil. However, history is not yet over, despite the famous pro-
nouncement of Francis Fukuyama. The challenge for all of us is, how do we find
the moral and ethical compass by which to live day to day?

The "nature" I wish to address is the "spiritual" nature or dimension, and the
kind of "authority" I wish to address is "power"—not economic, military or market power, but political power—whether legitimately or illegitimately attained. It
is thus important to recognize that I am addressing the exercise of political power
in liberal democracies as well as in non-democratic authoritarian regimes. And
thus my subtext is, "The Spiritual Dimension of the Exercise of Political Power,"
and my focus is not on "Who?" or "Whom?" but on "How?" and "Why?"

My involvement with politics began in the mid-1960s while I was working as
a young lawyer in New York at Milbank, Tweed, Hadley and McCloy. In 1968, I
was seconded to the Rockefeller family offices where I spent evenings doing volunteer work on the "Rockefeller for President" campaign, of which I later became
Treasurer. There I met Henry Kissinger and it was through this connection that
he asked me, in late 1969, to join the National Security Council (NSC) staff and
to work with him as his personal assistant. My prime qualification, to quote him,
was "because I can trust you."

Being Kissinger's Personal or Administrative Assistant involved three broad
areas of responsibility—14 to 16 hours a day:

- Scheduling and attending meetings and preparing follow up memoranda;
- tracking/monitoring the in and out flow of *all* papers and telephone calls; and
- attending to all support activities, and traveling almost continuously with
  Kissinger.

After about 18 months I became a Special Assistant with specific assignments from Kissinger, John Ehrlichman, the Assistant to the President for
Domestic Affairs, and the President. These assignments included:

- NSC representation on the Cabinet Committee to Combat Terrorism— (which was established in the wake of the killings of members of the Israeli Olympic team by Palestinian terrorists at the Munich games in 1972);
- the vetting of potential candidates for the United States Supreme Court;
- attendance at more high-level meetings, maintenance of records and staff support for various negotiations, including Vietnam, the Middle East and SALT;
- direction of the overhaul of the secrecy classification system throughout the government;
- direction of the Special Investigations Unit set up to try to stem the leakage of national security information in the wake of the Pentagon Papers case, which became popularly known as the White House Plumbers.

It is important to recall the intense atmosphere of those years—1968 to 1973. On the world stage, America and the Soviet Union were locked in a real nuclear standoff. The U.S was also enmeshed in an intractable war in Vietnam. Up to 500 Americans were being killed each week along with countless Vietnamese. The social cohesion of the country was strained to almost breaking point, and division across the nation was deeper than at any time since the Civil War 100 years before.

Vietnam was the first war fought on everyone's TV screens every night. As the country reeled from newscast to newscast, the stress on those in charge grew each day. Overall, it was a period of underlying pessimism, anger and extraordinary turmoil. In such circumstances, the challenges to one's character are unrelenting. In turn, this leads to vulnerabilities on matters of right and wrong. And in the midst of all this, one becomes aware of a level of human behavior and decision making that cannot be explained in conventional terms. One begins to sense that there is another dimension, for good or ill. I have called it a spiritual dimension, but call it what you will, it must be recognized. It is the nonrational side of the exercise of political power and therefore it is seldom talked about. Why? Because it doesn't fit with our self-image and self-confidence that we are in control and can explain everything logically and rationally.

My thesis, therefore, is:

- That the pursuit, exercise and retention of power is the *single most* important *goal* for anyone in the political arena;
- that to this end, the use of *secrecy* to *control* the creation and use of *information*, and thereby establish the most appealing *image* to one's constituency, is of paramount importance;

- that there is a *spiritual* dimension and mental dimension to the character of anyone exercising power;
- that the *character* of the *individual* human being as a whole is the single most important factor in how such power is wielded.

THE EXERCISE OF POWER: CONVENTIONAL DIMENSIONS

In preparing for the White House, I searched for something to read on what such a job might entail. The most interesting guide was a small book by President Kennedy's speechwriter, Theodore C. Sorensen, entitled, *Decision Making in the White House* (published in 1963). In trying to answer the question, "How does a President make up his mind?" Sorensen wrote: "It is my view that *three* fundamental kinds of forces influence most White House decisions, to be discussed in terms of presidential *advisors*, presidential *politics* and the presidential *perspective.*"

Sorensen then lists *five limitations* within which a presidential decision must be made; namely, those of: "permissibility, . . . available resources, . . . available time, . . . previous commitments, . . . [and] available information."

Sorensen was useful insofar as he went—and especially considering that he was in office at the time. But his little book did not address what I have come to believe is central to understanding the "exercise of power." Specifically, much attention is paid to the *physical* and *intellectual* dimensions of political decision making, especially in the White House, but little to the emotional, nonrational or *spiritual* dimension. In other words, we often address the demands of the exercise of the power on one's body and mind, but seldom on one's spiritual character. By *character*, I mean the individual human being as a whole person—including body, mind, spirit, emotions, ambitions, beliefs, prejudices, relationships, values, fears, etc. Indeed, the Hebraic concept of "soul," which views man as an integrated whole, created in the image of God, comes closest to what I mean by character.

Being a lawyer and looking for some precedent or parallel for my observation, I found myself recalling the famous lecture series on the nature of the judicial process given by Justice Benjamin Cardozo at Yale University in 1920. In the lectures, he agreed to simply put down his thoughts on "how" he, and by implication judges generally, make decisions. It was an historic series, for it seems to have been the first time that someone of stature stripped away the pretense of the law in a straightforward and comprehensive manner.

Cardozo's argument was that when the reasons of the written and common law alone "are nicely balanced" and do not yield an answer, then the judge's own judgment—subjective and subconscious as it may be—comes to the fore. Cardozo explained, "Deep below consciousness are other forces, the likes and dislikes, the predilections and the prejudices, the complex of instincts and emotions and habits and convictions, which make the man, whether he be litigant or judge."

To paraphrase Cardozo's thesis: These "subconscious loyalties" may have more do with how one decides the case than knowledge of the law. This view was later caricatured by those who said: "The law may thus depend on what the judge has for breakfast." I do not presume to liken my lecture to Justice Cardozo's except in one respect: our goals are not dissimilar. Just as Cardozo challenged his listeners to think unconventionally and admit there was another dimension to the legal process, so I wish to challenge you to consider that there is a further dimension to the exercise of power.

At the same time, our approaches are dissimilar in that Cardozo's analysis reduces the judicial process in many cases down to its more elemental factors— "inherited instincts, traditional beliefs, acquired convictions." Others have even taken this approach further by saying that the law is nothing but power, but class, but race, but gender, but sexual orientation, etc. Not surprisingly, the outcome is not only a debunking of the law (something of which I am sure Cardozo would disapprove) but a failure to explain properly human actions and decisions, whether judicial or political.

In contrast, I believe that the challenge is to move in the opposite direction— "up" rather than "down." In other words, I want to consider the impact of a higher level of factors—for good or ill—such as character, collective thinking, and spiritual conflict in the political process. It is my experience that "how" power is exercised is the result of the character of the individual. If we deny that there is a spiritual dimension to such character, I believe we limit our capacity to be fully human. As such, it is then possible to limit the significance of others, and eventually this type of thinking allows us to treat each other as less than fully human. Atrocities—whether in Germany's Third Reich concentration camps, Stalin's gulags, Cambodia's killing fields, or more recently, the uncovered mass graves in the Balkans—seem to be perpetuated when individuals are caught up in mass hysteria or collective emotion so that they no longer see others as fellow human beings. When such episodes pass into history, the remaining traumatized society is haunted by the question: How could this have happened?

F. Scott Peck's book, *The People of the Lie*, is very instructive here. Peck was the Harvard professor who was asked to examine Lieutenant Calley in the wake of the My Lai massacre in Vietnam in 1968. His conclusion was that the conventional explanations that Calley was either 1) psychotic or 2) neurotic were not applicable. Thus he began to find another explanation. In the end, Peck concluded that there was something else at work and he called it "Evil." Calley's own statement is telling:

> In all my years in the army I was never taught that Communists were human beings. We were there to kill ideology carried by—I don't know—pawns, blobs of flesh. I was there to destroy Communism. We never conceived of it as people, men, women, children, babies.

Scott went on to conclude logically that there must be "Good" if there is "Evil," and this was the beginning of his search, which eventually brought him to faith in God. My point is simply that just as Peck could not explain Calley's behavior within conventional analysis, so the nature of the exercise of power cannot be fully explained within a conventional two-dimensional—intellectual and physical—world alone. However, before we discuss the spiritual dimension we must examine the elements of conventional analysis, starting with "Power."

POWER: LORD ACTON WAS SURELY RIGHT

Man has always sought power. Such ambition is part of being human and can be a laudable trait if directed to right and good ends, and for the benefit of others as well as ourselves; however, when "appropriate ambition"—having achieved its end—becomes "inappropriate" and the self-interested pursuit of power comes to dominate, we come abruptly to Lord Acton's oftquoted observation that, "Power tends to corrupt and absolute power corrupts absolutely." To this one might add, "And a little power corrupts little men absolutely." It is important to understand the meaning of the word *corrupt* as much more than dishonest dealings. Rather, I believe Acton meant that the individual wielding the power loses his way, loses his bearings—behaves in a way he would not admit to or recognize in the cold light of day. This may be the ultimate kind of corruption resulting from the exercise of power.

Let us examine "The Exercise of Power" in terms of self-interest, image, information and control, credit and blame, and secrecy and truth.

Self-interest

As Garry Wills writes in his book, *Nixon Agonistes*, "The pursuit of self-interest is a kind of duty in America." The overarching question however is: To what end is political power sought? For the political leader, it is ostensibly to do what he thinks is in the best interest of the nation, state or organization, etc., for which he is responsible. Invariably, almost all leaders equate their desire to do what they think is in the best interests of their constituency with their gaining, exercising and retaining power. The argument becomes, "What's good for me is good for the nation. My self-interest is the same as the national interest." The great danger here is that it can lead to a belief that, as it is in the national interest that I be elected or reelected, *the end justifies the means.* In this pursuit of self-interest, then, what is it that enables one to gain, exercise and retain power? Besides ambition, what is it that facilitates this drive for power and the delusion that "what is best for me is best for the nation?" The answer is found in the creation of an image.

Image

Kissenger wrote in his memoirs: "Of course, every President carefully nurtures his own image; the obsessive pursuit of it, after all, brought him to where he is." Understanding the importance of a good image was not something unique to the Nixon White House. Indeed, we have no one better to thank than Machiavelli who so succinctly linked the roots of power to image. In today's world, Machiavelli might be hailed as the godfather of modern spin doctors. He set out so clearly both the "means" and the "ends" i.e., the right image begets power. His advice: a prince should appear to have such qualities "as are considered good."

> A wise prince then, is very careful never to let out of his mouth a single word not weighty with . . . qualities; he appears to those who see him and hear him talk, all mercy, all faith, all integrity, all humanity, all religion. No quality does a prince more need to possess—in appearance—than this last one.

Machiavelli further pointed out that negative qualities are necessary at times. For example, that cruelty prevail over mercy, stinginess over liberality, fear over love, duplicity over reliability, and so forth. He sums up: "For a prince, then it is not necessary actually to have all the above mentioned qualities as are considered good, but it is very necessary to appear to have them."

Every president hopes to appear in the first instance strong, sensitive, credible, self-confident, etc. The importance of these qualities can be seen in Kissinger's description of Nixon's admiration of John Connally whose "swaggering self-assurance was Nixon's Walter Mitty image himself." Of course, it would also be useful to have Machiavelli's appearance of being religious, faithful, trustworthy, humanitarian, charitable, etc.

To a large extent, these lists overlap with the qualities that most *electorates* admire and that all presidents and political leaders seek to emulate. The pursuit of an image detached from reality, however, is obviously a risky game. If it is pursued, there is no doubt that one has a better chance of projecting the desired *image* and preventing *reality* from interfering if *secrecy* is used to insulate one from the other. Hence, the preoccupation with secrecy and the critical role of information in most national executives.

INFORMATION AND CONTROL: CREATING AN IMAGE OF "GOOD" QUALITIES

All leaders, virtually without exception, want to create an image of the qualities identified by Machiavelli "as are considered good," and they in turn invariably embrace the values of secrecy and two fundamental related assumptions:

- The strong conviction that "information is power," but one must remember this is only so if it is relevant, timely, true, understandable and, most importantly, unknown by others;
- the assumption that information is power for a leader primarily when it is used to gain credit for achieving those things that enhance his or her image.

In turn, power flows back from the image because it is the image that is the key to the gaining, exercising and retaining of power—which in turn further facilitates the creation of information. Openness, of course, diminishes the capacity to control credit and blame.

CREDIT AND BLAME: GETTING ONE AND AVOIDING THE OTHER

But how does the prince/president/prime minister/CEO/board chairman manage to create such an image, that is, to appear all-wise, sensitive, understanding, tolerant, religious, kind, etc. The vehicle is essentially "words"—words that convey good news (and bad), good policies (and bad), good strategies (and bad), good results (and bad). The key, therefore, is to get credit for oneself when the news is "good" and shift the blame to others when it is "bad." The most effective way to do this is to have control of the words announcing the news, policy, idea, strategy or result. (For example, Vietnam withdrawals were usually announced by Kissinger or Nixon from the White House, while weekly casualties were usually announced by Secretary Laird or a member of his staff at the Department of Defense.)

INFORMATION POWER CIRCLE: ROUND AND ROUND IT GOES

The sequence is:

Information leads to Power→ Credit→ Image→ Power→ Information

Indeed, it is power that provides the capacity to create information to begin with, in which case the picture becomes a power-creating circle with information as the critical starting point.

The creation and control of information to get credit and shift blame is thus the key to the expansion of power, but it is also recognized that there is a limit to the amount of significant information that can be generated. Moreover, once used (that is, made public), its power-enhancing capacity evaporates. Thus the recognition of the need to constantly create information makes thoughtful politicians view their power at any given time as having definite limitations. Their power is the informational content of a zero sum game.

In my experience, this notion produced tenacious infighting and deliberate duplicity to gain access to and control information and a piece of the power pie. It also goes a long way toward explaining the sensitivity of virtually every White House Administration to leaks of inside information. Conversely, it seems that the reason why leakage surfaces in almost all administrations is because the bureaucracy, sensing that its share of the power pie is being reduced, becomes intent on curbing the power of the White House to create and control information.

When one considers that most presidents and their assistants spend a great deal of time cultivating relations with the press, we have a further explanation for their bias in favor of operating on their own without much assistance from the bureaucratic community. Kissinger's power through his positive image in the press enabled him to implement decisions and policies that otherwise might not have been possible, or at least would have required substantial bureaucratic cajoling. He often stressed, however, that his power was based only on the President's confidence in him. He frequently pointed out that if such confidence evaporated, he would be powerless. But the fact was that the President's confidence in him was, in large part, determined by the positive image that Kissinger had created of himself in the media—an image that later grew to overshadow the President's own. In sum, the confidence of the President and Kissinger's power, based on image, reinforced each other. The problem for each man, however, was in keeping track of reality as distinct from image.

To wield power based on image, one must remain interesting to the image builders. Retaining such interest can usually be accomplished by making oneself the exclusive source of reliable inside information, something in which Kissinger excelled. In the end, the image-makers accordingly found it difficult to criticize him for they would then be undermining their own credibility, since they were the ones responsible for creating the image.

SECRECY AND TRUTH: CAN ONE SUBVERT THE OTHER?

In showing the relationship between the use of words to create the right image and the goal of gaining, exercising and retaining power, I have intentionally left to the end the most crucial ingredient—that of secrecy. For it is secrecy that enables one to create image and insulate it from reality—and to make personal "self-interest" appear as part and parcel of the "national interest." Secrecy is at the root of the power base of non-democratic authoritarian regimes. It is the direct opposite of transparency and openness, but it thrives in liberal democracies as well. Secrecy thus plays a subtle but pivotal role in enabling power to be retained by those in power in all societies.

One of the most insidious things about secrecy is that it tends to bind together those who are privy to the secrets. Moreover, it has a tendency to make them more susceptible to a kind of group-think mentality—which creates its own plausibility—and in turn can be more easily detached from reality. As a result, rational people get trapped in a mind-set believing it to be the only one.

A certain level of secrecy may be critical to success in high diplomacy. For example, Kissinger made some 13 secret trips to Paris in the course of the Vietnam negotiations; and the success of Nixon's opening to China and the SALT negotiations were highly dependent on secrecy. Leakage, perhaps more importantly, can have the exact opposite effect to which it was intended; namely, instead of widening discussion, debate and advice, it narrows them and the creation and control of information gradually becomes concentrated in the hands of fewer and fewer advisors.

In sum, secrecy is the handmaiden to the creation and control of information in the pursuit of power derived from image. But it extracts a high price when practiced excessively because it raises tension and stress over all, spawning leakage by those left out and undermining departmental morale in general.

Of course, at the center of this game is "truth." That is, the use of secrecy is in large part an exercise in how and when to use or not use the "truth." Churchill once said the "truth is so precious that she must often be attended by a body guard of lies." This was of course in wartime, but once in power—war or no war—the self-identity of most political leaders with the national interest seems to become so strong that they feel justified in using the truth—by disclosure or nondisclosure—

to pursue their own ends, which are, as we have said, to get the credit and stay in power. In common jargon, this whole practice is called "spin" and it may or may not have anything to do with revealing the truth; but it certainly has much to do with secrecy, image, power, credit and blame.

THE SPIRITUAL DIMENSION: AN AWESOME BATTLE ABOVE THE WEST WING

The notion of a "spiritual dimension" to the exercise of power is not new. In 1888, in his famous book *Ecce Homo*, Friedrich Nietzsche wrote:

> For when Truth engages in struggle with the falsehood of ages, we must expect shocks and a series of earthquakes, with a rearrangement of hills and valleys, such as has never yet been dreamed of. The concept of 'politics' is thus raised bodily into the realm of spiritual warfare. All the mighty forms of the old society are blown into space—for they all rest on falsehood: there will be wars, whose like have never been seen on earth before. Politics on a grand scale will date from me.

Nietzsche's conclusion, that politics is a struggle between truth and falsehood and is a matter of "spiritual warfare," is at the heart of my thesis. In more recent times, Vaclav Havel said in an address in Tokyo in April 1992, "When I look around the world today, I feel strongly that contemporary politics needs a new impulse, one that would add a badly needed spiritual dimension."

There is, of course, another school of thought that seeks to reduce the notion of power to its more elemental aspects and that raises an interesting parallel to Cardozo's view of the judicial process. Such a view is epitomized in Mao Tse Tung's famous dictum that, "Political power grows out of the barrel of a gun," or Stalin's mocking quip in 1935 when urged to take a conciliatory view of Catholicism in Russia: "The Pope? And how many divisions does *he* have?" This is not to say that Mao and Stalin did not wield great power, but that power is not simply a matter of physical or armed might or the capacity to enforce one's will.

My most lasting memory of the White House is that those exercising political power did so in the midst of a spiritual battle. There were indeed days when I thought if I could only roll back the ceiling and roof over my office in the West Wing, and if I only had the right spiritual eyesight, I would witness an awesome battle in the heavens overhead—a battle not unlike the one in the hearts and minds of all those involved and so eloquently described by Solzhenitsyn at the beginning of this essay.

Before anyone thinks that I may have gone too far, let me remind you that throughout history great literature, such as Milton's *Paradise Lost*, Dante's *Inferno*, and noted artists such as William Blake, have all tried to describe and picture with extraordinary imagination the spiritual dimension of battles between the forces of good and the forces of evil. Indeed I would even say that the most accurate and concrete description of what I am talking about goes back almost 2,000 years to the Apostle Paul, who wrote in Ephesians 6:12, "For we wrestle not against flesh and blood, but against principalities, against powers, against the rulers of the darkness of this present world, against spiritual wickedness in high places." The fact that Nietzsche and the Apostle Paul agree that the exercise of political power is a matter of "spiritual warfare" must, at a minimum, challenge all of us to examine the possible reality of such a view.

STRATEGY AND TACTICS IN THE BATTLE

I am not a military man, but I do know that battles are about winning and losing— about attacking, defending, strategy and tactics, deception, surprise, support, courage, determination, confidence—and, most of all, about character. So how does the individual living in a three-dimensional world fare in the crucible of the exercise of political power at the highest levels? How does he or she cope with the spiritual forces of the battle? I have divided my thoughts on this into "Strategy and Tactics" and "Preparedness."

While the forces of evil may sometimes be on the defensive, it seems safer to assume that they are more likely to be on the offensive at the highest levels. This is so because they, as the patently weaker force over all, can only prolong the battle and cause maximum damage by following classical military strategy, for example:

- Concentrate forces on the enemy's most strategic positions/leaders (i.e., those wielding the most power);
- use surprise;
- use deception;
- take the initiative;
- be disruptive—don't let things get quiet, settled or calm;
- keep everything in a state of panic, crisis upon crisis;
- concentrate on the enemy's weaknesses;
- get the enemy to equate self-interest with national interest;
- the intensity of the spiritual confrontation is the direct proportion to the amount of political power at stake;

- those exercising such power are the strategic high ground targets on the spiritual battlefield. They are the "players."

Whether evil is on offense or defense, its strategy and tactics are likely to be pretty much the same. Where there is the greatest concentration of political power (that is, the opportunity to do greatest good or greatest harm), there one will find the greatest concentration of spiritual forces.

Another perspective on the spiritual dimension may be glimpsed by viewing the contending sides as a guerrilla force on one hand and large main force units on the other. Guerrilla movements may or may not have just causes, and may or may not deserve to win; that is not my point here, but rather to borrow a phrase from Kissinger: "The guerrilla wins if he does not lose, and the main force units lose if they do not win." In other words, the weaker attacking forces of evil can cause major disruption for the larger defensive forces of good, even though the former may be doomed to fail in the end. I do not want to stretch the analogy too far, but I think it provides a useful insight into the strategy and tactics on the spiritual battlefield.

PREPAREDNESS FOR THE COMING BATTLE

So, how do we prepare? How can one holding political power prepare for such battle? How can one defend oneself?

Before I left my job at Milbank, Tweed, Hadley and McCloy, I went to see John J. McCloy, head of the firm and my mentor. He was former Under Secretary of Defense in World War II, High Commissioner to Germany, and Head of the World Bank. Until his death a few years ago, he was confidant and advisor to every U.S president starting with Franklin Roosevelt. McCloy was one of America's truly great public servants of the twentieth century. I asked him for his advice and one of the things he said to me was, "Just remember, there will be a lot of intrigue in the palace when you get that close to the throne."

I mention this because "intrigue" at its heart implies "duplicity"—"to conspire or to make secret plots." One must recognize also that loyalty and trust among colleagues declines in proportion to the amount of power at stake. It is vital to be on one's guard. In this connection, it is more important to be aware of one's weaknesses than one's strengths.

In any event, here are some reflections on preparedness:

- Avoid getting drawn into the intrigue: Let your "yea" be "yea" and your "nay" be "nay." Or as it is stated in the scriptures (Matthew 5:37), "Anything more is from the evil one." Do not be equivocal. Do not complicate the notion of truth. (All of us know instinctively when we are not telling the truth about something we have seen or done or said. My recollection is that there were more Watergate convictions for perjury than for the acts charged.)

- Don't underestimate the value of loyalty (trust). Be loyal without compromising your integrity. (Don't try to serve two masters. Just as a house divided cannot stand, neither can a man.)
- Have a clear sense of who you are (strengths and weaknesses) and why you are where you are, but never let the position become more important to you than your own view of yourself. Have confidence and faith in your future regardless of what happens. Mr. McCloy's advice to me on leaving the White House in 1974 is pertinent here: "The most important thing for you to do is to maintain your integrity and credibility as a private citizen." In other words, do not let your self-identity get swallowed up by your job or position, however successful.
- Be sure that your self-identity and belief in yourself is not dependent on achievement, praise or power. These come down to a sense of hope and peace about the future. So regardless of how well or how badly things happen to be going, learn to live each day in a self-contained way. In my case, I benefited from my belief that God is the God of history. However brilliant, chaotic, foolish, delightful or tragic the circumstances I witnessed in the White House, I drew on this belief daily. As was written in the famous Desiderata Prayer in a Baltimore church in 1624: "Whether or not it is clear to you or me, the universe is unfolding as it should."
- Have a clear reference point and framework of moral values that provide a guide as to what is "right" and "wrong."
- Be alert and have the courage and confidence to do what you know or sense is right, even when it is against your own self-interest.
- When something does not seem right, trust your instincts and say so. Otherwise you may get co-opted, as silence is taken as assent. And once it is, it's very difficult to reverse.
- My ultimate reference point was/is my faith in God. Whether you agree or not, it behooves you to have thought through your own criteria for right and wrong and "why?" Once you are there, you don't have time to figure out what you believe in. As Kissinger often said, once in the White House, he was living off his intellectual capital. In a similar vein, we all live off of our moral capital in such circumstances.
- Be passionate about the truth—even in the smallest matter. There is a connection between mundane matters of truth and substantial matters of truth. When no one sees or hears, the truth is still the truth.

- Remember that "nothing is done for nothing," that is, everything has a price. Therefore, avoid being obligated whenever possible.
- Be faithful in mundane tasks. They may or may not lead to more responsibility, but do them because it is right to be diligent.
- Endeavor to maintain a calm, quiet, noncrisis, non-panic attitude regardless of circumstances.
- Be aware of the dangers of collective emotions leading to a group-think, irrational mentality, which is exacerbated when in an environment of secrecy.
- Recognize that you are in a spiritual battle that will test you as a whole human being—not just your physical stamina and your mental acumen, but your beliefs and values.
- Recognize that you need the support of others. In a word, one needs humility—humility to recognize that the rational and logical world does not have all the answers.

These ideas are not quick-fix answers. They make up our character—what we are when no one is looking—cultivated throughout our lives.

SO HOW CAN WE APPLY THIS?

As multinational corporations and financial institutions have continued to grow in recent years in the wake of—or as the instruments of—globalization, those in authority in such organizations exercise power not dissimilar to that of their political counterparts. As Bill Pollard wrote in *The Soul of the Firm*:

> Power in business is suspect, and not without reason. It is, I believe, because management often wields too much power, and there is no effective check and balance or governance either at the board level or from that diverse and distant population often referred to as "the shareholders."

Indeed, CEO's have their press officers—and spin doctors—who take care of their image. Their media are the security analysts and their audience—instead of voters—are their shareholders. They are therefore very much subjected to the same demands—and temptations—to put self-interest in place of corporate interest and play the game as those wielding political power.

The information power circle described above is also as applicable to CEOs as to presidents and prime ministers. Each has within his or her power the capacity to manipulate the information he or she is the first to know or create. Hence, with a little help from the creative side of accounting, unless things go disastrously wrong, "result" can usually be produced "in line with expectations." Of course, CEOs will have worked hard at creating the expectations that they are sure to meet in the first place.

While it is beyond the scope of this essay, I want to put down a marker here on the reference and impact of the internet to all I have been saying about the exercise of power. Image (correct or incorrect) as well as truth or falsehood can be global in milliseconds—and the impact can be constructive or destructive. The internet can promote transparency or it can promote terrorism. There is absolutely no doubt in my mind that it expands everything relating to communication both for better or for worse. It is as important to the future of politics and business as it is to the future shape of democracy and education around the world. In sum, it behooves us all to take the internet's ramifications very seriously.

While I have addressed things primarily from the perspective of the exercise of substantial political power, the principles apply to all relationships, and the reflections and lessons are applicable to more than the small circle of men and women around the world who run countries or major corporations and financial institutions. It is my belief that there is a spiritual dimension to how we work with colleagues, treat our husbands or wives, raise our children and relate to one another every day. It is my hope that, whatever your station or calling, these ideas may prove of value to each of you on a day-to-day basis.

RESPONSIBILITY

What is our responsibility in the light of all that I've tried to suggest? It is crucial to recognize *what* we—the onlookers/spectators (and even the participants) of the exercise of power—are admonished to do; namely, *"To pray for those in authority."*

In I Timothy, the Apostle Paul writes: "I urge that petitions, prayers, intercessions and thanksgivings be offered for *all men*, for *sovereigns* and *all in high office* that we may lead a tranquil and quiet life, godly and respectful in every way."

Moreover, we are not urged to pray only for the "good guys"—that is, only for those elected in legitimate democratic systems. It says pray for *all those in authority*—good and bad—legitimate and illegitimate. Why? Because they are both the players and the targets. They are the ones exercising the power, for better or for worse. If they lose their sense of right and wrong, and if their values get distorted and they make bad decisions instead of good ones, then the harm, damage, pain and loss that results is all the greater. The challenge today therefore is that we should be praying for Milosevic and Saddam Hussein as well as for Clinton, Bush, Gore, Blair.

CONCLUSION

Let me conclude with a story that poignantly illustrates my point. Lord Chesterfield, the famous English statesman, in a letter to his son dated March 5, 1749 wrote as follows:

> Closet politicians never fail to assign the deepest motives for the most trifling actions, instead of often ascribing the greatest actions to the most trifling causes, in which they would be much seldomer mistaken. They read and write of kings, heroes, and statesmen as never doing anything but upon the deepest principles of sound policy.
>
> But those who see and observe kings, heroes and statesmen discover that they have headaches, indigestions, humours and passions just like other people; everyone of which in their turn determine their wills in defiance of their reason.
>
> Had we only read in the Life of Alexander that he burnt Persepolis, it would doubtless have been accounted for from deep policy: we should have been told that his new conquest could not have been secured without the destruction of the capital, which would have been the constant seat of cabals, conspiracies and revolts. But, luckily, we are informed at the same time, that this hero, this demigod, this son and heir of Jupiter Ammon, happened to get extremely drunk with his whore, and by way of frolic, destroyed one of the finest cities in the world.
>
> Read men, therefore, yourself; not in books, but in nature. Adopt no systems, but study them yourself.

In sum, whether decisions are right or wrong, good or bad, it is not merely a matter of having good advisors or being an experienced and powerful leader. In the end, it comes down to the *character* of the individual acting within the mystery that God is the God of History, character shaped not just by physical and mental demands but by spiritual ones as well.

It is only when we grasp the reality of this spiritual dimension of character that we appreciate what it means to be fully human. This impacts both how we see ourselves, as well as how we treat others. It determines how we live our lives day by day, publicly and privately.

Most importantly, recognizing the spiritual dimension of character is an essential part of the foundation on which we must establish a moral and ethical reference point for the political and commercial marketplaces of this world. It is the creation of such a reference point that is going to be the basis of how we meet the enormous challenges ahead for all of us.

RESPONSE BY DONALD E. GIBSON

Dr. Gibson is an Assistant Professor, Yale University School of Management.

The idea that decision-makers are engaged in a spiritual contest, particularly as the power stakes increase, is important. And it comes as a surprise, because, as David Young points out, our political and business organizations are supposed to be places of rational decision making that leave out the spiritual, intuitive and emotional sides of human beings. After all, as Max Weber—as close to a patron saint for the management field as we're likely to get—writes about the ideal bureaucratic organization, it is "Without hatred or passion, and hence without affection or enthusiasm," and successful only to the extent that managers can eliminate "all purely personal, irrational, and emotional elements which escape calculation." We are better off, Weber asserts—and our MBA students are often taught—when the messy spiritual sides of people are left at home.

As one who teaches organizational behavior in Yale's School of Management to those MBA students, I would like to focus on the aspect of spirituality in business organizations. As Dr. Young emphasizes, corporate decision-makers, like political ones, are also living in situations that include uses of power, image, and information, critical allocations of resources, and life-changing outcomes—including the power to deprive or enhance another person's livelihood. This makes discussions of the spiritual forces behind such decisions essential. In my response, I will outline the often-contradictory view we have about introducing human spirituality into corporate settings, and why current market forces make talking about spirituality in organizations important and timely, and yet so difficult.

We who are in the business of generating management theory have long had a love-hate relationship with spirituality. On one hand, the economic models we constantly rely on are quite consistent with Weber's notion of bringing only the rational, calculating side of people to work. We even have a name for this idea, called "Theory X" (because we're too embarrassed to give it a real name) in which people who work in organizations are thought to be so passive that we need to reward, punish or control them to ensure that they behave correctly so as to fit the organization's needs.

On the other hand, we have long realized that encouraging people's spiritual sides can make for highly effective organizations. No less a theorist than Chester Barnard, an executive at AT&T who also philosophized about the nature of management in the 1930s, argued that there is inherent spirituality in the cooperation of people to attain a common goal. As he put it, "Among those who cooperate, the things that are seen are moved by the things unseen. Out of the void comes the spirit that shapes the ends of men." Management consultants and MBA instructors encourage people to bring their passion and spiritual sides to their creativity at work. We argue that participating on teams can be a spiritual experience, and we endlessly portray our best leaders as charismatic, suggesting that they are able to move the spiritual sides of their followers. We even say this about Bill Gates. Which is it to be then: are we better off when people leave their God at home, or when their God enters the organization on the side of—and in the service of—management?

Lately, this love-hate relationship has veered to the side of love. Recent popular articles point to a trend of CEOs bringing spirituality to their decision-making, and actually encouraging employees to discuss their spiritual sides. S. Truett Cathy, an evangelical Christian and chief executive of Chick-Fil-A, Inc. hosts a hymn-filled prayer service on Monday mornings for employees who want to take part. His fast-food stores are closed on Sunday, because Cathy believes in keeping the Sabbath. Aetna International Chairman Michael A. Stephen has extolled the benefits of meditation and talked with Aetna employees about using spirituality in their careers. The CEO of Timberland Co. is an orthodox Jew who says he uses his religious beliefs to guide business decisions. As an article in *Business Week* put it at the end of the 1990s, quoting Laura Nash, a business ethicist at Harvard Divinity School, "Spirituality in the workplace is exploding."

Why has the fire of spirituality suddenly inflamed the business elite? I think there are several trends that have contributed to this; I will focus on two. First, more people are spending more of their waking hours at work. With this shift in the allocation of time, work organizations now occupy more attention and time than institutions where spirituality has traditionally been emphasized, including the family, the church and civic organizations. The anchor of our lives may increasingly be our community of work relationships. We spend far more time developing those relationships than those with our children, our spouses, and our fellow church or synagogue-goers.

Second, at the same time, however, the expectation that organizations will help to foster people's needs for community is becoming fractured. The old expectations we used to have about work are now called the "Old Deal." The Old Deal was an agreement between employer and employee in which you agreed to bring your skills and expertise and, most importantly, your loyalty to me and my goal, and I agreed to pay you a reasonable wage and provide a place to work for as long as you wanted. It was a deal based on security and stability, "til death do us part." It was, in fact, not unlike a marriage, something like when I promise to bring my skill at doing home repair and lawn mowing, and you promise not to throw me out when you realize I'm embarking on an academic career. It was sometimes a dysfunctional marriage—the one between employers and employees—but a marriage, nonetheless.

This state of affairs is being replaced by the New Deal, in which the market permeates the veneer of the organization. Now the emphasis is on "employability" rather than employment security; I promise to provide you with skill training and a place to work for the short term; you promise to provide your skills in a way that helps me meet my near-term production goals. When your skills become outmoded for what I need, I will encourage you to sell them to the next highest bidder. As Peter Capelli puts it in a recent book on the New Deal, "if the traditional, lifetime employment relationship was like a marriage, then the new employment relationship is like a lifetime of divorces and remarriages, a series of close relationships governed by the expectation going in that they need to be made to work, and yet, will inevitably not last."

The onset of the New Deal may make people feel uneasy about their work, and a turn to spirituality may be happening precisely because it provides a sense that there is a higher being watching over us, protecting us from the New Deal's uncertainties. Substituted for loyalty to Mother Chase Manhattan, Ma Bell, and Father IBM, there is now a higher being, a God of my career, to fill the void of the relationship I used to have with my organization. The positive side of the New Deal is an increase in individual control; now I control my career and have more freedom to move from one organization to another to meet my needs. I can now be my own career—and spiritual—entrepreneur.

But there's a problem. The paradox in this new spirituality in the New Deal transition is that with increasing autonomy and individualism, what gets lost is that spirituality does not work well alone. True spirituality is based on community, a group of people working toward a common goal. This is precisely why Barnard stressed "cooperation" as the spiritual basis of organization. It's why our memories of spiritual awakening at work and away from work usually occur in groups. It's why church groups meet in sanctuaries and synagogues rather than in phone booths.

Spirituality implies a group infused with a spirit. Yes, spirituality may imply an individual journey and an individual relationship with a God. But a meaningful spirituality also implies supporting and understanding other people—it implies relationships not only with the spirit but also with others. This is especially true in the business setting, where teamwork and cooperative interdependence are inherent to accomplishing goals. What was wrong with the Old Deal was that it left out our spiritual sides in the quest for rational bureaucracy. With the New Deal, we have greater freedom to talk about our spiritual sides, but less of a forum in which to do it. We may lack the community that brings about true spirituality.

The New Deal's emphasis on market relationships has a downside: it makes the relationship people have with their organizations very tenuous, and therefore, I argue, less likely to be places where, as David Young urges, we are able to have a soul at work. In a true marketplace mentality, "soul" will only be important to the extent that it represents a tool toward higher productivity. This gives new currency to the term "sell your soul." If in the new Deal we "sell our skills" to the highest bidder, it may be just as true that now we will need to "sell our soul" to the most spiritual organization. I think this puts fresh pressure on our leaders to use this movement toward spirituality—if it is a real trend—to do more than simply advocate organizations that allow the spiritual sides of people to arrive at work. We also need organizations that generate commitment to something larger than the immediate task—commitment to the organization's values and goals, commitment to its leaders, commitment to other people in the organization. Out of that strong relationship, out of that community, can come a real appreciation for spirituality in decision-making.

RESPONSE BY THOMAS W. OGLETREE

Dr. Ogletree is a Professor of Theological Ethics, Yale University Divinity School.

David Young's essay confronts us with two starkly opposed ways of living: on the one hand, gaining and wielding power—whether political or corporate; on the other, pursuing a spiritual life. In the former we strive to gain control of positions of power so that we can impose our wills on others, thereby furthering our own interests. In the latter, we seek to develop character, even at the risk of jeopardizing our own interest. The contrast between these two life possibilities appears so sharp that the simultaneous pursuit of both would seem to be out of the question. We have to choose.

Will I seek high political office, and adjust myself to the inevitable intrigues, controls on the flow of information, and smooth spins on the truth that will be required for my effectiveness? Will I aggressively promote my own image, claiming credit for the good things that happen and finding ways to blame others for the bad, thereby securing my own hold on power? Or will I rather claim my identity as a spiritual being? Will I tell the truth? Will I speak up when I sense that something is wrong? Will I do what is right regardless of the cost? Will I further arm myself for spiritual battles, calling upon others for the support I need, and remaining calm no matter what I may face?

If I choose the spiritual life, I do not see how I could also wield power, given what it entails. Dr. Young's own references make this point clear. To begin with, if my identity as a spiritual being is wholly removed from any consideration of my worldly achievements, how would I ever muster the ambition I would need in order to gain a position of power in the first place, still less to maintain my hold on power amid the endless intrigues that swirled around me? Likewise, if I am disposed to tell the truth, and to speak up when I sense that something may be wrong, who would ever trust me enough to allow me into the "information power circle" in the first place? I would surely be viewed as a potential source of leaks that could undermine the public image of the leadership team. Yet a virtuous public image is itself necessary for the effective use of power.

To make matters worse, if I should become preoccupied with my spiritual life, will I not lose my ability to focus on the business at hand? Will not my ultimate spiritual destiny always take precedence?

In inviting David Young to be his assistant, Henry Kissinger said: "I trust you." I initially thought I knew what that meant. Later I was not so sure. Did Kissinger trust Dr. Young because he was convinced that Dr. Young was a man of integrity who would speak the truth, who would always do the right thing even if such actions would undermine his own effectiveness as a Presidential advisor? Or did Kissinger trust Dr. Young because he was satisfied that Dr. Young would accept the constraints of the "information power circle" and adjust himself to its "group-think?"

Dr. Young clearly does not wish to isolate the spiritual life from political and corporate offices. In fact, he states explicitly that what happens in the framework of power itself finally depends upon the character of the individual leader. Such character, he contends, is the single most important element in the exercise of power. The difficulty, however, is that he has not shown us how these manifestly disparate life practices can be brought together in a constructive and fruitful way. In this response I offer some suggestions that might supplement what Dr. Young has set forth.

First, I would suggest that we focus on the moral life rather than the spiritual life. As a person of faith, I do believe that our moral sensibilities ultimately have a spiritual foundation. Indeed, without that foundation our efforts to nurture and sustain moral commitments will themselves flounder. Nonetheless, Dr. Young primarily emphasizes what I would call moral themes: truth-telling, integrity, doing what is right, speaking up in the face of what is wrong—not spiritual themes as such.

Second, I would suggest that these moral themes are not finally alien either to the operations of democratic political systems or the corporate organization of economic activity. I do not in any way wish to minimize Dr. Young's emphasis on the intrigues that accompany virtually all uses of power. In this regard, moral evil is a pervasive feature of all human activities, even those that appear most worthy of our praise. When we devote ourselves to a life of integrity and honesty, we do have to prepare ourselves for spiritual warfare. The battles can be fierce and costly, and we will not always win, or even survive.

Nonetheless, political leaders who lose the public trust lose authority as well, and without authority, they can no longer effectively fulfill their public responsibilities. As Dr. Young himself observes, a concern for public image is a legitimate concern for a political leader. Effective leaders have to devote energy to getting their messages across. They will have to enable the wider public to understand and appreciate the policy initiatives that are under consideration, to see that broad human interests are well-served by those initiatives. Public image matters.

Even the Apostle Paul had to face this reality. He discovered that people following in his tracks were demeaning him, calling him self-serving, portraying him as one who undermined the will and purposes of God. Paul realized he had to challenge this reading of his activities if he was to remain effective as the apostolic leader of the young Gentile Churches he had established. Even within a spiritual vocation, public image matters.

In a liberal democracy, however, a positive public image cannot be sustained indefinitely by deceit and distortion, by concealments or misrepresentations of the truth. A deceitful leader may for a time succeed in fooling or misleading the public, but the public is not stupid. In time it will see through the "spins," especially in a government that protects basic civil liberties, and that maintains a separation of powers at the highest levels.

Similarly, I would contend that secrecy has a legitimate place in virtually all human relationships, including political and economic exchanges. No public official can pursue sensitive negotiations with representatives of a former adversary or a potential enemy without a cloak of secrecy. Secrecy provides a safe environment within which to explore ideas, especially ideas that could generate unintended social upheavals. In this respect, strict controls of the flow of information can serve the public good. The same point holds for corporations negotiating new contracts with labor unions, or exploring possible mergers with other enterprises, or seeking to resolve major lawsuits without resorting to the courts.

Actually, the term *confidentiality* may better capture this more positive and fully legitimate sense of secrecy, for the term *secrecy* connotes attempts to conceal wrongdoing, and to do so illegitimately. The central moral challenge is to discriminate between legitimate and illegitimate efforts to control the flow of information. Attempts to withhold information from parties who have a right to know, and to do so without strategically compelling grounds, must be challenged and exposed as morally unacceptable.

Third, by citing Machiavelli, Dr. Young creates the impression that all forms of power are essentially the same, without regard for the diverse ways in which particular political and economic systems are structured. In contrast, I would stress the importance of paying attention to variations in the basis systems of social organization. While it may be possible to identify tendencies associated with the exercise of power that are more or less common to all societal systems, whether democratic or autocratic, the operation of these tendencies is profoundly affected by the varying organizational principles of particular social systems.

To be specific, the so-called "information power circle" confronts limits in a liberal democracy that simply do not exist within a military dictatorship. When Richard Nixon's links to the Watergate break-in came to light, Nixon realized that his own information power circle had been irreparably shattered. All the king's horses and all the king's men could not put Humpty Dumpty together again. As a result, Nixon immediately resigned his office of President. A liberal democracy is not well-designed to advance the interests of a tyrant who would impose his will on the people. It is rather designed to hold public leaders fully accountable for their actions, for the sake of a broader public good.

In contrast, Slobodan Milosevic had at his disposal for more than a decade a wide array of state instruments to maintain control over information in Serbia and Yugoslavia. It is not altogether surprising, therefore, that he thought he could cling to power despite losing an election. It was only when the police were no longer willing to enforce his will that he confronted his defeat. The risks and the costs of attempts to remove a military dictator from office can be quite high, especially when the political challenge comes from a public leader who is not himself part of the military establishment.

Similarly, though American corporate law permits a highly centralized executive office, it also mandates levels of transparency that limit the possibilities of information power circles. Corporate law in the U.S. is further supplemented by contract law, tort law, and various levels of regulatory constraints on corporate activities. While such constraints may sometimes appear intrusive, they also establish public accountabilities that in themselves constitute a moral framework for corporate activity.

In contrast, the 'crony capitalism" that has taken form in many of the rapidly expanding new economies of Asia, Latin America, Africa, and Eastern Europe permits a level of collaboration with political leaders that assures virtually uncontested executive control of information power circles. In short, graft and fraud are far easier to uncover and prosecute under U.S. corporate law than under "crony capitalism." Yet firms built upon such cronyism are far from driving the world's economy. In fact, most will fail unless they can become more transparent to potential investors. The exception would be state-owned firms that control highly marketable yet scarce natural resources, such as oil or natural gas.

I would further contend that truth-telling is requisite for the success of profit-making corporations, at least in the long run. At its best, the market gives rise to mutually satisfactory exchanges between producers or retailers and their consumers. The lack of such results seriously hampers economic activity. The principal point is that the information power circle, despite its short-term effectiveness, or its practical usefulness in addressing a particular crisis within a limited arena of political or economic activity, is finally self-destructive. Sooner or later it undercuts its own operations.

My claim is that the moral standards noted in Dr. Young's account of the spiritual life are not wholly incompatible with a highly functioning liberal democracy or with well-managed corporate enterprises. This claim, I hasten to add, does not imply that we question the pervasiveness of intrigue, nor does it minimize the spiritual warfare that is likely to accompany our struggles for integrity as we carry out our public or corporate duties. If anything, it increases our accountability, for if truthfulness and integrity are themselves finally necessary for political and economic effectiveness, then any willingness on our part to tolerate deceit, intrigue, subterfuge, graft, and fraud, becomes all the most inexcusable.

Dr. Young observed that John J. McCloy, in alerting him to the presence of intrigue in government operations, gave him the best and the worst advice he received: the best, because it prepared him for some troubling realities; the worst, because it disposed him to accept far more duplicity and plotting than he would otherwise have tolerated. His comment reminds me of Reinhold Niebuhr's eloquent observation: "The more we live with a necessary evil, the more necessary it seems and the less evil." Neibuhr stressed the importance of political realism; but he also knew that democratic political systems require moral substance as well, however imperfect and incomplete it might be.

Finally, we must recognize that our most zealous attempts to construct fair and just systems of social organization will ever remain subject to corruption, even evil. Dr. Young's contrast between the information power circle and the moral substance of our spiritual quest remains vivid and compelling. Nonetheless, our commitments to moral integrity do not finally preclude our effective participation in the political and economic systems of our society. The task is to find ways of providing significant leadership that is also governed by a substantial moral framework. I trust that Dr. Young's involvement with Oxford Analytica is an attempt to address this challenge.

RESPONSE BY MIROSLAV VOLF

Dr. Volf is Henry B. Wright Professor of Divinity, Yale University Divinity School

Dr. Young's essay is rich and his argument complex, but his thesis is simple. Though much attention is paid today "to the physical and intellectual dimension" of the exercise of political power, little or none is paid to "the emotional, non-rational or spiritual dimension." And yet, argues Young, "it is the spiritual character of the individual human being as a whole...that has the greatest impact on how such power is wielded—for better or worse, for good or ill."

By underscoring the spiritual dimension of the exercise of political power, I assume Dr. Young is not claiming that "the physical and intellectual dimensions" of the exercise of political power are unimportant. I also take it that he is not suggesting that we disregard the structural and cultural environments in which political power is exercised. I also take it that he is not implying that it would be unnecessary to explore the role of "the spiritual dimension" precisely in the nexus of relations between the intellectual, physical, structural, and cultural dimension of the exercise of political power. I take it, rather, that Dr. Young is concentrating so single-mindedly on the spiritual dimension because its extraordinary importance remains unrecognized or at least underappreciated.

Within that framework, I certainly agree with his thesis. And if he is right on this matter, then the central question will be what one understands as the "spiritual character" of human beings and in particular how that spiritual character is related to a specifically political moral vision. In that regard, I cannot help thinking of Martin Luther and the Reformation he set in motion. The case of Luther both underscores the importance of the "spiritual character" and helps us open the question of a political moral vision. True, Martin Luther was not a politician; he saw himself as primarily a professor of the Holy Scriptures and a teacher of the church. The consequences of his activity were not just religious, however. He set in motion epochal changes in the culture and politics of sixteenth century Europe whose impact has helped shape in substantial ways the subsequent history not only of Europe but of the world.

Leave aside for a moment the merits of his astonishing accomplishment—say, whether he was a God-sent prophet of true Christianity in an age of religious decadence (as Protestants preferred to believe for centuries) or a "sex-crazed monk of furious temper, a liar and fraud willing to tumble down the great and beautiful edifice of the Catholic Christianity for no better motives than lust and pride" (as Catholics traditionally insisted); or whether he was a revolutionary figure in the history of human freedom (as Hegel and Marx thought) or whether, remembering especially the religious wars of the seventeenth century, he brought more misery than well-being into the world (as a recent biographer, Richard Marius, argues). Leave all these questions aside for a moment and pay attention to how Luther accomplished what he did. In particular, note on how slender a thread hung Luther's enormous subsequent impact.

In his book *Luther: An Introduction to His Thought*, Gerhard Ebeling makes the following comment on Luther's role in the dramatic events of the years 1517 to 1521 in which the Reformation was born:

The real drama of these years consisted only in a secondary sense of impressive, tense and critical scenes such as the hearing before Cardinal Cajetan in Augsburg in 1518, the disputation in Leipzig with Johannes Eck in 1519, the burning of the bull of excommunication in 1520 or the appearance before the Emperor and the Imperial Diet in Worms in 1521. This course of events was not one which, once set in motion, continued automatically. Each further step depended to an astonishing degree upon the word of a single person, who had unintentionally presented a challenge to the contemporary world. If he had recanted at Augsburg, if he had been fore cautious at Leipzig, if he had not rejected the judgment of the Pope, and if he had followed the advice of numerous well-intentioned friends and had been prepared to compromise, and if in some way he had come to an arrangement with the Imperial Diet, the course of the Reformation would have been different. During these years, Luther's responsibility for the word of God resolved itself simply into clinging firmly to this word—something that was simple and straightforward in essence, but which represented for Luther, who stood alone and whose endurance was being tested, an ordeal by fire with a thousand trials and temptations, in a constantly changing situation.

Incredible as it may sound, Luther's *word* determined the course of history. No doubt, other factors—other personalities and shifting constellations of political power—were essential, too, but Luther's word was indispensable. What made him cling to that work, all religious, cultural, social, and political pressure notwithstanding? Many explanations might be given, but ultimately we have to fall back on the mystery of his character. He became a reformer not because of his physical stamina or intellectual prowess, though these were formidable, but because of his character, because of his unique blend of emotional and spiritual traits.

Now, I have asked you to suspend judgment about the merits of Luther's achievement so as to concentrate on Luther's character which make it possible. But such a judgment cannot be suspended indefinitely. Ultimately we cannot be concerned simply about the scale and the "mechanics" of the impact, but must also assess its value. And it is here that the spiritual dimension in the exercise of political power becomes significant in a different, and much more important, sense. For spirituality can be a mere means of maintaining power and of better achieving political ends—whatever their moral content. Like Machiavelli's prince, a politician will then strive to *appear* "to those who see him and hear him talk, all mercy, all faith, all integrity, all humanity, all religion." Or she will sincerely strive after such qualities but will apply them only to the limited circle of her family, friends, and political allies; she might then act like a leader of the gang of robbers who is aware that her success depends on the loyalty, honesty, and self-sacrifice of the gang's members. If naked political success is not what ultimately matters, but rather the well-being of a political community in the context of the larger world, then politicians must not only have spiritual character as individual human beings, but that character must also be infused with amoral political vision.

Let me conclude with a contemporary example. Some years ago in Ireland, I was talking to Alex Bourain, an important political activist in the anti-apartheid struggle in South Africa and later a co-chair of the Truth and Reconciliation Commission, about Nelson Mandela's role in the dismantling of apartheid. He confirmed, in a rather different context from Luther's, the importance of the single word of a single individual in critical situations. In delicate but hard negotiations with the apartheid regime, when things could have gone either way, it was often Nelson Mandela's demand—his word!—to press on and not to give up that made all the difference. But his "word" dismantled apartheid not simply because it was a word of a man with personal integrity, but equally because it grew out of the spiritual character of a person who was guided by a compelling moral vision for a political community.

USC

MARSHALL

SCHOOL OF

BUSINESS

CHAPTER SEVEN

THE INTEGRATION OF FAITH IN THE WORKPLACE

By Donald G. Soderquist

In 1980, having been president of Ben Franklin Stores, Don Soderquist went to Arkansas to join Sam Walton at Wal-Mart. Annual sales were just over $1 billion then. Today annual sales exceed $260 billion. For most of those years, Soderquist was Vice Chairman and Chief Operating Officer. This lecture was given at the University of Southern California in 2001.

Talk of integrating faith in the workplace makes a lot of people nervous. Why should that be? In business, as well as in business schools, we like dialogue. We talk about economics, politics, science and medicine, even history, and how those fields relate to business. But we do not like to talk about faith or mention the word God. That is unfortunate. Because if we leave out faith and God, we have a harder time talking about what I think is an intrinsically related subject—ethics and ethical conduct in business.

Business schools do a superb job of teaching leadership skills and how best to use the abundant technological tools we have today. I worry that there isn't more of an emphasis on ethics. As I talk to business leaders and to university students, I am convinced that there is a great need to integrate faith in the workplace.

Let's start with some definitions:

- Character is who you are. The real you. The person behind the mask.
- Ethics are the things you do, especially in the way that you treat people.

- Values are characteristics that are desirable because they are intrinsically good.
- Faith is a set of beliefs rooted in a solid foundation.

Why are these attributes so important? Because a transformation has taken place in regard to ethical behavior in our country and in the world. In the past 15 months, I've talked with groups of students and business people across the United States, in Mexico, Central America, Canada, Britain, Germany and Switzerland. I frequently ask, how many think that ethics are better today than they were 10 years ago? The same as 10 years ago? Worse than 10 years ago? Hardly anyone raises a hand to say ethics are better. Very few say they're the same. Most people say ethics are worse. Moreover, their response is supported by what they read every day in newspapers: corruption, deceit, cheating, and lying. That ought to frighten us, as should national opinion surveys in our schools and workplaces.

I've looked at a number of these surveys and they're all pretty similar. Here's a compilation. Some 90 percent of students say they've lied to their parents in the last 12 months. Nearly 80 percent say they have lied to a teacher in the last 12 months. Around a quarter say they would lie to get a job. Some 70 percent admit to cheating on a test in the last year. Half of those say they have cheated on more than one. About 40 percent of males and some 30 percent of females say they stole from a store in the last year. Nearly half of U.S. workers say that workplace pressures have led them to commit one or more unethical or illegal acts in the past 12 months, And here are the scariest numbers: 47 percent of top executives, 41 percent of corporate controllers, and 76 percent of graduate business students were willing to commit fraud by misstating write-offs that would have an impact on profitability.

I teach a graduate class at John Brown University, a small school in Arkansas. In the section called Vision, Mission and Values, I often ask the students to take the next week to look in newspapers, magazines and on television for reports of any breaches of ethical behavior. It's mind-boggling. There hasn't been a week in which there were not scores of breaches of ethical behavior. The definition of right and wrong has become blurred. The idea of absolutes has been largely rejected. Decisions are not made on historically accepted ethical standards.

PROSPERITY HAS HAD A DOWNSIDE

What caused the change? I fear that prosperity has been a big part of it. The United States is arguably the wealthiest civilization in real terms that ever existed. The majority of people in our country are not struggling to meet the necessities of life. The next step, then, is a never-ending quest for luxuries. That in turn has created a highly competitive environment that can cause people to cut corners, to not tell the truth all the time, to deceive. This has nothing to do with competence. Retired General Norman Schwarzkopf believes this country has what he calls a vacuum in leadership, which he attributes not to a lack of competence, but to a lack of character. If that is true, business schools across the nation ought to be spending time on more than just competence, but on teaching character.

Warren Bennis, Professor of Business Administration at the University of Southern California, has studied leadership for more than 30 years. He has written 18 books on the subject. Said he, in an interview with an organization known as Behavior on Line: "I have never seen anyone derailed from top leadership because of a lack of business literacy or technical competence or conceptual skills. It's *always* because of lapses of judgment and questions about character." Bennis went on to say that "judgment and character tend to be ignored by those responsible for educating others and are arguably difficult or even impossible to teach." I agree with Bennis with one exception. I think that judgment and character are difficult to teach, but not impossible.

In the interview, he went on to quote Dr. Jan Halper, the behavioral researcher, on an important point: "Jan Halper has studied over 4,000 executives about how level and open they are in giving feedback to their direct reports. Almost none of them said they were as open and honest as they should or could be. So, all too often, management turns into a manipulative art where deception, spin, maneuvering, guided ambiguity and other small deceits and slights of the tongue replace straight-forward communication." This is unethical behavior.

John W. Gardner served as Secretary of Health, Education and Welfare under President Lyndon Johnson and was founder of Common Cause, an organization dedicated to bringing out the best in society. In his lectures and many books and other writings, Gardner sounds a consistent theme: that "a great civilization is a drama lived in the minds of the people." He calls it "shared vision, shared values, shared expectations, shared purposes." Note his emphasis on *shared.* "In any healthy, reasonably coherent community," Gardner writes, "people come to have shared views concerning right and wrong, better and worse. They define for their time and place what things are legal or illegal, virtuous or vicious, good taste or bad. Values are embodied in a society's religious beliefs and its secular philosophy. Values always decay over time. Societies that keep their values alive do so, interestingly enough, not by escaping the processes of decay, but by powerful processes of regeneration." If he is right, and I think he is, then what we are seeing today is part of that cycle of decaying values, that sense that things today are worse than ten years ago.

But Gardner doesn't end there. "Each generation must rediscover the living elements in its own tradition and adapt them to present realities." He's saying you can't stop the decay, but what you have to do is rediscover what is in your traditions and in the past and adapt them to the present realities. And he ends by saying, "To assist in that rediscovery is one of the tasks of leadership." I couldn't agree more.

If there is to be a rediscovery or regeneration, it must begin with leaders. I've spent an entire business life trying to live it. Now I'm spending my retirement sharing what it is I've learned. At John Brown University we've developed a center for business leadership and ethics. Every undergraduate has to have at least one course in ethical leadership. We've instituted two graduate programs, one an MBA with an emphasis in ethics and another, a master's in business leadership and ethics.

A HANDSHAKE MEANT A DEAL WAS A DEAL

I grew up in a world where there was a common understanding of right and wrong. There was a high level of trust among people. You pretty much knew where everyone stood. In business, a handshake meant a deal was a deal. In my early days at Wal-Mart, we did those kinds of deals all the time. We weren't worried about the technicalities of the law. What was important to us was our intent. We *intended* to keep contracts, not to find ways to break them through some technicality or error.

I grew up in a world where you could depend on the vast majority of people to keep their word. This phrase was very familiar: "His word is his bond." Parents supported teachers who disciplined their children. Character was more important than money. Reputation meant something. People who declared bankruptcy felt a continuing moral obligation to pay off what they originally owed. And the larger context of this was the common understanding of right from wrong. There was general agreement between parents and teachers, politicians and business people of what was black and what was white, what was right and what was wrong. But those two circles have moved together in the minds of many people into what they see as a big, blurry gray area.

Of course, the world then was far from perfect. There were problems in many areas of society. There was prejudice against minorities. There was little opportunity for minorities and women. But I believe we did have higher ethical standards in regard to integrity, honesty, trust and keeping promises. I would argue, in fact, that the seeds of the solutions to many of those societal problems grew out of higher ethical standards. I don't yearn to return to yesterday. But I do want to learn from the past and rediscover our ethical foundation. There's a Russian proverb that says, "He who lives in the past is blind in one eye, but he who ignores the past is blind in both eyes."

BUT WHAT IF "EVERYONE ELSE IS DOING IT?"

The major pitfall of our highly competitive business environment is the idea that you have to cut corners, you have to lie and cheat and push yourself ahead of others because everyone else is doing so. Then comes the rationalization. It's ok to lie and cheat and steal under certain circumstances, under certain situations. Don't believe it. And don't fall into the trap that if it's legal, it's ethical. That's a dangerous one. There is a difference between legal and ethical. In a real sense, the law is society's minimum standard. Many actions can be legal, but can also prove to be unethical because of detrimental consequences to communities or various groups of people.

To those who say you can't be ethical and be successful, I would point to Wal-Mart, where I worked for more than 20 years. When I joined the company, sales were $1.25 billion. Twenty-one years later sales topped $191 billion. No company has ever grown that fast in 21 years. This year we're going from $191 billion to over $215. Last year we were the second largest company in the world after ExxonMobil. [Editor's note: Soderquist was referring to 2001. In the 2002 Fortune 500 list, Wal-Mart surpassed ExxonMobil to become the world's largest corporation, with $219 billion in revenues.] Our workforce of 1.2 million people is bigger than that of any other commercial enterprise. At a time when layoffs are rampant across American business, we are adding people, 75,000 this year alone. We're going to add 40 million square feet of selling space in this country this year. And this was done by a company headquartered in Bentonville, Arkansas, a town of 15,000 people, and by a company dedicated—passionately dedicated—to ethical conduct from top to bottom.

The ethical conduct, in fact, was crucial. I can honestly tell you that in my years at Wal-Mart, I was never asked to do one thing that in any way was unethical or breached my own ethical values. Our success wasn't because we were smarter than everyone else or that we had some secret formula. It wasn't because we stepped on other people, or because of our size we could buy merchandise cheaper than everybody else. When we started out, we were not large. And it's not even because we have a large number of MBA's at Wal-Mart. I like the definition of leadership of Colin Powell, a soldier's soldier who served as Secretary of State under President George W. Bush: "The art of accomplishing more than the science of management says is possible." (And Powell is the man who entered the army through ROTC at City College of New York and rose through the ranks to become Chairman of the Joint Chiefs.) Nobody believed what we did at Wal-Mart was possible, not even us. If you had told me in 1980 when I joined the company that we would become the largest company in the world, I never would have believed it. The impossible is possible. That's why I challenge MBA students to dream big. But I also challenge them to be part of the regeneration of values in this country, and in the world.

"WE DIDN'T DO EVERYTHING RIGHT"

Our processes included all the basics taught in business schools and practiced at other companies. We've had various strategies over the years. Some remained the same from our very beginnings and others have changed. While strategies may change, values do not. Now, I must say that we didn't do everything right. We certainly weren't perfect. But the underpinning of our company and of our success has been a culture based on a sound set of values. I said earlier that values are characteristics that are intrinsically good. When I talk about values, I'm talking about basic things that we might all agree to: integrity, honesty, trustworthiness, fairness, keeping promises, respecting individuals, excellence, truth, faith. Within those values was our vision. Our vision was not to become the largest company in the world, or to make the most money. Our vision was to provide a shopping environment that no one else had provided before, and to attract a group of employees who could be considered family, who were loyal and dedicated and who shared the same vision. All the rest flowed from that.

In any business you have to start with a product. Ours was to serve all people across the country with access to general merchandise and the fairest prices. Then you have to have resources. Most people would put financial resources at the top of the list, but to us, people are at the top of the list. You have to take care of your people, motivate them, and be certain they feel they have a piece of the enterprise, that they are part of something that's never been done before. Most of all, you have to have confidence in your people. Of course, financial resources, technology, logistics, and merchandising skills are all important, but the top of the resource list is people. You can have a wonderful dream and vision backed up by values, but to execute those plans everyone in the organization has to know what they are. It isn't enough for the leaders to know; the people down the line need to know. Everybody needs to know what those values are.

As a result of what we have done, we consistently had outstanding financial performance. We have developed a base of loyal customers that tell us of their loyalty every time we do market research, and we do it monthly. We check the number of people in our trade territories, the stores that cover a particular trade territory, and consistently 90 percent of the people in our trade territories have shopped in a Wal-Mart in the last 30 days. That is an incredible base of loyal customers. We have a wonderful family of associates who believe in what we are doing, who are dedicated, who work hard, and have fun and are rewarded accordingly. We are a group of ordinary people, very ordinary people, who have been able to do extraordinary things.

ETHICAL STANDARDS MUST HAVE A FOUNDATION

The ethical standards we have established in Wal-Mart are based on our values, and our values have roots in Judeo-Christian principals. From the very beginning, the things that we did were embodied in those principals. I said at the beginning that people are afraid to talk about God in the workplace. That is true at Wal-Mart too. This is the point where some people get jittery. They will say, ethics is one thing, but you're not supposed to talk about God because this is a secular environment. They do tend to think of a commercial enterprise in terms of our country's separation of church and state.

What is interesting to me about this is that multiple surveys taken over the past ten years reveal that consistently between 94 percent and 96 percent of people surveyed in the United States say they believe in God. In fact, in the shadow of September 11, more and more people are talking about God. Business marquees read "God Bless America." At the World Series in the seventh inning, instead of singing "Take Me Out to the Ballgame," we had celebrities and heroes singing "God Bless America." The President has asked Americans to pray for grieving families of those who have been killed. He's asked us to pray for him and his advisors as they make difficult decisions that impact all of Americans. Church attendance rose after the attacks, as did the sale of Bibles. America is calling on God in a time of tragedy. I'm encouraged. In times of difficulty, where do people look? When they're at the end of the line, where do they look?

I'm also encouraged by an article that appeared recently in *Fortune Magazine* [July, 2001]. Here's part of it:

> Bringing spirituality into the workplace violates the old idea that faith and fortune don't mix. But a ground swell of believers is breaching that last idea in corporate America. Three dozen middle aged rebels in business suits are gathered for lunch in a conference room on the top floor of the LaSalle Bank building in Chicago. They have come for sandwiches and spiritual sustenance and before long they are floating radical ideas like 'work less,' 'slow down,' 'stop multi-tasking,' 'listen to your heart.' The burly long-haired man stirring up this talk is a 59 year-old scholar, theologian and health care consultant named Jack Shay. As the business people recount the pressures they face, Shay recalls a Latin phrase, 'Do what you do and do it with all of yourself.'

Strive for excellence. Work from your soul. That, too, sounds subversive, yet it is this goal that animates these executives who belong to a Chicago area group called Business Leaders for Excellence, Ethics and Justice. For more than a decade they've wrestled with big questions. How can business promote family life? What is a just wage? When are layoffs justified? They say the struggle to integrate faith with work is never-ending. Lately, they're finding numbers are increasing.

We all face ethical dilemmas every day. Some are really tough choices and I don't want to minimize that. We choose who we are really going to be and what it is we are going to do. We make that choice consciously or unconsciously by the way we act. That's why it's important to have a personal foundation of beliefs and know who you are. It's easy to have a double standard of judging others in terms of their character while judging ourselves in terms of our circumstances. We act as if it's OK for us to lie and cheat and steal, but we don't want others to do that to us. When I'm sitting across the table in a negotiation with someone, I want to trust what he says. I presume he wants to trust what I say. He doesn't want me to keep an important fact off the table. He doesn't want me to lie to him or deceive him and I expect the same of him. So when we look at ourselves sometimes, we say it's the circumstances. There may be a price to pay for being ethical and it may cost you your job. To be ethical in a company that does unethical things may be very lonely. In the first group of graduate students I taught three years ago, two people quit their jobs. When faced with the reality of what ethical behavior is all about, they couldn't stay where they were. I'm happy to tell you both of them got better jobs.

GET TO KNOW THE ROOTS OF YOUR OWN VALUES

Every person acts on a set of values. Even if they have not articulated them, their actions are a clear picture of what it is they believe. Every value is rooted in something and there are values that transcend culture. The basis for my values is the Bible. I find the standards in the Bible to be simple, clear-cut, reasonable, understandable, and a good picture of how I want to be treated by other people. The question is, what are your values? What are the roots of these values that you live by? What is the foundation of your values and do they represent how you like to be treated by others? How do your beliefs translate in your daily life into action?

We can pass over these things and we can talk about integrity and honesty and ethics and values and all the rest of it. And we can say it's for the other guy. But we would deceive ourselves. We use a team approach in teaching at our graduate school. We have a business practitioner as well as an educator. In one class, the educator, who was the former Provost of the school, told this story about himself:

> I went to Home Depot to buy some chain. I found the chain I wanted. It was right on the bottom shelf and when I looked at it, I could see the price was $1.94 a foot. I told the young man I wanted 10 feet. And so, he went to measure it off and cut it. And then he wrote out the slip that I was to take up to the counter and he wrote $3.94. As soon as he wrote $3.94, I said, "Wait a second, it's $1.94."
>
> He got down on his hands and knees and looked. "I'm sorry, sir, you're right. It is $1.94."
>
> I proceeded to the cash register and the cashier took the slip and she took the chain and entered it into the computer. "Ninety-four cents a foot."

And he said, to my amazement,

> I had to think before I said anything. It scared me about myself because I consider myself an ethical person. I had no problem stopping the young man who was going to overcharge me, but I had to stop and think when they were going to undercharge me.

We all pass those crossroads every single day. I do not try to convince others to adopt my values. But I do challenge others to think through what it is they really believe. You want to be successful. Then begin by building a solid foundation of values. Add to the foundation your skills, your experience, your education, your ambition. Develop interpersonal skills. Remember to treat others like you would like to be treated. When I talk to groups of senior executives, I tell them I'm going to give them a two-question quiz. First of all, write down the top three officers reporting to you. Write their names down in full. The next question is, write down the names of three of your janitors, the maintenance people. The average grade in the class is 50 percent. They don't know who the janitors are. One of the reasons that Wal-Mart has been successful is that we treat everybody with respect and dignity. We treat people like we would like to be treated and that is a key ingredient in the success of our company. I've been saying this for years and most business leaders don't get it. Treat people like you'd like to be treated. Sounds pretty simple. But it becomes complex because we have such big egos. We have importance and we have titles and we have power and we have influence. I can tell you the names of our janitors.

Reexamine what your values are. What is it you stand for? What are the constants in your life? What will you absolutely not compromise? Write them down.

Most people have never written down their values, but if you don't write them down they're not implanted in your mind. Get in the habit of looking at what your values are, then test yourself as you make daily decisions. Don't change because others have changed. Be a passionate voice for sound values. Stand for something. Don't be afraid to speak out for what you believe. Don't compromise something as important as your character. Make the right choices when you come to those ethical crossroads in your life. Behave as if everything in your life is really important, because it really is. Don't let popular opinion or ego stand in the way of principle. Have a passion to be the best at what you do. In Wal-Mart we're never satisfied. And that's not a negative thing. We always strive to get better.

Don't say what you believe. Show or live what you believe. The founder of ServiceMaster said it best; "If you don't live it, you don't believe it."

Let's go back to the beginning. The Integration of Faith in the Workplace. What does it come down to? It comes down to, first of all, not standing up and trying to convert others to my brand of religion. It is, however, men and women of character who recognize that they are not the center of the universe. Who recognize that it is important to treat everybody with respect and dignity because we've all been created in the image of God. To acknowledge that there is a God who is a loving but just God, who cares about us and cares about how we live our lives. It is men and women who choose to live honorable and productive lives—*choose* to live honorable and productive lives. Who understand what it is that is inherently right and wrong and to defend the truth at all costs. Who live their daily lives in accordance with a sound set of values. Who realize that faith is an integral part of how we are made and is something to be embraced and not something to be feared or avoided. And as a result of how they live their lives, these kinds of people are not only rewarded with the joy of unique reputation, but also the impact they can have on their company and the people around them in a transforming way.

RESPONSE BY WARREN BENNIS

Warren Bennis is University Professor and Professor of Business Administration at the University of Southern California. He has lectured widely on leadership and is the author of 18 books on the subject.

There's a Chinese proverb that goes like this. "I curse you. May you live in an important age." All of us are. And that's why Don Soderquist's essay is so timely and important.

I agree so much with him. I think we're all hungry spirits. We all want something out of work beyond stock options. What we want out of work, and what we want from leadership, is meaning. All the exemplary leaders whom I have studied, interviewed, researched or met over the last fifty years, all of them had a true moral compass. Character counts, especially now, in this crisis of war against terrorism.

But I want to address three questions to Mr. Soderquist, and I will end with a bit of disagreement with one of the things he says.

My first question begins with a quote from the philosopher Emanuel Kant; "From warped wood has man been made. Nothing straight can be fashioned." That's an interesting Judeo-Christian principle, that we are all born in sin. Wal-Mart and ServiceMaster have both done a great deal to create an ethical culture to bring out the best in us, our most creative selves, our most human selves, ourselves of faith.

So what I would like to ask Mr. Soderquist is, how did you spread and deeply embed those ethical principles into Wal-Mart? How did you create a culture where people were rewarded for them, where people believed in them, where people acted on them? Because we're all imperfect, we all need a culture that will help us develop those attitudes and spirit that will make us bigger and stronger and keep integrity in the workplace. How did you do this in this global company that reaches out all over the world? And what lessons did you learn?

The second question is a tricky and important one, especially now. It is one for which I don't have a good answer. I think religion, particularly when we consider the tragic event of September 11, 2001, may define our nation's century. Religion can be an exclusionary factor. Think of today's world, of Jews, of Christians, of Hindus, of Buddhists, of Shinto's, and Muslims. Then think of tomorrow's world. From what we can discern from demographics, by the year 2025, 50 percent of the world's population will be Muslim. When we talk about the Judeo-Christian ethic, who is excluded and how do we take those other groups into account in our wide tent of spirituality? In a *New York Times* column [November 27, 2001], Thomas Friedman wrote: "World War II and the Cold War were fought to defeat secular totalitarianism, Nazism, and Communism. World War III is a battle against religious totalitarianism, a world view that my faith must reign supreme and can be followed passionately only if all others are negated." That's Bin Ladinism, he writes. "But unlike Nazism, religious totalitarianism cannot be fought by armies alone. It must be fought in schools, mosques, churches and synagogues and can be defeated only with the help of imans, rabbis and priests." So, how do you relate that to Judaic and Christian ethics?

The third question is very much related to Wal-Mart. The antiglobalism protestors, among others, who use Wal-Mart and McDonalds in their fanatical attacks, think that Wal-Mart has brought about the eclipse of community by eliminating Mom and Pop stores. While I don't really believe this is true, and I believe Wal-Mart has brought more prosperity, I am curious to know how you respond to that question which is on many people's minds. Is opening a Wal-Mart, which could drive small shop owners out of business, an ethical act?

I want to end with what might be a disagreement. My sense of young people today, from teaching undergraduates at USC and a recent study that I just finished on leaders 30 years and younger, is that they are quite interested in giving back to society. They seem to me to be more interested in the environment, in work-life balance, in ethical moral issues than my generation was. My experience with young people today leads me to think that the marvelous cadre in business schools today seems to be more concerned with human values and ethical issues that in the past.

DON SODERQUIST RESPONDS TO BENNIS'S QUESTIONS

Concerning the first, as to what Wal-Mart has done to drive the ethical process deeply into the company, it starts at the top, with the leadership. You have to believe it in your heart. If you don't truly believe it, then the ethical system will not be passed down to the other people. The leaders have to be role models, leading by example, by how they live their lives. After that, you reward people who treat other people right and, I hate to say the word, punish people who don't. I remember a trip Sam Walton and I made to Nebraska to visit a small store. Sam always liked to walk around stores by himself. He went one way and I went another. We talked to people; we came out and talked in front as we usually did. Sam said, "Don, what did you think?"

I said, "Boy, there's a problem in the store."

And he said, "Don, there absolutely is. Did you see that people wouldn't look you in the eye and they were cautious about talking to you? Let's get the district manager in when we get back." Well, I hate to say this, but by Friday that store manager was out of the store. We did a survey of the people and they said he wasn't listening to them, he wasn't talking to them, and so we didn't hesitate to move him out of that store. Now, we didn't kick him out of the company, but we did demote him. I couldn't understand how someone who had been in Wal-Mart for six or eight years, hearing all of the things that we talked about, knowing about our culture, could get in and run a store and then not listen to the people or talk to the people. The issue was, that manager never believed in what we were teaching and what we were preaching. Not everybody is going to believe it.

Another example is the relationship our buyers have with our suppliers. In other companies, when samples are sent to the buyer, they become the property of the buyer and he can take them home or he can give them to his assistant or he can give them to people around the office. In Wal-Mart, samples become the property of Wal-Mart and they are either given away to unfortunate families or they are sold in our company store. That sends a signal that you don't take anything free from the vendor. In addition to that, our gift policy is that a buyer cannot accept a gift of cash, baseball or football tickets, or anything at all from a vendor. That includes lunch and dinner. Suppliers do not pay for our lunch or dinner; if anything, we pay for theirs. If a buyer violates that policy, the buyer may be terminated and we may not do business with that vendor again.

Unfortunately, in spite of how much we preach it and teach it, we have had to fire some buyers; we've had to stop dealing with some vendors. We've asked some vendors to take a particular person off the account because they were not trustworthy. Every vendor, when they come to do business with Wal-Mart, must sign an agreement that lists all of our policies. We keep it on record. It becomes one of the symbols throughout the organization that this is how we operate, this is who we are.

Furthermore, Sam used to visit every store every year. And as we got still bigger, we ended up doing satellite network to all the stores and we talked about this all the time. People in the home office would hear about it every single Friday and every single Saturday. It's not something you say once and then forget. We talk about integrity at least once or twice every year with all of our people. It's a constant job.

The second question relates to Judeo-Christian principles. I am not trying to convince people to accept my beliefs and values. What I am saying is, ask yourself the question, what is the basis for what you believe? What is the basis for your values? I find a lot of people haven't really thought about that subject and if they really think seriously about it, I think most people will say, I agree with integrity and honesty and forthrightness and trustworthiness and so forth. When I was speaking in Switzerland to university students from all over the world and 750 European business leaders, we were talking about this particular subject. A young man in the back stood up and said, "I'm from China and when I hear you talk about Judeo-Christian principles, I think, Confucius says the same things that Jesus said: treat people with respect and dignity, be honest." I said "That's it. You have a foundation, you have a foundation then on which you're building your life." I want people to examine what their foundation is and I would rather be inclusive rather than exclusive on that particular issue.

The last question is about Wal-Mart driving small businesses out. First of all, if you think of the history of retailing in the United States, there is an evolutionary process. Mom and Pop grocery stores have been largely replaced by bigger stores that offer convenience, assortment and better pricing. But there is more to it than that. When Wal-Mart comes to town many small businesses not only survive, but thrive. I opened the store in Western Denver, on the way out to the mountains, and a lady came up to me after the grand opening and said, "I want to thank you for coming and opening a Wal-Mart store."

I said, "You're very welcome. That's a common comment we get."

She said, "You don't understand. I run a little paint store over there. Since you've opened here and you've been on your dry run for the last two weeks, I've had the best sales I've ever had because you're bringing people here. I just want to thank you for it. And on top of it, yesterday a man came and said 'I understand you've got such-and-such kind of paint here.' I said I did and asked him how he knew. 'A guy at Wal-Mart told me they don't carry it but to go over to the lady who runs the little paint store over here. She's got it.'"

We believe in the free enterprise system. That's how we began. We believe in it very much. But it's the customers who put people out of business; Wal-Mart doesn't. In some of the towns we go into, shops have been closing at 5 p.m. When do people in two wage-earner families shop? They have parking meters downtown. You have to pay in order to shop. Sometimes stores are not open on Saturdays. We're open when the customers are going to shop, when they're available to shop, when they're not working.

We want small businesses in particular to survive. We want our competitors to survive. We run the best stores where we have the most competition. We run the worst stores where we have little or no competition because we get complacent and we don't take care of the customer the way we ought and we don't keep the store looking good and we don't stay in stock. We want competition. That's the free enterprise system. We believe in it.

Concerning Warren Bennis's view of today's MBA students, I do see that spark. I am just concerned about what I see taking place in business. That's why I am pleading with young people to take their concerns about environment and other issues and combine those concerns with ethical behavior. Unethical behavior can be more of a threat to this country than all other issues.

CHAPTER EIGHT

BUSINESS ETHICS IN SKEPTICAL TIMES

By James A. Baker III

James Baker, a corporate lawyer by training, has held high government positions in three Administrations. He was Undersecretary of Commerce for President Gerald Ford; Secretary of the Treasury, Chairman of the President's Economic Policy Council, and White House Chief of Staff for President Ronald Reagan, and Secretary of State for President George H. W. Bush. This lecture was given at the University of Michigan in 2002.

The backdrop of this essay is a period of intense scandal in American business, highlighted by the spectacular failure in 2001 of Enron, the Houston-based energy conglomerate. The outcry over the questionable accounting practices that contributed to Enron's collapse also brought down the venerable accounting giant Arthur Andersen. Other scandals, also involving accounting practices, followed in Enron's wake creating an almost unprecedented public revulsion against business, at least since the nineteenth century. These events have cast a shadow over our entire system of free market capitalism. My view of all this is highly personal, and intimately tied to who I am and how I came to be that way.

In 1970, in Houston, Texas, I was an apolitical lawyer whose grandfather had told him that if you want to be a good lawyer, you work hard, you study, and you stay out of politics. That was my grandfather's advice to all the young lawyers at Baker Botts, the family law firm that began in 1840 in Houston. So I stayed out of politics. Then I had a tragedy in my life. I lost a wife to cancer when she was 38. A very good friend of mine, with whom I did not at that time share a political philosophy, named George Bush, came to me and said, "You know, you need to do something to take your mind off your grief. How about helping me in my campaign for the Senate in Texas?" And I said, "Well George, I'd like to do that, but number one, I don't know anything about politics, and number two, I'm a Democrat!" And he said, "Well I think we can take care of that latter problem." And we did. I converted, and I helped him with his campaign. We won Houston, which is the biggest population center in Texas and was the area I was responsible for. Nevertheless, we lost statewide. One thing led to another and a couple years later I was invited to come to Washington to interview with the then new Ford Administration (Nixon having just resigned), and ultimately became Undersecretary of Commerce, the number two job in the Commerce Department. And again, one thing led to another and after only about seven or eight months, I found myself being asked by President Ford to go over to the President Ford Committee to run a delegate operation for him against a challenger named Ronald Reagan, the governor of California. And I did. And then one thing led to another, and in the fall I found myself being asked by President Ford to be chairman of his national campaign for election against Jimmy Carter. We lost very, very narrowly by 17,000 votes out of 81 million votes cast. If you turn 17,000 votes around in Ohio and Hawaii, Ford is elected and Carter isn't, and I said to myself, "What a wonderful opportunity. I've been involved in the closest presidential election in American history." And I never suspected there would ever be one any closer, and then of course there was. [In the 2000 presidential election, George Bush asked Baker to head the Republican legal team dealing with the disputed election in Florida that was ultimately settled in Bush's favor in the U.S. Supreme Court.]

I've always been more inclined to deal with practicalities than with theories. Some people used to refer to me in Washington as a pragmatist, and to some people in Washington that's a dirty word. To me it is not, as long as you say you're a principled pragmatist. You've got to get things done if you want to leave a mark. It doesn't do any good to have the greatest ideas in the world if you can't put them into action.

PROFOUND ISSUES OF ETHICAL CONDUCT

I think of this essay as a report from the field. I serve on the boards of two corporations listed on the New York Stock Exchange. I serve on the board of one family-owned private corporation rather widely held but not listed, and I serve on two large, non-profit or academic institution boards. So I have retired from government but I have not retired from governance, and I see my duties as a director a lot like my duties as a public servant. Both are intertwined with the most profound issues of ethical conduct. One of these issues is the independence of outside directors. It could reasonably be asked, how can Jim Baker be independent when he serves on the boards of two corporations that pay his law firm millions of dollars in legal fees? When I joined Baker Botts, the family firm, I was told, "We want you to serve on a lot of boards." And I said, "I'm sorry, that's not something I have in mind for my future, but I'll make a deal with you, I'll serve on two, you pick them." And so that's how I came to serve on the boards of two listed companies. My view is that despite the professional relationship between my law firm and these two companies, I believe that I am totally and completely independent. Now you can say, "Well it's very easy for you to stand up and say that, why do you think so?" I'm not sure that I can put this in a very delicate way, so I'll tell you why I think so as hopefully and in as non-arrogant a manner as I can, but 72-year-old former Secretaries of State who have enough money in the bank to do all the hunting and fishing and golf playing that they want to do, still do care about doing a good job and don't care if in trying to do that, they make somebody mad. I don't have anything to lose so I speak my mind.

ENRON: LESSONS FROM A SAD STORY

I contemplate the subject of business ethics in skeptical times with sadness because Enron is a Houston story, and Houston is my home. I know some of the board members. Some are friends of mine. I very much doubt that my friends set out one morning (certainly the ones that I'm thinking of right now) with the objective of misleading anybody or with planning a major-league conspiracy to mislead and injure. Yet, however good their intentions may have been, decisions were made about business, about accounting, and about disclosure matters that you simply cannot justify. Each bad decision, as it turns out, begat yet another bad decision. In the end the financial community understandably lost confidence and we saw Enron collapse rather dramatically. I can't remember a business failure in the United States that happened with such rapidity from the time it started to the time it was totally over in terms of the collapse.

As long as fallible human beings are in charge, we can expect more businesses to get into big trouble. Generally they're going to fail through bad luck or bad business judgment, but sometimes they're going to fail through negligence or active malfeasance or even active criminal behavior. The challenge our society faces is to study these events and to take lessons from them about ethical conduct personally and ethical conduct as representatives of our companies, and about public policy responses. I ask myself, what should I do differently in my job as a corporate director? What should my company do differently? What should our system of free market capitalism do differently? Consider these questions in the context of four general topics.

SKEPTICISM, THE FIRST DEFENSE

The first is the issue of skepticism. The collapse of Enron, along with other similar though less spectacular corporate scandals, has understandably triggered public skepticism. But we need to maintain some perspective. For business, all times should be skeptical times. The ultimate form of skepticism was Marxism, a system of government and economics based on the premise that capitalism abused workers and that central planners could do a better job. Marxism, of course, has failed, and the thing that it opposed, that thing called capitalism, has survived. Capitalism survived because with all of its faults, it generally works, and because on balance it treats everyone, including workers, better than any alternative system. To paraphrase Winston Churchill's famous statement about democracy, "No one pretends that a market economy is perfect. Indeed it has been said that a free market is the worst form of economy, except all those other forms that have been tried from time to time."

Even from within capitalism, however, we find skepticism. Theodore Roosevelt used to complain about the malefactors of great wealth, and he started the antitrust movement, a very good thing. Franklin Roosevelt blamed the Great Depression on economic royalists. I'm not sure that's true, but he was making those comments 75 years ago. Dwight Eisenhower warned us about the military industrial complex, and don't forget that Vice President Gore did win more than 48 percent of the popular vote in November 2000 with a promise to "stand up to the powerful forces in our economy," whatever that means. Now, add the 2.74 percent that Ralph Nader won, and you could argue that a majority of Americans support some form of economic populism. That's a philosophy that my old boss, Ronald Reagan, might have described this way, "If it moves, tax it, if it keeps moving, regulate it, and if it stops moving, subsidize it." Popular culture is even more unforgiving than the politicians. Hollywood has turned business bashing into an art form. The movie *Wall Street* gave us a typical business villain who famously declared greed is good.

My point is simply that the seed of Enron fell on very fertile soil. But while Marxism has been discredited, and while I disagree strongly with economic populism, I think we all need to understand that healthy skepticism is an essential element of both a sound market economy and a mature ethical perspective. For example, it is absolutely impossible to have a functioning market economy without the rule of law. If you don't believe that, just look at the problems Russia is having. The Russians really want a market economy, but they have yet to understand that first you must put the basics in place: a system of laws, private property, enforceable contracts, corporations, stocks, bonds, courts, and banks. You cannot do business without them. We can and should argue the details, particularly about some of the overly complex laws and regulations that govern business, the environment or taxes. But the principle is inarguable. The rule of law is an absolutely necessary and desirable precondition to a functional market economy. And what is the rule of law? It is nothing more than institutionalized skepticism about human nature. With the rule of law, property changes hands through voluntary sale or through inheritance. Without the rule of law, property goes to the neighborhood bully. Likewise, the conduct of business requires prudent skepticism, whether by investors, employees, officers, or board members.

Prudent skepticism is a critical business skill. In a business acquisition, for example, we call it due diligence. One problem at Enron in retrospect was that at critical points in the company's history there was either not enough skepticism or there wasn't any skepticism at all. To suggest the need for business ethics is to suggest that our system lacks something that must be supplied by men and women of good will who conduct themselves according to higher standards than those of the marketplace. That means that the rule of law, ordinary commercial prudence, and the impulse to act ethically in business all reflect a healthy skepticism about human nature. As a moralist, I certainly do not agree that greed is good, but as a realist, I understand that greed is—it exists.

WHAT IS THE GENIUS OF CAPITALISM?

That leads to my second point, the argument that free market capitalism is itself an ethical system. A genius of capitalism is to turn a destructive human characteristic (greed) into benign self-interest, something we know as incentive. It's hard to improve on the explanation that Adam Smith gives. "It is not from the benevolence of the butcher, the brewer, or the baker that we expect our dinner, but from their regard to their own self-interest," Smith wrote. "Under this system, every man as long as he does not violate the laws of justice, is left perfectly free to pursue his own interest in his own way and to bring both his industry and capital into competition with those of any other man." By pursuing his own interest, says Smith, he frequently "promotes the interest of society more effectually than when he really intends to promote that interest." Now, Smith's classic *Wealth of Nations* was published in 1776, the same year as the Declaration of Independence. It established the theoretical foundation for the free market. The

Declaration of Independence, on the other hand, set the American colonies on a path toward the form of Republican democracy established a few years later under our Constitution. Both capitalism, free enterprise, and republican democracy have succeeded beyond measure. I was Secretary of State of this wonderful country at almost the best time anybody could have been, because Communism collapsed, the Berlin Wall fell down, the 40-year struggle of the Cold War was over, everybody wanted to get close to the United States of America, and everybody around the world wanted to embrace democracy and free markets, save one or two little dictatorships.

James Madison wrote in *Federalist 51*, "What is government itself but the greatest of all reflections on human nature. If men were angels, no government would be necessary." Of course the American form of government is not perfect, among other things it failed to prevent our Civil War. On balance, however, it has worked marvelously. Consider the painful case of Watergate. President Nixon violated our trust. He abused the power in his office, and he challenged the rule of law. But the true legacy of Watergate is that our system identified and peacefully expelled an unethical president, an event that was in many ways unprecedented in human history. Our free press did its job exposing the wrongdoing, Congress cranked up the impeachment machine, and President Nixon had to resign. After Watergate, the people demanded higher standards and we had four presidents in a row with the very highest character. President Ford, whom I served, was one of the finest men ever to serve as President and he restored honor to the Oval Office. Jimmy Carter, in my view, was wrong on many policies and perhaps he was less skilled in governance than some, but nobody would ever question his honesty. And Ronald Reagan and George Bush were both men of the highest integrity. Watergate, like Enron, was an ethical failure. Like Enron, it created great skepticism about the system. But I think it's wrong to see Watergate solely as a failure of the system. Rather, it demonstrated the genius of our founders and the strength of the ethical system they created.

FIRST, LIKE THE DOCTOR, DO NO HARM

Now to my third point. I think we need to take great care that in our eagerness to avoid another Enron, and corporate scandals like it, we do not seek reforms that are inconsistent with the ethical structure of our economic system or that weaken that structure. To put it another way, the proper response to any corporate scandal is not a simpleminded rush to "do something" with little concern about what that something might be. Instead, the first concern of the business ethicist, like the doctor, should be to do no harm. Let me illustrate. The myth part of the

Watergate story is that politics is essentially corrupt and "everybody does it." The myth inspired two very fundamental changes in our system of governance. The first was the enactment of unrealistic and deeply flawed campaign finance laws. We've seen how deeply flawed they were and we've now gotten legislation correcting some of the problems. The other was the creation of the independent counsel's office, an office with prosecutorial power outside of the normal institutions of government.

On campaign finance laws, columnist Robert Samuelson sums up my view. Said he, "In the futile effort to regulate politics, the 'reformers,'" [and he puts the term reformers in quotes to signal his scorn] have manufactured most of the immorality, illegality, and cynicism that they deplore, and that's even before considering the conflict between these laws and the first amendment." The right answer, which is consistent with the Constitution and the ethical structure of our system of government, is not to somehow stay on this road of criminalizing our politics and thereby politicizing our criminal justice system, but to require full and immediate disclosure of all campaign contributions with extraordinarily severe penalties for those who fail to report or who file erroneous or misleading reports. This is the analog in politics to the honest disclosures that should be required in the world of corporate finance.

As for independent federal prosecutors, the consensus today in both parties and even among those who originally supported them, is that the cure proved far worse than the disease. The prosecutors were not subject to the checks and balances that the founders built into our system. Countless investigations produced very little evidence of smoke and even less of fire, but they did so at the cost of further weakening public confidence in the system and creating skepticism where none was justified. Still, I want to be absolutely clear about one thing. Though I have always opposed the independent counsel law, while it was the law of the land, the executive branch was absolutely obligated to cooperate with all of those investigations. The presidents I served did just that. I can't tell you, however, how many countless hours we spent being interviewed by the FBI or testifying on one thing or another, because all that was required by the independent council statute was an allegation. If you were a high enough government official, a mere allegation that you did something wrong resulted in the appointment of an independent counsel.

I have the same concern about this country's response to Enron and other corporate scandals. Our economy, like our political system, is self-correcting. We've just been through this with the political system, and we don't need to make that same mistake with our economy and with our business system. Enron and its leaders have been punished and they will be further punished. The punishment will justifiably be harsh. There was an enormous amount of what I would call collateral damage—to employees, many of whom lost their retirement savings, and creditors and other companies that had to take massive write-offs. But we shouldn't exaggerate the impact of what happened on the system itself. To my knowledge, not one home or business lost electricity or natural gas as a result of the failure, nor was there any significant turmoil in the market for those commodities.

In addition, justified market skepticism swept through our economy on a search-and-destroy mission against dishonest accounting and misleading disclosures, and that search-and-destroy mission is still under way, as any corporate director would tell you. I've seen this process from the inside and I can attest that it operates with stunning efficiency. Furthermore, I think there is little doubt that the Enron debacle is stimulating useful reforms in our general accepted accounting principles and perhaps more importantly, in what we view as generally accepted business principle.

I don't ask anyone to disregard or excuse the damage caused by the Enron episode. It did a lot of harm to a lot of innocent people, and it exposed some very serious weaknesses in our system. What I urge, instead, is that we evaluate that harm and those weaknesses in the proper context, which is that our market is an ethical system that is self-correcting. Further reforms should be designed to strengthen that ethical system and not to weaken it.

INDEPENDENT DIRECTORS ARE THE KEY

That leads to my fourth and final point: How should we review our own conduct and the conduct of our companies to strengthen them against the virus that infected Enron? Mostly, this should be aimed at my fellow directors. Most boards, of course, are self-perpetuating and CEOs recruit most directors. But directors should never forget that their sole purpose in being there is to represent the interest of the shareholders, and outside directors have a particular burden to be independent. This is not only a legal imperative, it is a moral obligation. Directors simply cannot do their job properly unless they are willing from the first day to oppose management if it is necessary.

When I joined one of my two corporate boards a few years back, I was appointed Chairman of the Governance Committee. Shortly thereafter I had to encourage the CEO, the man who had recruited me to the board and who had been with the company for 30 some years, to seek other opportunities. That was not an easy thing to do, but it was the right thing to do. On my other board, I took the lead in challenging management to come clean on all Enron-like accounting and disclosure issues. Now, in both cases I think I acted properly, and I know I acted with independence. Independence, of course, isn't any good unless you know what you're doing. In fact it could be bad if you didn't know what you were doing. And I'm speaking now about professional qualifications. They may differ from case to case, but I think the task always demands education, experience, and, maybe because I have a lot of these gray hairs up here, maturity. But it also demands courage, perhaps most importantly of all. It's not easy to cross management, particularly if you're relying on that directorship for whatever it might be, whether it's financial reasons or status. When you cross the CEO, you had better be ready to tell him, "Either you do this, or I'm out of here." Now this may demand qualities in addition to courage, but it certainly demands courage.

In addition, I believe directors should limit their board memberships. The job today is a lot harder than it was a few years ago. I'm aware of somebody who at one time served on 18 boards. I don't see how you can serve anybody well when you serve on that many boards. You can't meet the demands of the job if your attention is divided too many ways.

We also need to take another look at executive compensation. We are frankly paying some executives way too much, and we're doing it in ways that create perverse incentives for companies. Options have been the subject of a lot of discussion recently. They can have a place, but they are truly exposed as a hoax when they are re-priced again and again in the face of a falling stock price to guarantee that they can be exercised at a profit. They're also dangerous when they tempt executives to make questionable accounting and reporting decisions "just this once, just this once" to lift options above water. We should look for better ways to tie our executives' compensation to the long-term success of our companies, and not just to the quarterly results. This is a tough one. And the demand for short-term results in our system today is a difficult problem, and we need to examine that and see what needs to be done about that.

We should also be alert to accounting and reporting decisions that follow the letter of the law but violate the spirit of the law. Accounting rules today are often so esoteric and difficult to understand that you might be literally within the legal constraints of a particular rule, but way outside the spirit of it. The temptation is strong, but it ought to be resisted. The ultimate ethical value here is simple honesty. It could probably cost a few points in a stock price today, but it is the right thing to do, it's the right thing in the long run because the market rewards honesty and it rewards credibility. And in this context, it is crucial to remember that ever more complex regulation sometimes encourages ethical corner-cutting by suggesting that just legalistic compliance is sufficient. That is what we might call the moral hazard of over-regulation. In business as in politics, credibility is tough to acquire and extraordinarily easy to lose. So a lot of work needs to be done on our accounting standards. That work is under way, it's going to be done. Rules that were written for a brick-and-mortar economy years ago don't work for the new economy today.

Finally, there is no substitute for electing men and women of character and integrity to corporate boards and to our executive suites. This is not inconsistent with the idea that free market capitalism is an ethical system. Our founders understood that public virtue was absolutely essential. "Of all the dispositions and habits which lead to political prosperity," George Washington said in his farewell address, "religion and morality are indispensable supports." That is the same impulse that compels us to consider the moral and ethical framework of the marketplace. The business firm was not simply an economic entity to maximize profits, it was also a vehicle for the development and the growth of people as they served their customers and their communities. George Washington had it right.

RESPONSE BY PROFESSOR C. K. PRAHALAD

C. K. Prahalad is a professor at the University of Michigan's Ross School of Business.

I wear two hats. First, for 22 years, I was a full-time professor at the University of Michigan, and I still am. That gives me a sense of perspective, studying large companies. I am also active in management. I am on two corporate boards and the board of a large non-governmental organization that operates around the world. In addition, I am chairman of a small startup company.

In his essay, James Baker raised four points: skepticism as a critical element of our system; the rule of law as a precondition for markets to function; the probability that reforms can over-correct; and the proper response to corporate scandals.

I prefer to think of skepticism as checks and balances. In our economy and society, there are competing interests that must be explicitly balanced. There is always tension inherent in the system, and that is what makes it so vibrant. If we ever destroy the vibrant quality of tension, we destroy the system. Sometimes the system will get out of balance because of the very nature of tension. Therefore I believe there is always skepticism of the moment. The recent corporate scandals, of which Enron has been the most prominent, have produced what I would call skepticism of the moment, not a fundamental disagreement with the system itself. Balance must be brought back.

Central planners and Marxists have always assumed that the excesses of capitalism can be solved by wishing away the tension. I grew up in a system like that [in India], and I can tell you everyone assumed central planning would take care of the tensions. Planning *will* make appropriate resource allocation choices. I believe the desire to eliminate tension and checks and balances, however, is what results in inefficiencies.

DISSENT IS FUNDAMENTAL

A fundamental factor in bringing back balance is to guarantee legitimacy of dissent. I wish more companies understood why legitimacy of dissent is critical for them to have an internal due process, to provide share of voice, and to create structural impediments to the concentration of power. Companies often fail when they destroy the structural impediments to the concentration of power. I see the board, auditors and even consumers as providing checks and balances to the excesses of companies. As a board member, my job is to challenge the CEO and senior managers on key issues, not on trivialities.

On Mr. Baker's second point, that the rule of law is a precondition for the efficient function of markets, nobody should disagree. The idea is increasingly getting the support of scholars around the world, especially in the developing world. It is fundamental to creating a vibrant global economy. But on Baker's view that we must be very careful to insure that reforms do not over-correct, I disagree. I believe reforms *will* over-correct, and that they *should*. Over-correction is a result of not knowing what the correct balance is. If you over-correct like the swing of the pendulum, you can always change and reduce the dysfunctional elements of the correction. But if you do not go far enough, it is hard to know what is the appropriate response. I believe we *will* over-correct in the Enron case as well, and I'm not overly worried because in the short-term it may be a problem, but if you look at a 10-year perspective, we will re-correct. Trial and error in improving the system with apparent friction and frictional losses is the sibling of checks and balances of our society. Trial and error is how we build consensus, how we experiment, and how we improve. And therefore some trials will over-correct, and I do not believe one can exist without the other.

So how should we react to Enron? I like to take a stronger position. I want to say that this is not just Enron. We are going to see a wide variety of firms under SEC scrutiny. This is a much broader problem. Large numbers of options with re-pricing schemes have been unearthed and will be unearthed. Enron just happened to be the lead player, but with time we'll unearth more. I'm convinced it will happen. But you can ask why so? Why is this happening now? I believe that the disclosures, one more damaging than the other, have their roots in three basic causes. One, I believe, is the complexity of business itself. Second, is the inherent limitations of the current checks and balances, and the third, the violation of ethical guideposts. Unless you're in touch with your own personal values, no system can solve the problem.

But start with the complexity of business. It is very common to have a global corporation today that operates in 100 countries with 20 businesses and 50 to 100 separate partnerships and alliances. The number of transactions, both routine and unique, can boggle the mind. No single person understands and manages the details of the entire organization. Senior managers on the board must depend on systems, culture, and the senior management team to enforce appropriate controls. But this is not as easy or as straightforward as it seems. Consider some specific examples, some of it from my own experience.

The first question to consider: what is the process for revenue recognition in multi-year software contracts and projects in a global economy? This is a very complex accounting problem. More interestingly, should the Japanese subsidiary follow your standards? I remember this coming up in one of my board meetings, and the CEO took a very strong view; Japan will follow American standards because we are an American company. I said, "We'll lose some business." He said, "So be it." And it was not easy to push this approach down the throats of managers from the Asia operation. But the good news is, we didn't lose any business.

A second question is how dependent are mangers on uniform systems around the world? What if we have 25 systems with different approaches to revenue recognition that came with acquisitions. How do we insure quality? What do we audit? Transactions, systems, or both? Where are the latent risks? Does the competition for talent and low-cost capital drive managers to create incentives that are dysfunctional?

VALUES THAT HAVE STOOD THE TEST OF TIME

There is a simple framework for looking at these kinds of issues inside a company. Imagine a hard core at the center of our ethical consideration. I call it the core of ethical behavior that is an invariant, that does not change with time, context, circumstance, or business demand. That's what I like to call the invariants. These are values that have stood the test of time: integrity, personal accountability, I will put due process in the same place, respect for the individual, property rights, and the rule of law. They do not change with circumstances. Violating them is unethical behavior, pure and simple. On the other extreme are the new emerging circumstances where these values are going to be tested. For example, Napster, the software that allowed people to download music without paying for it, tested the limits of property rights in the Internet age. A new technological capability imposes a new demand. This is an example of pushing the limits of the envelope, if you will. So at the core are the invariants, and on the periphery are those areas where we experiment as society and as businesses. There is a ring in-between, if you will, and that is the most interesting one.

This middle ground is where we have precedents and an emerging consensus, but not total agreement. Different views can persist. Foreign corrupt practices was a big debate 10 years ago. Slowly there is an emerging consensus, it might not be always practiced correctly, but there is an emerging consensus. Pooling of interest accounting is another. So we may have some rules, we may have some law, but we don't have total consensus on this as an invariant tested over time. So I look at altering the middle ground where there is an emerging consensus, that is where the legal procedures stake precedence over what you like and what you don't like. Core invariants to me are ethical values. Emerging consensus is often represented by legal requirements. Pushing the envelope is about innovation. Use of the new technologies is for experimentation and creating new capabilities. As a society we need this portfolio. We cannot progress without experimenting at the margin.

So in categories two and three, the emerging consensus and in pushing the envelope, I can imagine misjudgments and misunderstanding. I will let you decide what Enron represents. We do not have all the facts, we certainly have enough sensationalism, but if it is a violation of core invariants, let us say so. It is not misjudgment when it is a violation of core invariants for me. We cannot and should not hide behind misjudgment of our core invariants in senior positions in public life, neither should there be a question of interpretation of accounting rules. As we evolve and as our economy goes through a process of this continuous change—deregulation, globalization, convergence of industries, Internet, and biotech—we will face multiple ethical dilemmas. I believe it is an essential tension we must accept as an integral part of progress. Experimentation is critical to progress. However, moral lapses and violation of core should not be confused with evolving uncertain business domains. We need innovation, we need to have our anchors clean and clear. And to me, if there's one message I can give, it is don't forget your values. Ultimately, business is about values. If that is lost, everything is lost.

AFTERWORD

So the words have been spoken. How will the truth of what has been said translate into action and right behavior?

There is agreement that:

1. The business firm should be a moral community to help shape human character and behavior.
2. There are absolute moral standards.
3. People are imperfect and we all reflect the crooked timber of humanity in which self-interest and the propensity for greed reside.
4. Morality cannot be legislated. More rules and process will not provide all the answers.
5. Leadership can make a difference.
6. Leaders who want to make such a difference should have a moral compass and know what they believe with the courage and conviction to resist evil and provide an example of right behavior.

But what have we learned about the source for this moral authority? Is God the ultimate source? If so, how does this fit the world of making money and running a business? As a number of the lecturers noted, Western society has been greatly influenced by Judeo-Christian culture and tradition. This culture and tradition recognizes that there is a God and that He is the ultimate authority. We are all subject to Him and there is value in seeking His truth. Such was the thought expressed by John Locke almost 300 years ago and etched in stone on the floor of the Chapel of Christ Church College at Oxford University: "I know there is truth opposite falsehood and that it may be found if people will search, for it is worth the seeking."

But God and His truth are not accepted by all. The business corporation today must operate in a pluralistic and diverse world. It is not the role of the firm to impose or mandate any one person's faith or belief. In fact, for those of us who believe in God and are followers of Jesus Christ, we also must recognize that different people with different beliefs are all part of the world God created and the world He so loved. The business corporation then, as a moral community, must be inclusive. It is not a church, synagogue, or place of worship. The ultimate litmus test for any of its moral standards or actions should be the resulting effect upon people. Do such standards and practices reflect the dignity and worth of every individual? Do they encourage the development of the whole person—a person who has economic, social and spiritual needs? Do they promote the development of human character and behavior as people work together to accomplish a common goal? Will they provide an environment where there is freedom to explore truth, including the question of God and His role in transforming the belief and actions of people?

It was C. S Lewis who said: "There are no ordinary people. You have never talked to a mere mortal. Nations, cultures, arts, civilizations —these are mortal and their life is to ours as the life of a gnat, but it is immortals whom we joke with, work with, marry, snub and exploit." The moral standards and practices of a business firm must begin by placing a high value on people—people, every one of whom has been created in the image and likeness of God—people, every one of whom needs to belong and grow within a community—people, every one of whom is searching for the meaning of life. But the virtues reflected in these moral standards, including the virtues of honesty, character, integrity, and putting the interest of others ahead of one's self, must become more than just statements in a code of ethics if they are to become practices of the firm. They must become a part of who people are and who they are becoming if the community of the firm is to function beyond the rules and codes and do what is right even when no one is looking or measuring and even when the people of the firm are faced with the challenges of a changing dynamic market.

I raise this issue not as a philosopher, educator, or religious leader, but simply as a businessperson—someone who over the past 25 years has participated in the leadership of ServiceMaster during a period of rapid growth and expansion. As I have now retired from those leadership responsibilities and look back, I can add up the numbers that show significant growth in profits, customers served, and a premium return for our shareholders. While these figures are part of a normal business assessment of performance, the conclusion for me cannot be limited to these money or value-creation measurements. The real and lasting measurement is whether the results of my leadership can be told in the changed and improved lives of people I have led.

As a business firm, we wanted to excel at generating profits and creating value for our shareholders. If we didn't want to play by these rules, we didn't belong in the game. But I also tried to encourage an environment where the workplace could be a community to help shape human character. I wanted an open community where the question of a person's moral and spiritual development and the existence of God and how one related the claims of faith to the work of the firm were issues of discussion, debate and, yes, even learning and understanding. I considered the people of our firm as, in fact, the soul of the firm. We were about the process of soulcraft.

My experience confirmed Peter Drucker's conclusions: that people work for a cause not just a living and that mission and purpose were important organizing and sustaining principles for the firm. Our corporate objectives were developed under the leadership of Ken Hansen and Ken Wessner before I joined the firm. They were simply stated: To honor God in all we do; To help people develop; To pursue excellence; and To grow profitably. Those first two objectives were end goals; the second two were means goals. We didn't use that first objective as a basis for exclusion. It was, in fact, the reason for our promotion of diversity as we recognized that different people with different beliefs were all part of God's mix. The fact that we had these goals did not mean that everything was done correctly. We experienced our share of mistakes. We sometimes failed and did things wrong. But because of a stated standard and a reason for that standard, we could not hide our mistakes. Mistakes were regularly flushed out in the open for correction and, in some cases, for forgiveness. Leaders could not protect themselves at the expense of those they were leading. The process of seeking understanding and application of these objectives at all levels of the organization was a never-ending task. It involved matters of the heart as well as the head and it was not susceptible to standard management techniques of implementation or measurement. While at times it was discouraging, it also was energizing as one realized the continuing potential for creativity, innovation, and growth. The focus was on development of the whole person.

Now for me as a Christian, a follower of Jesus Christ, this environment provided an opportunity to live my faith in such a way so that it was not imposed upon my colleagues and fellow workers, but instead could be examined, tested, understood and, in some cases, embraced by them as they sought not only to do things right but also to do the right thing. One of the best ways that I found to lead our firm as a moral community was to seek to serve as I led. My model was Jesus as he washed his disciples feet to teach them that no leader was greater or had a self-interest more important than those being led. In seeking to so serve, the truth of what I said could be measured by what I did. My ethic became a reality as I was able to serve those I led.

Servant leadership has been a learning experience for me. It has not come naturally. The first thing I had to understand was what it meant to walk in the shoes of those I would lead. This was a lesson that I would learn as I first joined the ServiceMaster team. My predecessors in the business, Ken Hansen, who was then Chairman, and Ken Wessner, who was then President and CEO, were both involved in recruiting me. They wanted me to come and initially head up the legal and financial affairs of the company, reporting to Ken Wessner. In the selling of the job, it was suggested that I, along with others, would be considered in the future for the job of chief executive. The interviewing process took several months and as we were coming to what I thought of as the final interview to confirm compensation and starting date, I decided that I needed to know more about what it would take to be CEO of ServiceMaster. As I pressed the point and tried to get some assurance of how I could become CEO, Ken Hansen stood up and told me the interview was over. Ken Wessner then ushered me to the front door. As I left ServiceMaster that morning, I concluded that it was over. I had blown the opportunity.

A few days later, Ken Hansen called to ask me if I wanted to have breakfast with him to discuss what had happened in his office. When we sat down for breakfast, he simply said: "Bill, if you want to come to ServiceMaster to contribute and serve, you will have a great future. But if your coming is dependent on a title or position or ultimately the CEO's position, then you will be disappointed. To be successful at ServiceMaster, you will have to learn to put the interest of others ahead of your own." His point was very simple. Never give a job or a title to a person who can't live without it. Determine at the front end whether the leader's self-interest or the interest of others will come first. Know whether he or she can define reality by being willing to do what they ask of others. Test whether they have the conviction of their faith or belief. I took the job and Ken, in his own way, tested my commitment and understanding of what he had told me. I spent the first six weeks of my ServiceMaster career out cleaning floors and doing the maintenance and other work which was part of our service business. There were lessons for me to learn, the most important of which was my dependence upon and responsibility to the people I would lead. The experience also reminded me of the reality of my own imperfections and the need to admit my mistakes and ask for forgiveness.

Later on in my career the faces of our service workers would flash across my mind as I was faced with those inevitable judgment calls between the rights and the wrongs of running a business. The integrity of my actions had to pass their scrutiny. When all the numbers and figures were added up and reported as the results of the firm, they had to do more than just follow the rules or satisfy the changing standards of the accounting profession. The numbers also had to accurately reflect the reality of our combined performance, a result that was real and that would reflect the true value of the firm. Otherwise I was deceiving myself and those whom I was committed to serve. Drucker has referred to this type of leadership as reflecting the ethic of prudence—prudence that demands that leaders be an example by what they say and by the way they live. In Drucker's judgment, the leader has only one choice: between direction or misdirection, between leadership or misleadership. Responsible leadership requires the choice of an ethic of service and example of right behavior. In seeking to lead an organization as a moral community, one should recognize that it is not always comfortable. At times it feels like you are in a rowboat rowing upstream. There will always be an abundance of skeptics with questions raised regarding a goal that mixes the principles of faith and work, God and profit. For me, there certainly were times of adversity and doubt. But my faith in God provided a special strength and peace as I knew that the One who was the object of my faith not only loved me but also loved the skeptics and gave of himself in service to others.

What is a business without people? What is corporate governance without integrity? What is leadership without the example of service and an ethic of right behavior? For me, seeking to serve as I have led has been the salt and light of what I believe—the reality of my faith and my God.

C. William Pollard
Chairman Emeritus
The ServiceMaster Company

INDEX

A

abandonment, principle of, 52

accountability, 65, 89, 137, 141-42, 173. *See also* leadership, accountability

accounting; complex, 31, 203; dishonest, 47, 164, 195, 202, 203; pooling of interest, 207; revenue recognition, 206

acquisitions, 66, 206

Adams, John, 104

advertising, 80, 114

Applebaum, Arthur, 70

Aristotle, 70, 104, 133, 145

arrogance. *See* hubris

Arthur Andersen, 195

Augustine, 74

B

Baier, Scott, 119

Baker Botts, 195

Baker, James, 30-31

Bankruptcy, Barons of, 13

Barnard, Chester, 167

Bellah, Robert, 82

Bennett, William, 85

Bennis, Warren, ix, 181, 188

Bible. *See* Christianity

biotechnology, 207

Black, Sir James, 146

board monitoring. *See* corporate governance

bottom line, triple, 141. *See also* environmentalism; profit maximization; self-interest

Bourain, Alex, 176

Buffett, Warren, 40, 53, 68

Bush, George H. W., 196, 200

business; as calling, 97, 113, 132; complexity of, 205-206; cultural attitudes toward, 92-93,102, 109, 143, 195, 198; as educator, 111-12, 134-35; inherently moral, 99, 101-02, 114, 116-17, 145, 199; and international development. *See* constructive engagement ; as key social institution, 38, 54, 76; as moral community, 18-20, 25, 38, 63, 71, 77, 124, 209-11; public pressure on, 135-36, 195; responsibility to employees, 16, 60, 94-95; responsibility to society, 23, 33, 66, 71, 92, 97-98, 110-12, 126, 143, 204; society's need for, 98, 112, 134; as source of values, 18, 23, 98, 134-35. *See also* values, fostered by business

Business Enterprise Trust, 82

Business Leaders for Excellence, Ethics and Justice, 186

businesses, small, 30, 190, 192

C

Calvin, John, 113

Capelli, Peter, 168

capitalism; corrupt, 173; and democracy, 20-22, 79-88, 97-101, 137-38; distinguished from "free market", 98; emerging, 93; morality of, 21, 59-60, 199; reputation of, 60, 109, 195; superiority of, 79-80, 198; a threat to virtue, 105; threatened by immorality, 80. *See also* capitalism, reputation of; and totalitarian states, 22, 98-101, 109-112

Cardozo, Benjamin, 152

Carter, Jimmy, 141, 200

Categorical Imperative, 49

Catholicism, 60, 61, 80, 102-103, 113-14, 117, 131; John Paul II, 60, 114; Pius XII, 102

Cathy, S. Truett, 167

Chami, Ralph, 116

character, 170, 175. *See also* values; virtues ; defined, 163, 179; in leadership, 181, 189

charitable giving, 33, 126, 134, 191

checks and balances, economic, 204

Chesterfield, Lord, 165

childcare centers, 119

Christianity, 25, 211; as a source of values, 25, 29, 84, 89-91, 141, 162, 164-165, 171, 174-

Investcorp, 47

Islam, 43-44, 130-31, 189

J

Jefferson, Thomas, 105

job security, 71. *See* employment security

Johnson, Elmer, 18-20

Judeo-Christian thought. *See also* Catholicism; Christianity; faith; values, religious; decline of, 26, 142; and pluralism, 188; and sin, 189; as source of values, 18, 25, 28-29, 43, 47, 60, 69, 130-31, 152, 185, 191, 209

justice, 48, 51

K

Kant, Emanuel, 189

Kay, John, 143

Kellogg Foundation, 82

Kirdar, Nemir. *See also* monotheism

Kissinger, Henry, 150, 155, 156, 157, 158, 161, 162

Kung, Hans, 129

L

Lavengood, Lawrence G., 20, 75

law; natural, 42-43. *See also* Tao, The; spirit of the, 203. *See also* legislation, inadequacy of

layoffs. *See* downsizing

leadership; accountable, 21; characteristics of, 70, 86, 183, 205; and communicating values, 27, 34, 36-37, 87, 182; current lack of, 181; as examples of values, 53, 190-91, 196-97; importance of character, 27, 112, 209; not limited to office, 85-86; requirements for, 72, 84, 94, 181, 203, 204; risks of, 164-65; servant, 36, 72, 126, 211-12

Lear, Norman, 82

leave, family, 119

legislation, 14, 172; campaign finance laws, 201; inadequacy of, 14, 26, 61, 117, 126, 137, 209; as minimum standard, 16, 137,

183; need for, 198-99, 205; overly aggressive, 31, 200-01, 201, 203. *See also* overregulation

Lewis, C. S. , 17, 42-43, 114, 128, 210

liberalism, economic, 102

"license to operate", 136

local businesses. *See* business, small

Locke, John, 209

Lorenz, Konrad, 39

loyalty, 67, 125, 163, 184

Luther, Martin, 28, 115, 174-76

M

Madison, James, 199

management, centralized, 62

Mandela, Nelson, 28, 176

Mandeville, Bernard, 126

Marius, Richard, 175

market, free. *See also* capitalism; and human equality, 20; global, 24, 54, 67, 205. *See also* globalization; negative consequences, 115-16, 192. *See also* self-interest; potential perfection of, 75; preserving principles of, 80-88, 91; promotes civilization, 105-106; self-correction, 30, 31, 118, 201-202

Marx, Karl, 39, 44, 56, 175

Marxism, 198, 204

materialism, 83

McDonalds, 190

meaning, found in work, 189

mediation; between individual and state, 76; between self-interest and public interest, 76

middle management, 66

Milosevic, Slobodan, 172

mistrust, 73-74. *See also* skepticism; trust

Montesquieu, 106

moral; authority, 15, 16, 25, 209. *See also* values, sources of; discernment, 72; leadership, 22-24, 72, 133. *See also* leadership, characteristics of; practices, immoral vs. amoral,